Global Trade in the Nineteenth Century

In this engaging new study, John D. Wong examines the Canton trade networks that helped to shape the modern world through the lens of the prominent Chinese merchant Houqua, whose trading network and financial connections stretched from China to India, America, and Britain. In contrast to interpretations that see Chinese merchants in this era as victims of rising Western mercantilism and oppressive Chinese traditions, Houqua maintained a complex balance between his commercial interests and those of his Western counterparts, all in an era of transnationalism before the imposition of the Western world order. The success of Houqua & Co. in configuring its networks in the fluid context of the early nineteenth century remains instructive today as the contemporary balance of political power renders the imposition of a West-centric world system increasingly problematic and requires international traders to adapt to a new world order in which China, once again, occupies center stage.

JOHN D. WONG is an assistant professor in Hong Kong Studies at the University of Hong Kong. His research interests focus on transnational business history.

Global Trade in the Nineteenth Century

The House of Houqua and the Canton System

John D. Wong

The University of Hong Kong

CAMBRIDGE
UNIVERSITY PRESS

CAMBRIDGE
UNIVERSITY PRESS

University Printing House, Cambridge CB2 8BS, United Kingdom

Cambridge University Press is part of the University of Cambridge.

It furthers the University's mission by disseminating knowledge in the pursuit of education, learning, and research at the highest international levels of excellence.

www.cambridge.org
Information on this title: www.cambridge.org/9781107150669

© John D. Wong 2016

First published 2016

Printed in the United States of America by Sheridan Books, Inc.

A catalogue record for this publication is available from the British Library

ISBN 978-1-107-15066-9 Hardback

For Linda

CONTENTS

Figures

Acknowledgments

Since its inception, this project has taken more than eight years to reach its present form. Many have accompanied me on this long journey and to them I will be forever indebted. A team of senior colleagues shepherded this project in its first incarnation. Michael Szonyi not only provided a guiding force every step of the way but also assumed the impossible task of helping with the many life problems of this "mature" mentee. Hue-Tam Ho Tai offered generously her insightful comments and helped with the logistical challenges. In addition to inducting me into the study of financial history, Niall Ferguson served as my model of productivity in research and teaching. Elisabeth Köll demonstrated for me time and again how to approach business history when I could not be sure if I was a businessman or a historian.

Many other intellectual creditors have also advanced my work on this project. At Harvard, Peter Bol, Mark Elliott, Henrietta Harrison, William Kirby, Philip Kuhn, and Michael Puett helped with its formulation. In Hong Kong, I enjoyed the warm welcome of the History Department of the Chinese University of Hong Kong, as well as the Hong Kong Institute for the Humanities and Social Sciences, the History Department, and the School of Modern Languages and Cultures at the University of Hong Kong. For this, I owe my gratitude to John Carroll, David Faure, Kendall Johnson, and Angela Leung. Paul Van Dyke not only provided invaluable guidance on research in Macao and Guangzhou but also munificently shared with me his data on the Hong merchants. At Sun Yat-sen University, Liu Zhiwei and May-bo Ching, along with their colleagues in the History Department, offered insights on local studies of the Pearl River Delta. Liu Wenpeng facilitated my research in Beijing. In Taiwan, Ch'en Kuo-tung shared with me his tremendous experience researching this topic. Zhang Kan at Xiamen University provided local support for my research in Fujian. In Singapore, I enjoyed the hospitality of the Asia Research Institute at the National University of Singapore and the wise counsel of Wang Gungwu. Frederic D. Grant Jr., fellow enthusiast of the Hong merchants, shared with me his collection of U.S. legal cases involving Houqua. During my stay in London, Debin Ma and Kent Deng at the London School of Economics offered me their advice. The Centre for History and Economics arranged for my research at Cambridge University. Thanks also to Patrick Conner, Joshua Derman, James Fichter, Chiara Formichi, He Wenkai, Denise Ho, Loretta Kim, Li Ren-Yuan, Matthew Mosca, Niccolò Pianciola, Winnie Wong, Lawrence Zhang, and the many friends and colleagues who offered comments on this project at various stages.

Spanning three continents and innumerable research sites, this project would not have been possible without the tremendous institutional support I received. My various research visits were funded by a Fulbright Institute of International Education grant, an IHR Mellon Pre-dissertation Fellowship in the Humanities, a Frederick Sheldon Traveling Fellowship, a Mellon Prize Research Grant in History and Economics, a New England Regional Fellowship Consortium (NERFC) grant, as well as study grants from the South Asia Initiative, the Asia Center, and the Fairbank Center at Harvard, and a Hsu Long-sing grant from the University of Hong Kong. In addition to these institutional sponsorships, the project required access to historical materials. Matheson & Co. Ltd. kindly granted me access to the Jardine Matheson archives. I would like to thank in particular the dedicated archivists and librarians at the Baker Library at the Harvard Business School, the Massachusetts Historical Society, the John Carter Brown Library, the Number One Historical Archives in Beijing, the National Palace Archives in Taipei, the Sun Yat-sen Library of Guangdong Province, the British Library, the National Archives of the United Kingdom, the University Library at Cambridge, and the library at the University of Mumbai. The Hongkong and Shanghai Banking Corporation Limited, the Ipswich Public Library, the Museum of Fine Arts (Boston), and the Peabody Essex Museum not only facilitated access to their holdings but also granted me permission to include images of their paintings in this book. The team at Cambridge University Press offered critical support during the production stages of this book and for this, I am grateful to Lucy Rhymer, Rosalyn Scott, and Claire Sissen. Nancy Hearst proofread the manuscript. Two anonymous reviewers provided insightful critiques.

My family experienced an eventful period during my work on this research project. In addition to offering encouragement as a fellow journeyman in academia, my brother Andrew also served as a source of mutual support during this time, which witnessed the passing of one

parent and the broken leg of the other. My sons Gregory and Ian have
provided great impetus to my work as they inquired incessantly about
the completion of my "homework." My wife Linda has been a constant
source of support and companionship. To her, my lifelong partner and
loyal critic, I dedicate this book.

Introduction

In the closing months of 1842, when the Qing court and the British government had just concluded the negotiations that ended the Opium War, the Chinese Hong merchant Wu Bingjian, known to his Western partners as Houqua,[1] was already becoming immersed in the business of reactivating his trade network. On December 23, 1842, from his base in Canton, Houqua wrote to his American associates, John Murray Forbes and John's brother Robert "Bennet" Forbes: "My dear friends, / I cannot let the *Akbar* go off without a few lines to you." The ship the *Akbar* had served as a conduit for the frequent dispatch of messages and cargo between Houqua and his American partners. As the ship stood ready to return to America, Houqua prepared a note to acknowledge his receipt of letters from John and Bennet that another American associate, Mr. King, had interpreted for him. He had no time to respond to the particulars in these letters; however, he hurried to compose a quick message to accompany his shipment on the departing boat. "I send you by the *Akbar* about 500 tons of Teas all of good quality, & nearly all imported by myself from the Tea country. I have invoiced them low, & hope the result will be good." Why the rush? Houqua had received market intelligence that the U.S. government might impose a heavy duty on tea imports, but that "ships leaving here [from Canton] before January may get their cargoes in free." He limited his specific instructions to the brothers thus: "If a fair profit can be realized I am inclined to recommend early sales & returns, and with this remark for your consideration, the selling will be left to your discretion." In the global tea market, speed was of the essence. Houqua indicated his preference for a speedy sale of the cargo, but in his instructions to his trusted confidants, with whom he had engaged in transactions for years, he allowed ample latitude in the execution of the trade. "The *Akbar* has loaded quickly & Capt. D. if he has usual luck, will be among the first ships with you," Houqua hoped.

---

[1] His name is sometimes written as "Howqua." I have used "Houqua" throughout this volume because this is how he signed his name.

1

In this update for his associates in America, Houqua took care to include his intention of also shipping to England, the other important market for tea. "I am sending to London by the *John Moore* about 10,000 chests of Tea, & about 7,000 of the same to FF&Co. & the balance to BB&Co." From this shipment to England, Houqua did not expect high profits, but he thought "the chance better to ship than to sell here [in Canton] by & by." Houqua understood that his American partners needed more than mere details about his plans for the U.S. market; they wanted privileged information about Houqua's dealings in other important markets, thus allowing the team in America to coordinate its actions in the global marketplace.

In addition to his export shipments from Canton, Houqua explored the options regarding remittance of the proceeds. He believed that the Forbes brothers would send a ship from America bound for Canton. The ship would "come direct with cotton & lead, and if bought low these articles may pay a good remittance." Unlike the outbound cargo, which consisted primarily of tea for the China trade in Canton, the return shipment would be assembled based on the profit opportunities that the various commodities offered at any particular moment. Houqua would, of course, welcome specie, but even the different forms of silver had unequal profit potentials. "I prefer Old Head Dollars to any thing [*sic*] else if to be had at or under 6% premium."[2] In mid-nineteenth-century Canton, the various Spanish silver coins had different values in the market. The global trader Houqua had to communicate the latest pricing information to his overseas associates in order to reap the most financial gains.

By the outbreak of the Opium War, Houqua had already held court for decades in Canton's nexus of international trade. During the closing years of the eighteenth century, he had entered the China trade in Canton, which at the time was the sole port of call for Western traders. As early as the 1810s, Houqua had already earned sufficient clout in the commercial world to be recognized as the preeminent Chinese merchant in the Canton system. However, in the aftermath of the Opium War, the Treaty Port system would alter the terms of international engagements for Houqua and other enterprising merchants. Nonetheless, Houqua, with half a century of experience in international business and the fortune he had amassed from the China trade under the Canton system, continued to charge ahead in the world of trade and finance in search of

---

[2] MHS Houqua Letters, December 23, 1842.

profitable avenues of exchange, much in the same manner that he had since the turn of the nineteenth century.

Wu Bingjian, whom the West would come to know as Houqua, was born in the thirty-fourth year of the reign of Qing Emperor Qianlong, the third of four surviving sons of Wu Guoying.[3] Although the Chinese would reckon Houqua's year of birth as the year of *jichou* in the sexagenary cycle, according to the Western calendar Houqua was born in 1769, "the same year [as] Napoleon and Wellington," as one of his Western trading partners notes in his memoir.[4]

Houqua was born in Canton merely twelve years after the Manchu court of the Qing dynasty declared that Canton would be China's sole port of call for Western traders. The political turmoil brought on by the Manchu conquest in 1644 had intensified the movement of people, goods, and capital along the Chinese coast and in Southeast Asia. The ensuing conflicts dragged on, and it was not until the mid-eighteenth century that conditions became sufficiently stable for Sino-Western trade to be conducted with some regularity. The establishment of Canton as the sole legal port of call for Western traders facilitated a steady flow of goods between China and many Western countries, channeling the various parties to negotiate their interests in the city. These economic motivations, along with the evolving geopolitical landscape of the times, brought to Canton merchants from the West and from elsewhere in China, including Houqua's family and other enterprising Chinese traders. With their Western counterparts in Canton, Houqua and these select Chinese merchants interacted in their respective capacities as the licensed China traders, the so-called Hong merchants.

During the century that followed, the fates of Houqua, Napoleon, and Wellington, three men born only months apart in 1769, would intertwine. Napoleon's military conquests in continental Europe would alter the balance of international trade and Wellington's accomplishments would push British power to new heights. In response, Houqua maneuvered strategically and successfully to account for the changing partners arriving at his port of Canton. In fact, Houqua's commercial successes owed much to the political realignment in Europe, half a world away from

---

[3] Wu Quancui, ed., *Lingnan Wushi hezu zongpu* (Complete Genealogy of the Entire Wu Clan in Lingnan) (1934), 2a:44a. Wolfram Eberhard relies on this version of the Wu genealogy in a case study of the clan in his *Social Mobility in Traditional China* (Leiden: E. J. Brill, 1962). The present study extends the exploration into the Wu clan by examining multiple genealogies, which not only provide more detailed information on the various generations but also explain the mechanisms behind family and business maneuvers framed in the idiom of kinship.

[4] William C. Hunter, *The "Fan Kwae" at Canton before Treaty Days, 1825–1844 by an Old Resident* (London: K. Paul, Trench, 1882), 50.

Canton. The political realignment, in which Napoleon and Wellington played critical roles, provided Houqua an opportunity to build his business and to consolidate his commercial power in Canton. Although he did not command military power or transform the political landscape in the manner of Napoleon or Wellington, Houqua proved to be instrumental in shaping the playing field for international commerce as he steered the flow of both goods and capital. His achievements pivoted around his ability to circumvent the ascending power of the British, epitomized by the Duke of Wellington, Napoleon's archrival at the Battle of Waterloo. As the British military elevated the East India Company (EIC) to a dominant position, Houqua countered by recasting his trading partners. Long after Wellington had thwarted Napoleon's ambitions to dominate continental Europe, Houqua still remained prominent in the world of trade, living out his last years by holding court in the emporium of Canton.

During this period before the imposition of Western rules of engagement for global exchange, enterprising businessmen had to fashion social connections for the flow of information and to deploy their goods and capital along the sinews of their networks to further their financial interests, all in the absence of a universal standard unit of account or a commonly accepted international court of law to mediate disputes. Houqua, the Hong merchant who dominated Sino-Western trade in the early nineteenth century, was an exceptional Chinese trader. The importance of his story lies not in his ability to represent the experience of an average Chinese player in global trade and commerce. Rather, it was his extraordinary ability to balance his interests with those of his partners from America, England, and other parts of the world that allowed him to play a pivotal role in configuring trade networks as global connections intensified. As he identified and pursued profit opportunities, he redirected the traffic of goods and capital around the world and, in the process, he altered the balance of commercial power on the other side of the globe, just as the Rothschilds tilted the playing field for political contenders in Europe.

Directing the development of trade in Canton, Houqua succeeded in navigating the turbulent waters of international commerce for nearly half a century. His death in 1843 coincided with the beginning of the Treaty Port days. However, his successors were unable to circumvent British military and commercial hegemony as successfully as Houqua had been able to do during the Canton era. During the ensuing power shift in international commerce, the command over the flow of capital and goods that Houqua's family had once enjoyed would be eclipsed by the mounting forces of the British, along with others of the Western world. This shift in the power structure has clouded our understanding of the earlier period of global exchange when Chinese merchants exerted as much control as, if not more than, their Western partners over the flow of goods and capital. Colored by Western dominance during the later period, any memory of Houqua's criticality in international commerce (and that of other Chinese participants) has faded to such an extent that today people around the world still remember Napoleon and the Duke of Wellington, but almost no one, even in China, recalls Houqua's story of success.

In 1769, however, no one could have predicted this eventuality. A confluence of events was brewing that would provide the backdrop for the course of action charted by these three men. In China, as the troubles along the southeastern coast caused by what remained of the preceding Ming dynasty had subsided, Qing subjects living in the coastal provinces busied themselves with the trading opportunities in China's New World, which stretched from these coastal provinces to the ports of Nanyang, or the South China Sea. On the other side of the globe in the New World of the Europeans, fomenting trouble would soon turn British attention toward the East and create another contending power in North America.[5] At the turn of the nineteenth century, in the cosmopolitan city of Canton, the colliding forces of these New Worlds brought together a motley crew of characters whose search for wealth and power would alter the course of the development of international politics and economics.

This book presents an account of Houqua's business enterprise not only to showcase the economic dynamism in China prior to the advent of the Treaty Port days but also to demonstrate the influence of this prominent Chinese merchant in constructing global networks of trade and finance as the flow of goods and capital accelerated in the emerging modern world. This study of Houqua's commercial and financial enterprise is intended to be a business history. It explores the social and cultural history of the players in China trade under the Canton system and traces the changes in the aftermath of the Opium War. In following the development of Houqua's business, I have three goals. First, I seek to restore the criticality of Houqua and the trade in Canton in the web of global commerce during the first half of the nineteenth century. Houqua fashioned his trading network as an international business enterprise predicated not on production capabilities but on connections and affiliations. Second, I investigate the means by which Houqua and his partners sustained

---

[5] On the redirection of British interests, see James R. Fichter, *So Great a Proffit: How the East Indies Trade Transformed Anglo-American Capitalism* (Cambridge, MA: Harvard University Press, 2010).

their system of trust and credit before the advent of the international order dominated by the Western powers. Third, I analyze how Houqua's descendants handled the new system of trade during the Treaty Port era and how the network that Houqua had constructed began to unravel in the second half of the nineteenth century. The overarching purpose of the study is to trace China's crucial role in the emergence of a dynamic global economy and its subsequent decline.

Houqua's business success stemmed from his ability not only to carve a space in the world of commerce but also to maneuver into a central position in the network of trade. That Houqua managed to expand his business enterprise globally defies the notion that the Canton system was a constricting arrangement that confined the Chinese Hong merchants and limited their ability to exert an influence beyond this one Chinese city. Houqua's ability to adroitly balance the powers of his Western partners and his insistence on actively charting his course of trade challenge the prevailing interpretation of the development of international trade as the unrelenting imposition of Western-style capitalism to which Chinese businessmen and China's economic system eventually succumbed. Without setting foot outside of his base in Canton, Houqua played an instrumental role in shaping international commerce and finance. The process by which he extended his global reach underscores his contribution in forging international trade as geopolitics transformed the commercial landscape.

Houqua in Chinese and Global History

Through the lens of a single prominent merchant house and its leading figure, this project explores the economic dynamism in early-nineteenth-century Canton. This study of Houqua and the Canton trade system adopts a global perspective. Such a global approach, overlooked by previous generations of scholars, seeks to underscore the commercial vitality and transnational exchange during the era of the Canton trade.[6] Each

[6] A recent publication, Eric Jay Dolin, *When America First Met China: An Exotic History of Tea, Drugs, and Money in the Age of Sail* (New York: Liveright, 2012) brings to the attention of the popular reader the global dimension of this exchange. The present study will extend beyond the oft-cited anecdotal examples based on Dolin's selected memoirs with a view toward building a critical understanding of the business dealings of these global traders. In a recently published monograph, Frederic Delano Grant Jr., *The Chinese Cornerstone of Modern Banking: The Canton Guaranty System and the Origins of Bank Deposit Insurance 1780–1933* (Leiden: Brill Nijhoff, 2014), introduces a different dimension of the global influence as he traces the origins of modern banking insurance across time and space to the Canton Guaranty System.

generation of earlier scholars of the Canton trade has focused on the decline of the Qing by interpreting historical issues through the lens of scholars of the respective eras. In the early part of the twentieth century, when China was struggling to find its footing on the international scene, research began to chronicle the rise and fall of various Hong families, but without capturing the dynamic economic exchanges in which they participated.[7] Similarly, scholars who wrote before China's recent economic takeoff have focused on the cases of insolvency among the Hong merchants as their studies reflected on China's prolonged economic struggles.[8] Balanced assessments of the Canton system have only begun to appear more recently.[9] Extending the analysis to the China trade of the nineteenth century as the impact of geopolitical forces escalated, through the individual stories of Houqua and his partners this study explores the dynamic global networks of commerce in the decades prior to the Opium War.[10]

[7] Liang Jiabin, *Guangdong shisanhang kao* (An Investigation into the Guangzhou Hong Merchants) (1937; rpt., Guangzhou: Guangdong renmin chubanshe, 1999).

[8] See Dilip Kumar Basu, "Asian Merchants and Western Trade: A Comparative Study of Calcutta and Canton 1800–1840" (PhD diss., Department of History, University of California, Berkeley, 1975) and Kuo-tung Anthony Ch'en, *The Insolvency of the Chinese Hong Merchants, 1760–1843* (Taipei: Institute of Economics, Academia Sinica, 1990). There is a similar trend in the scholarship on the Western traders. Reacting against Western imperialism, Jacques M. Downs depicts the American traders operating in the Canton system by highlighting their role as traffickers in the illicit and immoral opium commerce. See Jacques M. Downs, *The Golden Ghetto: The American Commercial Community at Canton and the Shaping of American China Policy, 1784–1844* (Bethlehem, PA: Lehigh University Press, 1997).

[9] Paul A. Van Dyke, *Merchants of Canton and Macao: Politics and Strategies in Eighteenth-Century Chinese Trade* (Hong Kong: Hong Kong University Press, 2011) and Paul A. Van Dyke, *The Canton Trade: Life and Enterprise on the China Coast, 1700–1845* (Hong Kong: Hong Kong University Press, 2007). Van Dyke views the Canton system as a sophisticated arrangement through which the Qing court managed the growing trade and generated significant revenue for the court, succumbing to Western imperialism only after the arrival of Western steamships and gunboats.

[10] With respect to writings on Houqua, there has been surprisingly little scholarly coverage. Ch'en, in *The Insolvency of the Chinese Hong Merchants*, refers to Houqua, but he does not prominently feature this successful merchant, largely because his focus is on the insolvency of many other merchants. As for Chinese-language materials, until recently writers have shunned Houqua as a politically problematic individual. His connections with Western traders called into question his political allegiance. His family's financial contributions to the Qing state's suppression of the Taiping Rebellion, which many Communist historians view as a harbinger of the peasant revolution spearheaded by the Chinese Communist Party in the mid-twentieth century, rendered Houqua an enemy of the masses. In contrast, English-language coverage has celebrated Houqua's accomplishments, perhaps too much so when written from the romanticized perspective of the Old China Trade. See, for example, W. Cameron Forbes, "Houqua, the Merchant Prince of China, 1769–1843," *Bulletin of the American Asiatic Association* 6, no. 6 (1940): 9–18.

Known today as Guangzhou, the Chinese city of Canton served as a dynamic node for transnational commerce until the demise of the Canton System in 1842. Tracing the footprint of its trading networks, this study includes archival work in Guangzhou, Hong Kong, Macao, Beijing, Taipei, Singapore, Boston, Providence, England, and India. The investigation covers genres of literature ranging from business records, family papers, personal correspondence, gazetteers, genealogies, government documents, travelogues, and anthologies of literary works. These sources are highly complementary. Whereas the Chinese court documents explain the Qing bureaucratic mechanisms of the Canton trade and the British East India Company (EIC) databank chronicles the ascending commercial prowess of England, the American records shed light not only on the business transactions but also on the personal stories of the individual traders. The genealogies of Houqua's family, in addition to tracing the lineage of the Wu clan, also detail Houqua's strategy for business succession. As the scattered historical records are reconnected, the emerging picture demonstrates the success of Houqua and his trading partners in sustaining their economic exchange on a global scale long before Western imperialism ushered in the era of international trade in the Euro-centric modern world at the turn of the twentieth century.

In the early nineteenth century, certain economic actors in Qing China, especially those in Canton, had become so involved in the world of commerce and finance that it is impossible to isolate their "Chinese experience" from the development of global processes. Their stories, however, reflect not only the "impact of the West," as these Chinese traders were not passive reactors to Western forces; rather, they were enterprising strategists furthering their economic interests in view of the shifting geopolitical landscape. To appreciate the interactions among the various players in this dynamic, multipolar trading world, one needs to go beyond not only the Fairbank model of the "Western Impact–Chinese Response" but also the later paradigm of "China-centered history."[11] The ever-evolving equilibrium in the nineteenth-century Canton system pivoted precisely around the traders' ability to navigate the turbulent waters brought about by the colliding regimes. As a central player in the world of commerce and a crucial figure in the geopolitics of the first half of the nineteenth century, Houqua offers a unique perspective on global development at the decisive juncture when China's fortunes began to diverge. His story allows us to explore how the divergence of business

---

[11] For an extended discussion of this historiography, see Paul A. Cohen, *China Unbound: Evolving Perspectives on the Chinese Past* (London: RoutledgeCurzon, 2003).

development on a macroeconomic scale pivoted around the talents and inclinations of specific individuals. Of course, even the most successful entrepreneur had to function within the geopolitical context of his times, but the fortunes of empires were contingent on the strategies of exceptional individuals in charting their course of business.

This analysis of Houqua's enterprise intervenes in the major debates that have preoccupied economic historians. Much has been written about the Canton system as a precursor to the Opium War and the subsequent demise of China. These scholarly analyses, usually privileging political and diplomatic developments, highlight the mounting incompatibility of Western and Chinese models of interaction and the reversal of the silver flows to which the Chinese merchants supposedly succumbed.[12] The story of Houqua and the Canton trade makes it clear that the Chinese economy did not merge with the routes of international trade with the advent of the Opium War. By the time of Houqua's rise to prominence at the beginning of the nineteenth century, the merchants in Canton had already weathered half a century of geopolitical turmoil around the globe.[13] Through the work of the sophisticated Hong merchants operating under the Canton system, China became integrated into the global economy well before the arrival of the gunboats that altered the terms of transnational engagement. Houqua's ability to sustain his interactions with global players for decades in the field of commerce defies the conventional assumption of an ossified Chinese system that failed to adjust to international developments and that doomed Chinese participation in the integration of the world. By reviving this story of economic vibrancy, we return to the juncture when the commercial equilibrium fell apart with the collapse of the Canton system. The focus on this moment of historical contingency reshapes our understanding of China's critical role in the formation of a global network of trade and finance prior to the Opium War.

---

[12] *The Cambridge History of China* on this period, for example, focuses on political developments and emphasizes the system of power in which the merchants were supposedly subordinate to a "corrupt" official hierarchy. See Frederic Wakeman Jr., "The Canton Trade and the Opium War," in *The Cambridge History of China*, eds. John K. Fairbank and Kwang-Ching Liu, vol. 10, pt. 1 (Cambridge: Cambridge University Press, 1978), 163–212. Although the hierarchy in which the merchants operated under the auspices of the officials nominally underwrote the system of exchange, the trade in Canton entailed a pragmatic exercise of constant negotiations among merchants and bureaucrats over the ever-changing practices in global trade against the backdrop of the constantly shifting geopolitical landscape.

[13] In 1757 Canton became the sole legal port of call for China traders arriving from the West. This system persisted until the conclusion of the Opium War in 1842, when the era of the Treaty Ports was introduced.

A better appreciation of how the system unraveled provides a new perspective to examine China's economic divergence from the West during the subsequent period. Economic historians have debated how the West escaped stagnation whereas China lagged behind, primarily from the perspective of industrial development.[14] Some studies have linked the issue of economic growth to the role of the Chinese state, but few have constructed a comparative analysis of this early period to explore how different configurations in the alignment of the interests of the state and the business sectors led to economic divergence. In studies of the British experience, early scholarship focused on the role of finance as a facilitating device, but more recent analyses highlight finance and commerce as independent activities that contributed to economic growth independent of domestic industrial expansion.[15] This realization of the contribution of finance and commerce to the British imperial enterprise redirected scholars' attention to the social networks of bankers.[16] It was precisely in the successful redeployment of capital by "gentlemanly capitalists" to generate healthy investment returns that the financial sector earned its prominent position in the economics of the British Empire. Such a revelation of the contribution of finance and services independent of industry should have invited comparisons with the East Asian experiences. But thus far comparative analyses involving East Asia have seldom extended beyond Japan and such comparisons have been limited to assessments of the role of finance in the successful transformation of Japan into an industrial power.[17]

---

[14] See, for example, Mark Elvin, *The Pattern of the Chinese Past* (Stanford, CA: Stanford University Press, 1973); Philip C. C. Huang, *The Peasant Family and Rural Development in the Yangzi Delta, 1350–1988* (Stanford, CA: Stanford University Press, 1990); R. Bin Wong, *China Transformed: Historical Change and the Limits of European Experience* (Ithaca, NY: Cornell University Press, 1997); Kenneth Pomeranz, *The Great Divergence: China, Europe, and the Making of the Modern World Economy* (Princeton, NJ: Princeton University Press, 2000); Kent G. Deng, "A Critical Survey of Recent Research in Chinese Economic History," *Economic History Review*, new series, 53, no. 1 (February 2000): 1–28.

[15] For studies focusing on the role of finance as a facilitating device, see R. S. Sayers, *Central Banking after Bagehot* (Oxford: Clarendon Press, 1957); E. Victor Morgan, *The Theory and Practice of Central Banking, 1797–1913* (Cambridge: Cambridge University Press, 1943); C. A. E. Goodhart, *The Business of Banking, 1891–1914* (1972; rpt., Aldershot, UK: Gower, 1986). For an analysis highlighting finance as an independent contributor to economic growth, see Michael Edelstein, *Overseas Investment in the Age of High Imperialism: The United Kingdom, 1850–1914* (New York: Columbia University Press, 1982).

[16] See Youssef Cassis, *City Bankers, 1890–1914*, trans. Margaret Rocques (1984; rpt., Cambridge: Cambridge University Press, 1994), and P. J. Cain and A. G. Hopkins, *British Imperialism, 1688–2000*, 2nd ed. (1993; rpt., New York: Longman, 2002).

[17] See, for example, Kozo Yamamura, "Japan, 1868–1930: A Revised View," in *Banking and Economic Development: Some Lessons of History*, ed. Rondo Cameron (New York:

As this study extends its focus on the role of merchants in facilitating China's exchange with the outside world, it also highlights their relations with the state. Existing scholarship on this topic shows that the court in Qing China, preoccupied with its imperial expansion along its north-western frontier, adopted a continental posture that promoted property rights more actively in the landbound regions where the state had to open up territories rather than along the maritime frontier of the southeast coast.[18] Zelin and others demonstrate a clear definition of property rights in China and the state's role in enforcing these rights.[19] However, except in cases in which assurances of no state appropriations served the needs of the Qing state for land reclamations along its expanding landbound frontier,[20] the state safeguarded property rights among its subjects but not between the state and its subjects. Although the state facilitated the use of contracts in the vibrant markets along the southeastern coast, protection of private wealth from the confiscatory state remained weak.[21] The constant pressure from the state and the ill-defined financial obligations to national and local needs engendered among successful traders deep-rooted suspicion of any gains from investing alongside the state. Such misgivings deterred cooperation between the Chinese state and the wealthy merchants in redeploying capital toward economic development in a manner that would have generated financial returns to the investors and that would have remained consistent with the Qing's imperial agenda. In this respect, the experiences of Houqua and the other Hong merchants contrast sharply with those of Western financiers, such as the Rothschilds.[22] This contrast underscores the potent power of financial resources for the political expansion and economic growth of empires, power unleashed most effectively when those with financial capital can maintain a certain level of autonomy from the state. The reluctance of

Oxford University Press, 1972), 186–197. Although he does not present his test cases as Asian models of gentlemanly capitalists, Richard Grace examines the lives of William Jardine and James Matheson against Cain and Hopkin's model. See Richard Grace, *Opium and Empire: The Lives and Careers of William Jardine and James Matheson* (Montreal: McGill-Queen's University Press, 2014).

[18] Paul A. Van Dyke argues that the policies of the Qing state inhibited the geographical scope of the Hong merchants' activities. See *Merchants of Canton and Macao: Success and Failure in Eighteenth-Century Chinese Trade* (Hong Kong: Hong Kong University Press, 2016), intro.

[19] Madeleine Zelin, Jonathan K. Ocko, and Robert Gardella, eds., *Contract and Property in Early Modern China* (Stanford, CA: Stanford University Press, 2004).

[20] Anne Osborne, "Property, Taxes, and State Protection of Rights," in *Contract and Property in Early Modern China*, ed. Zelin, Ocko, and Gardella, 120–158.

[21] Hill Gates, *China's Motor: A Thousand Years of Petty Capitalism* (Ithaca, NY: Cornell University Press, 1996).

[22] Niall Ferguson, *The World's Banker: The History of the House of Rothschild* (London: Weidenfeld & Nicolson; New York: Viking, 1998).

the Hong merchants to redeploy their capital in conjunction with the Qing court's economic initiatives lends support to institutional theories of economic divergence.[23]

Houqua's story extends beyond the scope of the existing literature that has predominately highlighted economic activities within China proper. His extensive and complicated global transactions required an elaborate system of trade that defies any simplistic analysis of business organization. Not only did Houqua have to structure his business in China in the idiom of Chinese family relations,[24] but he also had to engage his international partners in Canton according to Western conventions and to extend his reach overseas by developing networks of trust.[25] This study demonstrates that a large measure of Houqua's success stemmed from his ability to maintain an intricate balance between his commercial interests and those of his Western counterparts, all during an era of transnationalism before the imposition of a Western world order.

Houqua's business dealings also shed light on the macroeconomic issue of silver flows. This analysis of the business of individual merchants enhances understanding that has hitherto been confined to macroeconomic investigations of the trade balance and Western accounts of the galleon trade.[26] Silver was not simply a form of payment; it was also a

---

[23] Douglass C. North and Barry R. Weingast, "Constitutions and Commitment: The Evolution of Institutions Governing Public Choice in Seventeenth-Century England," *Journal of Economic History* 49, no. 4 (December 1989): 803–832, and Douglass C. North, *Institutions, Institutional Change and Economic Performance* (Cambridge: Cambridge University Press, 1990).

[24] David Faure, *China and Capitalism: A History of Business Enterprise in Modern China* (Hong Kong: University of Hong Kong Press, 2006).

[25] Many scholars who have analyzed trading networks have offered cultural explanations that build on the diasporic employment of social devices as the basis for business interactions. See, for example, Avner Greif, "Contract Enforceability and Economic Institutions in Early Trade: The Maghribi Traders' Coalition," *American Economic Review* 83, no. 3 (June 1993): 525–548, and G. William Skinner, "Creolized Chinese Societies in Southeast Asia: In Honour of Jennifer Cushman," in *Sojourners and Settlers: Histories of Southeast Asia and the Chinese,* ed. Anthony Reid (St. Leonards, Australia: Allen and Unwin, 1996), 51–93. The diverse ethnic background of Houqua's trading network challenges these assertions. By examining the process through which Houqua and his partners transcended cultural barriers and established their system of credit to cope with the risks and uncertainties of long-distance trade, the current research contributes to our understanding of transnational networks.

[26] Dennis O. Flynn, Arturo Giráldez, and Richard von Glahn, eds., *Global Connections and Monetary History, 1470–1800* (Aldershot, UK: Ashgate, 2003); Akinobu Kuroda, "Concurrent but Non-integrable Currency Circuits: Complementary Relationships Among Monies in Modern China and Other Regions," *Financial History Review* 15, no. 1 (2008): 17–36; Man-Houng Lin, *China Upside Down: Currency, Society, and Ideologies, 1808–1856* (Cambridge, MA: Harvard University Press, 2006); Richard von Glahn,

trading commodity that generated tremendous profits. Houqua's business dealings show that different forms of silver provided arbitrage opportunities for transnational traders. In challenging simple assumptions of stocks and flows of silver, the analysis also extends to the credit market. Compared to simple aggregations of data at a national level, Houqua's financial dealings across time and space provide the basis for a more nuanced understanding of global economic development prior to the period when Western systems came to dictate the terms for the accounting and clearance of international trade and credit.

Outline of the Chapters

Each period of global exchange involves its own pattern of connectedness with which the participants must negotiate. The China trade focusing on early-nineteenth-century Canton is no exception. Chapter 1 explores *the structural context* that gave rise to the business opportunities and challenges in Canton during this period. The chapter investigates how the Europeans' expansion into the New World and beyond intersected with the movement of diasporic Chinese along the southeastern coast of the Qing Empire and the Southeast Asian ports. Houqua's family had moved to Canton in the previous century when, by the mandate of the Qing state, the city became the nexus where seafaring traders from the West would interact with commercially savvy Chinese entrepreneurs of the South China Sea. This study situates the relocation of Houqua's family to Canton in the context of the geopolitical situation that led to the emergence of the international port of Canton.

Entrepreneurs must establish themselves within the existing *institutional frameworks* and develop a sufficient power base before altering the rules of the game to their advantage. Chapter 2 examines the important business institutions for Sino-Western trade in early-nineteenth-century Canton and the business strategy that Houqua employed to establish a presence in the China trade to consolidate his power and, eventually, to outsmart the overpowering British merchants. The waves of international trade in Canton were accompanied by the commercial impact of the reshuffled political powers in Europe. Just as Houqua was achieving prominence in commercial circles in Canton, the French wars, in conjunction with the British Commutation Act, which discouraged

Fountain of Fortune: Money and Monetary Policy in China, 1000–1700 (Berkeley: University of California Press, 1996); William S. Atwell, "International Bullion Flows and the Chinese Economy circa 1530–1650," *Past & Present*, no. 95 (May 1982): 68–90.

smuggling from continental Europe by drastically reducing customs and excise duties on tea in Britain, disrupted China's trade with continental Europe and allowed Britain to garner the lion's share of the trade in Canton. Keenly aware of the ascendancy of Britain, Houqua moved to consolidate his share in the business of the EIC. Although trade with the EIC provided a solid bedrock for his business, Houqua still had to counteract hegemonic British interests in Canton. Houqua accomplished this feat by redefining the terms of his business. Expanding beyond his role as a supplier of Chinese goods, he maneuvered into a pivotal position by becoming a critical source of funds for the British, thereby restructuring the division of the economic gains from trade and capturing an increasing share of the profits.

Patterns of global exchange are not static, and participants in the exchange actively transform these patterns to their own benefit. Chapter 3 examines how Houqua transformed his *trading network* and charted new courses from his home base in Canton. As he explored trading with the newly arriving Americans, Houqua faced a different set of challenges in his international dealings. He confronted these challenges with a pragmatic approach to business. Houqua redirected the flow of his goods and capital and positioned his business for the emerging U.S. market. By allying with his trusted American partners, Houqua not only entered U.S. markets but also tapped into investment opportunities in the financial centers that were burgeoning along the British sinews of capitalistic exchange. At a time when Westerners were still struggling to extend beyond their foothold in Canton into the interior of China, Houqua, by directing traffic from Canton, had already managed to access many overseas markets. Such a formidable accomplishment required that Houqua surmount significant legal and linguistic hurdles and, more importantly, assess and balance his risk exposure in the expanded time and space that his business encompassed.

To fashion new patterns of exchange and to extend trading networks require that enterprising traders cultivate trust and credit with their partners. Houqua's strategy in developing mutual *trust* with his partners is the crux of the discussion in Chapter 4. Houqua's success depended on his ability to maintain an intricate business balance on a global scale. In addition to carefully positioning his capital and goods around the world, he also secured a network of trust with his international allies. He sustained this network through the continuing physical presence of his closest partners in Canton, the exchange of token gifts with associates abroad, as well as the distribution of his portraits along the sinews of his business empire. Underlying the long-standing relationship in Houqua

& Co. was the shared pursuit of profits. This impressive international network not only allowed Houqua to access many trading centers in the West but also enabled him to protect his assets for the next generations and to safeguard his capital during the ensuing politically tumultuous periods.

Managing Houqua's elaborate business design required the sagacity of a dynamic entrepreneur. Development of the business subsequent to Houqua's demise in 1843 resulted as much from the ever-shifting geopolitical landscape as from the capabilities of the family members who inherited Houqua's estate. Chapter 5 studies the *reconfiguring of the world of business* in the aftermath of the Opium War and the attempt by Houqua's son to reorganize the family enterprise, even as the various components of his elaborate design were falling apart. Compared to his father who was ever eager to capture additional profits by regulating the currents of commercial traffic, Houqua's son was more interested in shoring up the status of Canton than in partaking in a recharting of the family's business flows worldwide. This heightened interest of Houqua's family in local development highlights the centripetal forces of the Sinocentric culture, which ultimately led to the recoiling of the family from the global reach that Houqua had attained.

Withdrawal from active participation in business does not precipitate an immediate dissipation of assets. Despite his descendants' retreat from international trade, the immense capital that Houqua had amassed continued to generate profits for his descendants, albeit through investments that also served the business needs of the American partners. Chapter 6 highlights the pioneering *transnational investments* of a portion of Houqua's estate. The most important element of Houqua's legacy was his decision to entrust his American partners with long-term overseas investments, a decision that reflects the unique challenges facing a business based not on the productivity of physical assets but also on the profitable deployment of liquid assets predicated on the flow of information. Contrary to our conventional emphasis on Chinese wealth accumulation through investments in physical assets and the weakness of the Chinese capital market, Houqua's strategy forces us to rethink how his farsighted risk management program and entrepreneurial instincts enabled him to overcome the political barriers to doing business in late imperial China and to leverage the boundaries to structure his investment approach.

In addition to his investments in land and properties, the most significant assets that Houqua bequeathed to his descendants were his investments in capital markets that he had entrusted to his handpicked

American partner. Decades after Houqua's death, this partner continued to remit funds to Houqua's family due to a desire to honor his personal ties to Houqua rather than due to any institutional obligations. From the perspective of the deployment of capital, his American partner became the true inheritor of Houqua's business from which Houqua's family continued to profit. Over time, Houqua's family became merely the financial beneficiaries of his estate as his American partners leveraged Houqua's capital for investments well beyond the confines of China. Rather than viewing this subsequent period as a usurpation of Houqua's business enterprise, I regard this development as evidence of Houqua's foresight in separating management from ownership of assets to take advantage of information flows, a critical factor in the business of trade and finance. As the second half of the nineteenth century unfolded, Houqua's plan proved to be effective. The sustained success of Houqua & Co. in navigating international trade transcended national boundaries and defied the simple binaries of the West and the Rest.

This study of Houqua's business sheds light on the dynamics of global exchange configured around nineteenth-century Canton as it explores the structural context within which Houqua operated, his strategy to establish his business and to transform the institutions of trade, his efforts to expand his trade network and to cultivate trust among his partners, as well as the lasting legacy of his heir's reorganization of the family enterprise and the enduring impact of Houqua's innovative transnational investments. This pattern of interconnections, like any other pattern of global interconnections, assumed a unique configuration that involved both regional and global economies. Houqua, as well as his China trade partners, worked within this configuration and forged new ties to transform it as they negotiated the structural and institutional frameworks for their own benefit. In their search for profits, they fueled the development of linkages around the world in a manner that was distinctive to the times.

Records of the accomplishments of Houqua and his partners in driving the commercial vitality of and the global interactions in old Canton faded only because we have allowed our image of this former emporium to be clouded by China's weaknesses beginning in the mid-1800s. The subsequent period of exchange underwritten by the rules of international exchange that the Western powers imposed on operators worldwide hardly lasted a century, thus barely matching the longevity of the Canton system. Houqua's story reshapes our understanding of China's economic experience in a global context. The success of Houqua & Co. in configuring its networks in the fluid context of the early nineteenth century remains instructive for us today as the contemporary balance of political power renders the imposition of a West-centric world system increasingly problematic and requires that international traders adapt dynamically to a new world order in which China, once again, occupies center stage.

1 A Study of the Structural Context
The Colliding Worlds in Canton

The convergence of the trading parties in Canton involved various currents of geopolitical developments in China and the West. As the Europeans' maritime explorations led them to find sustainable channels of exchange in Asia, people residing in the coastal provinces of China extended their reach to the ports of Southeast Asia. The movement of people, goods, and capital along the Chinese coast and in Southeast Asia intensified with the political turmoil brought about by the Manchu conquest of 1644. Once the conflicts subsided in the mid-eighteenth century, Canton became the sole legal port of call for Western traders. Motivated by the promise of profits from global trade, enterprising Chinese traders and their Western counterparts converged in the city. The paths of these China-trade participants, however, were conditioned by divergent state agendas toward their migrant-explorers and dissimilar political imperatives toward their respective New Worlds. This was the structural context from which Houqua emerged at the beginning of the nineteenth century.

A Family on the Move

Just as the Europeans departing for the New World found new economic opportunities in the Americas, Houqua's ancestors relocated to Canton in the second half of the seventeenth century from their native Fujian to capitalize on the reconfiguring trade networks. Wu genealogies record that Houqua's great-great-grandfather, Wu Chaofeng (1613–1693), relocated to Canton during the reign of Kangxi (1661–1722), registering in the jurisdiction of Nanhai, a county in the Canton area. To mark the relocation of this branch of the Wu family, Wu Chaofeng reinterred his mother and father on the Mountain of the Flying Goose in the city of Canton. Since then, Wu Chaofeng's descendants have honored Chaofeng's father as the founding ancestor of the Cantonese branch of the Wu family and have resided in the Xiguan area of Canton along the banks of the

Pearl River.[1] It was here that one could find the foreign factories of the Canton trade, the nexus of the Sino-Western trade over which Houqua would preside during the first half of the nineteenth century.

Genealogical records of Houqua's Wu family grafted their lineage onto the ancestral records of the Wu family in Fujian.[2] Despite disagreement about the generational count,[3] latching their lineage to the Wu family in Canton and their roots to Fujian helped the Wu family that resided along the Pearl River to construct a story that situated their origins during the initial period of Chinese civilization. Their family in Canton had come from the town of Jinjiang in the province of Fujian. These ancestors in Fujian had, the Wu genealogies claim, moved from Kaifeng, the

[1] Wu Quancui, ed., *Lingnan Wushi hezu zongpu*, 1:12a; 9:45a; Wu Ziwei, ed., *Wushi ru Yue zupu* (Genealogy of the Wu Family that Moved to Canton) (1956), vol. 1.

[2] Following the genealogies of the Wu family in Jinjiang, Fujian, from which Houqua's branch in Canton sprang, the record of the Wu clans in the Lingnan region, which encompasses both Guangdong and Guangxi, claims that they descended from a certain ancestor Can, through his great-grandson, Wu Zixu, who was a renowned minister in the late Spring and Autumn Era (circa fifth century BCE) (Wu Quancui, ed., *Lingnan Wushi hezu zongpu*, 1:12a; Wu Ziwei, ed., *Wushi ru Yue zupu*, vol. 1). Can's forty-ninth–generation descendant, Shi, is said to have earned the examination degree of the "presented scholar" (*jinshi*) in 1109 and to have relocated to Putian county in Fujian in 1125 (Wu Quancui, ed., *Lingnan Wushi hezu zongpu*, 2a:25a). The father of Wu Chaofeng who relocated to Canton and initiated a branch of the family there is said to be the thirteenth-generation descendant of Shi (Wu Quancui, ed., *Lingnan Wushi hezu zongpu*, 2a:42a).

[3] The same passage in the aforementioned genealogy that counts Chaofeng's father as a thirteenth-generation descendant of Shi who flourished in the twelfth century also considers Chaofeng's father to be a fifty-second–generation descendant of the founding ancestor Can who lived during the fifth century BCE. This second claim is most likely erroneous; it is more likely that there were thirteen generations between the twelfth-century Shi and the seventeenth-century Chaofeng, not three generations (as indicated by the second claim that Chaofeng was the fifty-second generation, as opposed to Shi being the forty-ninth generation). For the most part, the record in the larger genealogical project undertaken in 1934 to account for the Wu family residing in the two southern provinces matches the details provided in the 1956 genealogy, which focuses more specifically on the branch of the Cantonese Wu family to which Houqua belonged. This 1956 genealogy is the third edition of the work that Houqua's eldest brother, Wu Bingyong (1764–1824), initiated in 1824. The second edition, compiled by Bingyong's third son, Zhaoguang (1814–1887), was printed in 1884 (Wu Jiali's 1956 preface, in Wu Ziwei, ed., *Wushi ru Yue zupu*, vol. 1). This more focused genealogical record asserts that Chaofeng's father, whom the Cantonese Wu family honors as their founding ancestor, was an eleventh-generation (instead of a thirteenth-generation) descendant of Shi (see the genealogical table, in Wu Ziwei, ed., *Wushi ru Yue zupu*, vol. 1). This unresolved dispute probably stems from the missing link in the genealogical records for the two generations after Shi, a fact that the more focused genealogy compiled in 1956 duly notes in two instances (Wu Ziwei et al., 1956 preface, and notes to the record of the second generation, in Wu Ziwei, ed., *Wushi ru Yue zupu*, vol. 1). Unable to fully trace its linkage to the illustrious ancestor Shi, the compilers infer from the record of another Wu branch in Canton their proper place in the genealogical ranking (Wu Ziwei, ed., *Wushi ru Yue zupu*, vol. 1). The discrepancy in these genealogies indicates that descendants of Houqua's branch of the family maintained their different calculations into the twentieth century.

capital city of the Northern Song dynasty (960–1127). Tracing the roots back another millennium, the narrative links the Wu family to the genesis of the Sino-centric culture through their ancestors in Wuling in the kingdom of Chu and further to the story of the mythological God of Agriculture in prehistoric times. Acknowledging the lack of evidence for the earlier period, Houqua's brother, who compiled the family genealogy in 1824, nevertheless expressed his strong conviction about their ancestry in Fujian. This genealogical project, which he undertook with the help of Houqua and another brother, represented a celebration of their heritage and a testimony to the ties between the Wu family in Canton and that in Fujian.[4]

If we follow the genealogical claim asserted in the record that was prepared by Houqua's branch, Houqua was a sixty-fifth–generation (49+11+5) descendant of Can, the founding ancestor of the entire Wu clan, who lived half a millennium before the Common Era. Calibrated to the family's relocation to Fujian in the twelfth century, Houqua was a sixteenth-generation (11+5) descendant of Shi, who had relocated to Fujian. Focusing on the Wu branch in Canton, Houqua was a fifth-generation resident in the city since the establishment of the branch in the second half of the seventeenth century, not including the generation of Chaofeng's father who was reinterred in the city (see Figure 1.1).[5] What is important is not the accuracy of this account (in fact, the earlier segment of this genealogical record is most probably fabricated, similar to other cases of genealogical compilation projects of Fujianese and Cantonese families that aimed to claim ties to the Central Plains in China and thus deep-rooted family pedigrees within the framework of a Sino-centric culture). Far more important were the sociopolitical and economic contexts that such claims revealed.

The relocation of the Wu family to Canton took place during the tumultuous period when China was extending its reach down the coast of the South China Sea toward Southeast Asia. The genealogy compiled by the Wu family in Canton does not indicate the precise timing of the relocation to Canton. Nonetheless, the reference that this relocation took place "during Kangxi's reign" (1661–1722) indicates that the Wu family was probably among those families dislocated by the coastal relocation policy of the Qing court.[6] During the opening decades of the Manchu

---

[4] Wu Bingyong's 1824 preface, in Wu Ziwei, ed., *Wushi ru Yue zupu*, vol. 1.

[5] The claim in the 1934 genealogy that Chaofeng's father was a thirteenth-century descendant of Shi is more reasonable arithmetically as it implies an average of some thirty to forty years between succeeding generations. The assertion maintained by Houqua's branch yields a calculation of almost forty-six years between two generations.

[6] Wu Quancui, ed., *Lingnan Wushi hezu zongpu*, 2a:42a.

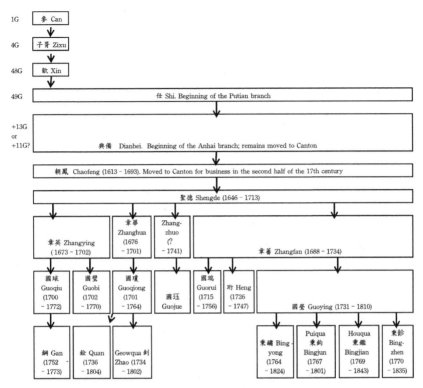

Figure 1.1. Schematic Representation of the Key Figures in the Genealogical Records of the Wu family up to Houqua's generation.

administration that entered Beijing in 1644, the grip of the court was far from certain and its territorial control was uneven. Along the south-eastern coast, the forces of Koxinga (Zheng Chenggong), who had fought as a Ming loyalist, plagued the newly established Qing court in Beijing. Determined to eradicate Zheng's forces, the Qing court escalated restrictions on maritime activities in the 1660s and eventually issued an order for a coastal evacuation to cut off supplies to Zheng's troops that had established a base in Taiwan.[7] These military expeditions and the associated economic embargo devastated the coastal area in southeastern China. Fujian, formerly a stronghold of the Zhengs, suffered tremendous losses.

---

[7] See Ralph C. Croizier, *Koxinga and Chinese Nationalism: History, Myth, and the Hero* (Cambridge, MA: East Asian Research Center, Harvard University, 1977), ch. 2.

Along with Fujian, the province of Guangdong also suffered from the displacement of residents due to the coastal evacuation order. The situation had subsided briefly when troubles in the late 1660s resumed as Canton, along with the rest of Guangdong and Fujian provinces, became embroiled in the Revolt of the Three Feudatories, lasting from 1673 to 1681. Not until the lifting of the ban on maritime activities in 1684 did the two decades of dislocation and destruction in the area come to an end. Just as the Qing court desired to redevelop economic activities in this region, people residing in the area were eager to participate in the rebuilding of business networks as commercial activities could now be revitalized in the aftermath of the warfare, both within China proper and in the ports of the South China Sea. The Wu family that resided in Jinjiang, Fujian, and lived through this period of turmoil and the relocation of a branch of the family to Canton, paralleled the process of reconstruction in the area when the Qing court lifted its evacuation order as it consolidated control during the ensuing decades.

Residents in the coastal areas, such as the Wu family, demonstrated a long-standing maritime orientation as they had to supplement the products of their agricultural labor with income from trade. Houqua's forefathers from Fujian thus decided to settle in Canton, the southernmost port of importance in the Qing Empire. Connected to Canton and their ancestral home in Fujian were, however, many coastal cities beyond the realm of the Qing Empire that had received generations of Chinese migrants, like those from Houqua's family. In fact, the migration of the Wu family from Fujian to Canton covered but a segment of the vast area that extended from the southeastern Chinese provinces of Fujian and Guangdong to the ports in China's New World in Southeast Asia.

China found its New World in Southeast Asia in the ports to which Houqua's fellow-countrymen from Fujian and Guangdong had migrated for centuries. Wang Gungwu has coined the term "merchants without empires" to describe Fujianese sojourners in Southeast Asia.[8] What makes the two Chinese provinces of Guangdong and Fujian appropriate for comparison to Britain is their shared orientation toward their respective "New Worlds" and their common commercial heritage. What distinguishes the Chinese search for a New World from the case in the West is that, unlike the separation of the Old and New Worlds by the Atlantic Ocean in the West, Chinese migrants observed no clear delineation between the sending community and the receiving community. Transcending jurisdictional boundaries of various political powers in the

[8] Wang Gungwu, "Merchants without Empires: The Hokkien Sojourning Communities," in *China and the Chinese Overseas* (Singapore: Times Academic Press, 1991), 79–101.

region, the migration patterns of the Wu family and other Chinese coastal residents reveal that they considered Canton as but one of the ports dotting the shoreline of China proper and beyond, forming a continuum of possibilities for migrants in search of opportunities that on occasion would arise precisely because of enforcement of different policies. As the state mandated that certain businesses be transacted in designated cities, these cities became possible destinations for potential Chinese migrants, where they could strategically position themselves to maximize profits for their families. Therefore, the Canton system that Houqua would come to dominate in the first half of the nineteenth century was not an exceptional case of China's trading connections with the world at large; instead, it grew out of the long-standing junk trade that extended along China's coast to various ports in Southeast Asia.

The ancestral origins in Fujian of Houqua and many of the other Hong merchants in the Canton trade underscore the process by which Chinese coastal dwellers exploited opportunities in an expanding world of commerce and capitalized on business possibilities created by political changes. For these enterprising traders, the Canton system was embedded in a system of exchange that encompassed Southeast Asia, and their presence in Canton situated them in the outlet for Chinese products to the Western world.[9]

The analogy of China's New World to its Atlantic counterpart can only extend so far, however. The Chinese experience differed considerably from that of the European "explorers" in terms of their mode of entry and the economic configuration that their New World encounters engendered. Under Manchu leadership during the Qing dynasty, China marched west to exert political control over vastly expanded territories. However, the Qing state did not sail south. Furthermore, Chinese migrants in Southeast Asia did not exert control over the productive resources of their receiving communities. Instead, this Chinese diaspora structured profitable trade on Chinese junks among fellow-migrants in the region and among their brethren in their ancestral homelands.

By the late eighteenth century, however, the junk trade among Chinese had yielded to the superiority of the Western vessels. Suffering from both direct and indirect limitations imposed by the Qing government, Chinese junks did not develop sufficient operational efficiencies to compete with the ocean-faring Western ships that had come to rule the seas with their

---

[9] Chin Keong Ng stresses the sustained vitality of merchants of Fujian ancestry in the aftermath of the congregation of Sino-Western trade at the port of Canton in 1757. See his *Trade and Society: The Amoy Network on the China Coast, 1683–1735* (Singapore: Singapore University Press, 1983).

more advanced sailing techniques and knowledge of new routes.[10] Situated in Canton at the crossroads of China and the West, Houqua and his fellow Hong merchants stood to benefit from the economic exchanges between China and the West. However, Western traders had established control over the sea routes for the delivery of tea, the bulk commodity that required express shipment to the Western markets. In Houqua's world of the early nineteenth century, the Western powers had yet to usurp the role of the Chinese in Southeast Asia. However, before their assertion of territorial dominance, Western navigators had already taken over the fast sea lanes, a reality with which Houqua had to contend from his base in Canton.

This was the conundrum that Houqua faced in Canton. He was situated at a port that afforded China a key interface with Southeast Asia. However, endogenous issues within this system encompassing both China and Southeast Asia had not allowed rice to come forth to serve as a binding element for sustainable commercial exchange and to fuel economic growth.[11] Exogenous to China's involvement in the economic system in Southeast Asia was the growth of the market for Chinese tea in the West. Other Chinese merchants in Canton, and in cities along the southeastern coast, would continue to pursue the junk trade with partners in Southeast Asian ports, but from his base in Canton, Houqua would come to specialize in the lucrative Sino-Western trade. Facing the challenge of operating when the sea routes were controlled by the West, Houqua leveraged his centrality in Canton, the nexus in the global flow of goods in and out of China.

Forming the Nexus of International Trade in Canton

For the Wu family and other enterprising Chinese migrant families, the appeal of Canton as a trading port grew as court policy, which favored

---

[10]   See Paul A. Van Dyke, "New Sea Routes to Canton in the 18th Century and the Decline of China's Control over Trade," in *Studies of Maritime History*, ed. Li Qingxin (Beijing: Shehui kexue wenxian chubanshe, 2010), 1.57–108; Paul A. Van Dyke, "Operational Efficiencies and the Decline of the Chinese Junk Trade in the Eighteenth and Nineteenth Centuries: The Connection," in *Shipping and Economic Growth 1350–1850*, ed. Richard Unger (Leiden: E. J. Brill, 2011), 223–246; and Van Dyke, *Merchants of Canton and Macao: Success and Failure in Eighteenth-Century Chinese Trade*, intro.

[11]   For a detailed analysis of rice trade, see Jennifer Wayne Cushman, *Fields from the Sea: Chinese Junk Trade with Siam during the Late Eighteenth and Early Nineteenth Centuries* (Ithaca, NY: Southeast Asia Program, Cornell University, 1993). Cushman argues that the China trade with Southeast Asia, in particular with Siam, owed its success to the Qing court's perception and justification of this trade as an extension of the domestic coastal junk trade, distinct from the tribute missions.

Canton as the port of call for foreign traders, tightened. Balancing concerns about domestic stability with the appeal of economic benefits, the Qing court restricted Western trade to the single port of Canton in 1757.[12] This move proved important to Qing finances. Revenue from customs constituted an important and reliable annual contribution both for the Emperor's purse under the institution of the Imperial Household and for state revenues collected by the bureaucratic body of the Board of Revenue. The Imperial Household and the Board of Revenue were the coffers of the imperial family and the state, respectively, and the Emperor was the master of both. Both these treasuries received annual contributions from the maritime customs in Canton.[13] The court issued customs quotas for each area, which totaled 2.26 million taels per year for the period between 1798 and 1821. Of this total, maritime customs from Canton accounted for 855,500 taels per year, or some 40 percent, making it the single largest contributor to customs collection and a material portion of the total proceeds to the imperial coffers.[14]

The strategic location in Canton allowed for tighter control over the movement of trading vessels and hence permitted more reliable surveillance and customs collection.[15] Canton is located on the banks of the Pearl River, which empties into a broad bay thirty-two miles downstream. This bay opens into the South China Sea some fifty additional miles from the entrance to the bay. In this region there are numerous small islands. Macao is located on one side of the bay. Ships approaching Canton would enter the bay at Macao. At the entrance to the bay, which points toward Canton, ships would need to clear the "mouth" of the Pearl River, a strait formed by a protrusion of land from either side a "little more than a

---

[12] For a detailed discussion of the role of the state in China's maritime expansion and the decision to restrict Western trade to Canton, see Gang Zhao, *The Qing Opening to the Ocean: Chinese Maritime Policies, 1684–1757* (Honolulu: University of Hawai'i Press, 2013).

[13] On the magnitude of this income stream to the Emperor's treasury, one scholar notes that "before the mid-nineteenth century [such income] as often as not exceeded the income of the Board of Revenue of the government." See Chang Te-Ch'ang, "The Economic Role of the Imperial Household in the Ch'ing Dynasty," *Journal of Asian Studies* 31, 2 (February 1972): 244. Other income streams flowing into the Imperial Household treasury included rents from the imperial estates, designated transfers from the Board of Revenue, income from the salt monopoly, customs from other bureaus, confiscations, and expropriations and fines, as well as profits from economic activities, such as the ginseng trade. See Preston M. Torbert, *The Ch'ing Imperial Household Department: A Study of its Organization and Principal Functions, 1662–1796* (Cambridge, MA: Council on East Asian Studies, Harvard University, 1977), ch. 4; Qi Meiqin, *Qingdai neiwufu* (Imperial Palace of the Qing Dynasty) (Beijing: Zhongguo renmin daxue chubanshe, 1998), ch. 5.

[14] Chang, "The Economic Role of the Imperial Household in the Ch'ing Dynasty," 258.

[15] Ibid.

musket-shot apart," as noted by a nineteenth-century British observer.[16] Known as Bocca Tigris ("Tiger's Mouth") to the Europeans, and Humen ("Tiger's Gate") to the Chinese, this formation afforded the Qing government a natural strategic stronghold. Foreign vessels were allowed to proceed another twenty miles upriver and to anchor at Whampoa, the "road" of Canton. These vessels were banned from proceeding farther and had to rely on boats to cover the remaining ten miles upstream to the city.[17] The narrow strait of Bocca Tigris and the officers stationed at Whampoa provided the Qing court with a reliable mechanism to regulate the traffic of foreigners, a tool it would firmly hold on to.

By the mid-1780s, the court had finally succeeded in aggregating foreign-trade traffic in Canton and in defining its collection expectations (see Figure 1.2). In 1789, customs revenue in Canton surpassed the million-tael mark, double the peak annual collection before the court orchestrated its concerted effort to derive economic benefits from Sino-Western trade. During the period, total state income was in the range of 40 million taels.[18] By the closing decades of the nineteenth century, maritime customs revenue had become an important and stable income stream for the court in Beijing.

The International Port Takes Shape

About this time, Houqua came of age and embarked on a career in international commerce from the port of Canton. This vital international port, which also served as the provincial capital, was a sprawling city. The expanding role of the city resulted in an ever-growing footprint of enclosed territories dotted by a government presence. With each phase in its expansion, the city did not metamorphose to assume a new shape. Instead of shedding its previous rings of protective city walls, the city grew into an organic formation of inner and outer walls, flanked by additions in the east and the west. A late-nineteenth-century gazetteer traces the inner wall of the city to the 1380 reconstruction efforts during the early years of the Ming dynasty. The outer wall, dating from 1563, extended from the southern side of the inner wall and ran a perimeter of 3,786 *zhang* (12,620 meters). At the top, this outer wall was 10 meters thick, and at its base, it measured over 11.5 meters thick. Eight gates punctuated the continuous

---

[16] "Some Account of the City of Canton, Part I," *Saturday Magazine* 10, no. 310 (London: John William Parker West Strand, April 1837): 162.

[17] Ibid.; Liang Tingnan et al., comps., *Yue haiguan zhi* (Gazetteer of the Maritime Customs in Canton) (rpt., Taipei: Wenhai chubanshe, 1975), 5:1a.

[18] Guoshiguan (Academia Historica), ed., *Qingshigao jiaozhu* (A Draft of the Dynastic History of the Qing, with Annotations) (Taipei, 1986–1990), 132: 3618–3619.

Figure 1.2. Maritime Customs Revenue Collected in Canton.
For issues related to year-to-year comparisons because of the inter-calary month, see Ch'en Kuo-tung, "Qingdai qianqi Yue haiguan de liyi fenpei (1684–1842): Yue haiguan jiandu de juese yu gongneng" (The Accrual of Benefits in the Maritime Customs in the Early Qing [1684–1842]: The Role of and Function of the Hoppo), *Shihuo yuekan* (Shih-Huo Monthly) 12, no. 1 (April 1982): 19–33; Zhongguo di 1 lishi dang'an guan (Number One Historical Archives of China), *Qinggong Yue Gang Ao shangmao dang'an quanji* (A Complete Collection of the Archival Documents on the Trade in Canton, Hong Kong, and Macao from the Qing Palace) (Beijing: Zhongguo shudian, 2002), 31–32; Liang Tingnan et al., comps., *Yue haiguan zhi* (Gazetteer of the Maritime Customs in Canton) (rpt., Taipei: Wenhai chubanshe, 1975), 10:7b–16b.

stretch of the outer wall: one each in the east, the west, the south, and the southeast, and four in the southwest.[19] The concentration of these city gates in the southwest pointed to the commercial heart of Canton that fueled the circulation of Chinese merchandise in the international marketplace. During his youth, Houqua witnessed how Canton became not only an indispensable contributor to the finances of the imperial

[19] Li Guangting, *Guangxu Guangzhou fu zhi* (Gazetteer of the Prefecture of Guangzhou Compiled During the Reign of Guangxu) (1879; repr., Shanghai: Shanghai shudian, 2003), 64: 1–4.

court in Beijing but also a vital engine in the flow of global commerce. In due time, Houqua would come to direct this flow of goods and capital around the world.

In the eyes of a Westerner stopping in Canton, at the turn of the nineteenth century this was an exciting cosmopolitan city located at the intersection of China and the West. In his account of the 1793 Macartney Embassy to China, George Staunton reported that "Canton, like a sea-port or a frontier town, bears many marks of the mixture of foreigners with natives." Traders from the West had established themselves in this frontier city and traders from various countries had set up shops in the designated area outside the walled city that marked the seat of the Qing government. These "handsome factories of the different nations of Europe trading to [Canton]" lined up neatly along the Pearl River, which year after year carried Western vessels in and out of the city, forming one of the end-points in their arduous journeys across the oceans. Although the Chinese Hong merchants might have only recognized each of these "factories" as the bureau of a European trading company or the office of an entrepreneurial trader from the West, Staunton saw a distinctive national identity in these factories, "each with its national flag flying over it." Yet, these clear marks of various European nations that Staunton observed did not yet seem to conflict with Chinese interests, as the foreign factories "contrast with the Chinese buildings, and are an ornament to the whole."[20] By the last decade of the eighteenth century, the Europeans had firmly established their presence in this seaport along the coastal border of Qing China, and this area where the foreign factories were located was witnessing large-scale transactions of international trade on a regular basis.

Westerners like Staunton were not allowed into the walled city. However, they often defied this prohibition. Through their visits as well as their vivid imagination, they saw the energy of commerce permeating the immense city of Canton, both inside and outside the city walls. "Canton, if we may judge by the Chinese maps, or by the suburbs, must be a city of great extent," noted an officer who traveled on board a British trading vessel to Canton in 1804. In his interminable wandering around the suburbs of Canton, he observed that a Westerner would be required by Chinese laws to turn back when coming upon a city gate. However, from the long perspective that these gates afforded the Westerner into the streets of the city proper, he noticed little difference between the scenes

---

[20] George Staunton, *An Authentic Account of an Embassy from the King of Great Britain to the Emperor of China, Including Cursory Observations Made, and Information Obtained, in Travelling Through that Ancient Empire and a Small Part of Chinese Tartary*, 2nd ed. (London: Printed for G. Nicol, Bookseller to His Majesty, 1798), 3: 366.

on either side of the gates, where one could see "the same bustle, the same kind of shops, and the same general appearance." To this British officer, the narrow streets of Canton were paved with little round stones, "like those of *North Yarmouth*." The streets in Canton were comparable in width to the rows and lanes of English towns, "*Market-row in North Yarmouth*, bearing striking similitude to the generality of the streets in this city, with respect to dimensions, the height of the houses excepted." A visitor could hardly fail to notice the vitality of this commercial city. Along these narrow alleyways, the great volume of foot traffic made it difficult to negotiate around town even during daytime.[21]

One could not see many dwelling areas from the streets in Canton because the spaces opening to the streets held precious commercial value. Buildings were often two stories high, with the lower or ground floor serving as a shop and the remainder of the building serving as storage space. In the middle of the shop was a door with a window on each side. Near one of the windows one would find a counter with some writing materials. The rest of the space was crammed with samples of whatever the store had to sell. The person sitting at the counter was always busy writing, or calculating with his abacus, "on which instrument a Chinese will perform any operation in numbers, with as much, or more celerity, than the most expert European arithmetician," observed our British reporter in 1804.[22]

In the area where the Westerners operated, foreign factories were arrayed along a considerable stretch on the banks of the Pearl River. These factories were set back about two hundred feet from the water's edge. In the eyes of the British officer, that was a row of "very elegant houses." This 1804 reporter and Staunton, who had described the scene a few years earlier, both mention the national flags hoisted from sunrise until sunset opposite the gate of each factory.[23] It was a scene of activity and prosperity with "strangers to be seen in the suburbs, . . . their ships are unloading and loading in the river." To a discerning European such as Staunton, these strangers' "various languages, dresses, and character-istic deportment, would leave it almost a doubt, if a judgment were to be formed from that part of the town, to what nation it was belonging." In Canton, each factory flaunted the national colors of its homeland and the traders revealed traits of their sending communities that Europeans would have no problem identifying. For Staunton, these foreign elements

---

[21] James Johnson, *An Account of a Voyage to India, China &c. in His Majesty's Ship Caroline, Performed in the Years 1803–4–5, Interspersed with Descriptive Sketches and Cursory Remarks by an Officer of the Caroline* (London: R. Phillips, 1806), 66–67, 69.
[22] Ibid.   [23] Ibid., 65.

did not disrupt the peace at this interface of China and the West. Rather, they formed a picture of harmony in the kaleidoscope of international commerce.[24] However, not all Western observers would agree with this judgment. The rising power of the British at the expense of their continental European rivals was palpable by the beginning of the nineteenth century and this shift in the power dynamics would soon present new challenges to Houqua and his fellow Hong merchants.

In the bustling cosmopolitan city of Canton, Houqua and his family established their home and grew their business into a formidable factor in global trade. In 1803, the family secured land on the banks of the river in the area where Houqua's father, as the elder in the family, had erected an ancestral temple for the Wu family,[25] just as his great-grandfather, Chaofeng, had constructed a new tomb for his parents. In this new ancestral temple, the deceased Cantonese Wus received incense and offerings presented to them by their descendants on a regular basis, forming in Canton an integral branch of the Wu family with a view toward a prosperous future in the city that they had adopted as their hometown a century and a half earlier.

The journey of the Wu family to Canton, in particular the later part of the journey, which is narrated with less artistic license in the genealogies, followed the legacy of opportunistic migration by the coastal people in southeastern China. Just like their fellow-countrymen who had dispersed and would continue to disperse to other Chinese cities, as well as to ports in Southeast Asia, Houqua's family moved to Canton in search of commercial opportunities. Their migratory path knew no political boundaries. In fact, they were often attracted to frontier regions where they could exploit their intermediary function to the fullest. Nevertheless, they maintained their ties to the cultural center in the north, asserting in their textual records their roots in China's central plains. Hence, the centrifugal forces that drew them for economic reasons into the pales of civilization as they knew it were balanced by the centripetal power of the Sino-centric culture. This set of countervailing forces conditioned the commercial orientation of these enterprising merchants and influenced how they positioned themselves in the global network of trade.

By ensconcing themselves in Canton, Houqua and his family situated their business at the interface of China and the West. To serve its dual needs of containment and revenue generation, the Qing court sanctioned

---

[24] Staunton, *An Authentic Account of an Embassy from the King of Great Britain to the Emperor of China*, 3: 365–366.

[25] See Houqua's 1835 inscription on the Wu ancestral temple, in Wu Ziwei, ed., *Wushi ru Yue zupu*, vol. 1.

China's trade with the West in this city at the southern tip of the empire. Official policies on the Canton trade intertwined with the unsettling military struggle in southeastern China in the seventeenth and early eighteenth centuries, disrupting the preexisting trade networks that linked the coastal cities in China to Southeast Asia and beyond. However, for Houqua's family and other resourceful merchants, this reconfiguration also offered opportunities. In the seventeenth century, the Cantonese Wu family fled from Fujian to escape political turmoil. But by the beginning of the nineteenth century, they made a deliberate decision to firmly establish the family in Canton because the city was the center of international commerce.

The clash between East and West would erupt in this city in southern China, but it would not occur for another four decades. In the meantime, the meeting of the New Worlds engendered a dynamic commercial environment where fortunes were made and lost many times over. By the beginning of the century, it was already evident that the New Worlds colliding in Canton were developing along different paths. Although commercial ties bound China and Southeast Asia, these ties did not flourish into the economic specialization of Europe and its New World in the Americas, a critical step in the enhancement of productivity. More importantly for Houqua and his fellow Hong merchants in Canton, by the mid-eighteenth century Western vessels had managed to chart new courses around the South China Sea. Although the Chinese Hong merchants held a monopoly over the supply of Chinese tea, they could only deliver the products to markets in the West through their Western trading partners. These were the business opportunities in Canton and the challenges with which Houqua had to contend.

In Canton, strangers were at the gates but they too were busy establishing a foothold in this nexus of trade. Houqua and other Chinese merchants were eager to work with them and even the court, despite its deepening resistance to foreign interactions, welcomed the economic benefits of this international exchange. Together in Canton, the international trading partners fostered a vibrant global trading network that promised to generate tremendous profits for astute participants.

By 1800, the volatile military situation in southern China had long subsided, thus providing Houqua and his fellow Chinese merchants with a stable environment to build their businesses. Half a world away, however, political upheaval in Europe and the birth of an aspiring power in America were tilting the tides and making new waves in the sea of commerce in Canton.

Lodging in an Existing Institution
Taming the Lion at Home

Houqua's emergence on the scene of the Canton trade coincided with
the beginning of British ascendancy in the world of commerce. Political upheavals in Europe transformed the trading conditions in Canton as
the increasing share of British purchases, at the expense of its continental
European rivals, allowed the British East India Company to dictate the
terms of trade with the Chinese Hong merchants. To Houqua's budding
business enterprise in the closing years of the eighteenth century, this
reshuffling of Western buyers in Canton meant opportunity. However,
the mounting power of the British also presented challenges to the profitability of Houqua's business. How did Houqua establish his business
among the existing institutions to ride the rising British wave and to prosper in the face of a difficult partner? After he gained traction with the
established British trade institutions, Houqua patiently developed and
consolidated his capital base as well as a critical mass of market share.
When the time was ripe, he dexterously changed the rules of the game.

The Rising Tide of the British Empire

Participants on both sides of the Canton trade were concerned about
any potential imbalance resulting from a concentration of power in the
hands of either buyers or sellers. The Co-Hong (or the merchants' guild),
which operated from 1760 to 1771, was often seen by foreign traders as
a strategy on the part of Chinese sellers to form a cartel arrangement to
control prices.[1] However, intervention by the Qing government, which
was eager to foster foreign trade in Canton, made it difficult to sustain

---

[1] Van Dyke argues that the purpose of the establishment of the Co-Hong was not to
serve as a monopolistic arrangement to eliminate competition and disadvantage foreign
traders. Rather, the introduction of the Co-Hong, Van Dyke shows, represented an
effort by two players to subvert a consortium of the three houses that had come to
control an increasing share of the market by the late 1750s. Qing officials allowed this
institution to continue because the arrangement promised stability and promoted a fair
and competitive environment among the Hong merchants. In 1771, the death of the key
players upset both the balance and the system, and, having served its purpose, it was

Figure 2.1. View of the Foreign Factories in Canton, circa 1805. Reverse painting on glass. Courtesy of the Peabody Essex Museum, Salem, Massachusetts.

any concentration of market share in a single Chinese merchant. As for the Western traders, competition among the various European trading companies served to diffuse any threat of excessive bargaining power. By 1800, however, the escalating British market share in tea exports had developed into a near-monopoly (for details, see later, especially Figure 2.2). As a result, the British East India Company became the dominant institution in the China trade. However, the structure of the tea sellers' network kept in check the concentrated buying power of the British EIC. Therefore, the configuration of the tea sellers in Canton had significant implications for China trade market dynamics in the nineteenth century.

This shift in market dynamics was palpable in Canton and noticeable in the attitudes of Western visitors. Westerners visiting the port of Canton in 1800 would have found it difficult to deny the economic vibrancy of the city (see Figure 2.1). Their perceptions of the source of this commercial vitality in Canton, however, were beginning to shift as the European

abolished, never again to be revived. Van Dyke, *Merchants of Canton and Macao: Politics and Strategies in Eighteenth-Century Chinese Trade*, 2–4.

political powers were reordered. The emergence of the British commercial powerhouse, backed by its military might, was keenly felt in Britain's growing share of the China trade. Britain's mounting commercial interests altered the power dynamics between China and its Western trading partners, fostering a new attitude among certain Westerners toward China.

Henry Ellis, a commissioner in the British Embassy in the early nineteenth century, was impressed by the prosperity of the port of Canton:

Canton, from the number and size of the vessels, the variety and decorations of the boats, the superior architecture of the European factories, and the general buzz and diffusion of a busy population, had, on approaching, a more imposing appearance than any Chinese city visited by the present embassy; nor do I believe that in the wealth of the inhabitants at large, the skill of the artificers, and the variety of the manufactures, it yields, with the exception of the capital, to any city in the empire.[2]

To this British observer, the vibrancy of the port of Canton, fueled largely by the seaborne traffic, was second to none in all of China, save perhaps the capital of Beijing. Nonetheless, this remarkable city, in his mind, was an exception to the general economic conditions in China. In fact, "[t]he traveler who only sees Canton will be liable to form an exaggerated opinion of the population and wealth of China." For Ellis, the phenomenal trade in Canton did not necessarily result from the sheer achievements of the Chinese.

Ellis was quick to point out the indispensability of foreign involvement in the economic activities of Canton: "The whole effect of foreign commerce is here concentrated and displayed." However, the Qing court did succeed in aggregating China's trade with the West in Canton and the impact was readily observable. The Chinese government had specified the location of this international exchange but, according to Ellis, it was the Western traders who were responsible for the prosperity of Canton. To the traffic generated by the European merchants, the residents of Canton should owe their gratitude, Ellis asserted. "The employment which the European trade affords to all classes of the inhabitants diffuses an air of general prosperity, not to be expected where this powerful stimulus does not operate."[3] Ellis maintained that the residents in Canton were indebted to international commerce for their prosperity. Moreover, they should be grateful not to the European trade in general, but to the trading

---

[2] Sir Henry Ellis, *Journal of the Proceedings of the Late Embassy to China, Comprising a Correct Narrative of the Public Transactions of the Embassy, of the Voyage to and from China, and of the Journey from the Mouth of the Pei-ho to the Return to Canton*, 2nd ed. (London: John Murray, 1818), 1: 174–175.

[3] Ibid.

volume generated by his fellow British merchants, whose ascendancy in global commerce was palpable even at the beginning of the nineteenth century.

In these early years when Houqua was just beginning to build his trading empire, it was already noticeable among the changing cast of Western merchants arriving at this center of global trade that the powers in the West were shifting. In 1804, a British officer depicting the scene in Canton noted that with only the one exception of the French, the national colors flying in front of the factories in Canton represented the European maritime powers. Among these powers, "the English factory, or rather series of warehouses, exceeds all the others both in elegance and extent." To the proud British trader, the grand British factory was but a manifestation that in Canton, "this great and remote commercial city, the mart of European trade seems to be fixed at the British factory." Such representation behooved him to describe at length the expanse of the compound of the British factory, which extended "nearly down to the water's edge," comprising an "elegant verandah" "raised on handsome pillars, flagged with square marble slabs." Such was the evidence not only of British wealth but also of its ostentatious display. The site of this British factory was fittingly imposing as it commanded "an extensive view of the river, east and west, the Dutch and French Follies, the suburbs, the southern bank of the Tigris, and a considerable scope of the country in that direction." From this verandah and the panoramic view it commanded, the officers of the British East India Company could retreat to the long room where they could enjoy their king's supper at the Company's table and also could plot their commercial exchanges with the Hong merchants in Canton.[4]

Upheavals in continental Europe proved to be highly disruptive to the aggregate volume of tea trade. These disruptions can be readily discerned in the saw-toothed shape of the graph of overall tea exports in Figure 2.2. The early period shows that the British Commutation Act of 1784, which reduced the tax on tea from over 100 percent to 12.5 percent, not only removed the incentive for smuggling tea from continental Europe into Britain but also stimulated a general increase in tea consumption. Continental European representation persisted throughout much of the 1780s until the general upward trend in the trade volume was interrupted by the several freefalls following the political upheavals in Europe. The unsettling impact of the French Revolution is evident in the sharp drop in 1790 and, from then on, the market share of the continental European shippers dwindled to negligible levels as political turmoil mounted back

---

[4] Johnson, *An Account of a Voyage to India, China &c.*, 65.

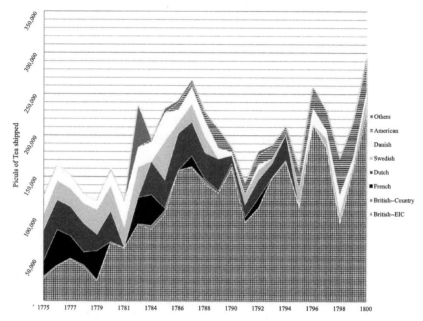

Figure 2.2. Market Size and Market Shares of Tea Exports from China, 1775–1800 (data are missing for 1782). *Source:* Hosea Ballou Morse, *The Chronicles of the East India Company, Trading to China, 1635–1834* (Oxford: Clarendon Press, 1926–1929), *passim*. My analysis of Louis Dermigny, *La Chine et l'Occident: Le commerce à Canton au 18e siècle, 1719–1833* (Paris: S.E.V.P.E.N., 1964) reveals similar trends.

home. While the political episodes in Europe eliminated many continental trading powers and reconfigured order on the continent, the currents of global trade carried to the port of Canton the effects of these changes in Europe, bringing to the Chinese Hong merchants a new structure of the relative importance of tea among European buyers in Canton.

In the last quarter of the eighteenth century, the volume of the British East India Company's tea purchases in Canton registered a fivefold increase, from 26,918 piculs in 1775 to 148,250 piculs in 1793, or from 3.6 million pounds to 19.8 million pounds.[5] During the same period, total tea exports from Canton also increased, but only by some 50 percent. In other words, the tremendous growth of the British East India Company's business, fueled partly by an increase in British demand for tea, resulted also from its market-share gains, at the expense of those of

---

[5] 1 picul equals 100 catties, which equals 133 1/3 pounds.

the French, the Dutch, the Danes, and the Swedes. In 1775, the British East India Company only accounted for 21.5 percent of total tea exports from Canton, behind the Dutch, which handled 29.5 percent of the trade, and not substantially ahead of the Danes (at 17.0 percent). But by 1793 the British East India Company had expanded to lead the market with an overwhelming 78.8 percent share of total tea exports from Canton, as the Dutch share dwindled to a mere 9.1 percent and that of the Danes was negligible.[6] The balance during the last decade in the eighteenth century would witness the continued dominance of the British East India Company as it held on to a steady 70 to 80 percent of tea exports from Canton, while the continental trading companies struggled to maintain a foothold in the market. Political turmoil in Europe had wrecked havoc to the trading system of continental Europe and had provided the conditions for British ascendancy in international trade, as evidenced by the escalating market share of the British in the volume of trade in Canton.[7]

The British East India Company Flexes Its Muscles

By 1808 Qing officials had already noted the dominance of British representation among European vessels calling in Canton.[8] Their observation proved astute. Shortly thereafter, the British attempted to occupy Portugal-governed Macao after Napoleon took Portugal. This crisis was averted when the Portuguese court relocated to Brazil and remained a British ally.

The enduring impact of British ascendancy was most evident in the power dynamics between the British EIC and the Chinese Hong merchants in what amounted to a barter trade. The EIC had long searched for a commodity to appeal to the Chinese market, but to no avail. For the lack of a better option, it continued to send to Canton woolens, a commodity that the Chinese Hong merchants would not have taken had the deal not been bundled with the Company's promise to buy tea from them. Thereafter, the British EIC, together with Pan Zhencheng, known in the West as Puankhequa, whose financial stability and ability to handle Chinese officials made him the most trusted merchant of the Company at

[6] Hosea Ballou Morse, *The Chronicles of the East India Company, Trading to China, 1635–1834* (Oxford: Clarendon Press, 1926–1929), 1: 11, 2: 205.
[7] For a discussion on the impact of the French Wars on European trade, see Fichter, *So Great a Proffit*, ch. 3.
[8] Zhongguo di 1 lishi dang'an guan (Number One Historical Archives of China), *Qinggong Yue Gang Ao shangmao dang'an quanji* (A Complete Collection of the Archival Documents on Trade in Canton, Hong Kong, and Macao from the Qing Palace) (Beijing: Zhongguo shudian, 2002), 7: 3715.

the end of the eighteenth century,[9] formalized a system of exchange that linked the allocation of the EIC's tea purchases to purchases of woolen products by each Chinese Hong merchant. This practice of tying import purchases to export sales, called "truck," became increasingly embedded in the Canton trade by the 1770s with the end of the Co-Hong.[10]

The British Company had long paid for its tea purchases partly with the woolens it exported to China. As the Company experienced a period of difficulty in generating liquidity to fund tea purchases in 1785, its managers in Canton worked out a solution with Puankhequa, whereby the woolens would be divided in proportion to the Company's indebtedness to each merchant. Two years later, Puankhequa engineered an agreement among the Hong merchants, tying their respective woolen intake to the amount of tea each merchant was to deliver to the EIC.[11]

The agreement to take woolen products from the EIC usually entailed a financial loss, but, more often than not, the loss was offset by profits from the Chinese merchants' sales of the tea that they procured from Fujian, one province up the coast from Guangdong (for more on the calculation of profitability, see later). Keenly aware of this economic quid pro quo, Puankhequa served as the middleman between the EIC and the Chinese Hong merchants and formalized the arrangement whereby the British Company would contract a designated proportion of its annual tea purchases according to the share of British woolens that each Hong merchant agreed to buy from the Company.

It should come as no surprise that the allotment of the coming season's tea contract was the means by which the Company calibrated its relations with the various merchants. After all, tea accounted for the preponderance of the Company's business with the Chinese merchants. Among the Company's exports from Canton during the 1792–1793 season, tea accounted for 86 percent of the total invoice cost. In comparison, nankeen cloth and raw silk only accounted for 11 percent of the total.[12]

---

[9] Morse, *The Chronicles of the East India Company*, 2:45, 3:38. For a detailed account of Puankhequa's business, see Van Dyke, *Merchants of Canton and Macao: Success and Failure in Eighteenth-Century Chinese Trade*, ch. 3.

[10] Other European trading companies adopted similar policies. I thank Paul Van Dyke for alerting me to the timing of the adoption of such practices.

[11] EIC R/10/21.

[12] Earl H. Pritchard and Patrick J.N. Tuck, *The Crucial Years of Early Anglo-Chinese Relations, 1750–1800* (Pullman, WA, 1936; rpt., London: Routledge, 2000), 396. Morse's data reveal a similar pattern: in 1792, black tea accounted for three-quarters of the total export value of 4.6 million taels, and green tea accounted for another 14 percent. Nankeen cloth and raw silk accounted for 11 percent of the total, whereas chinaware, rhubarb, cassia, and sugar did not account for any appreciable significance in the value of goods shipped out of Canton. The situation was similar among traders from other countries exporting from Canton. In the aggregate, the non-English traders, comprised

The importance of tea to the Company is even more apparent from the broader perspective of the overall operations of the British East India Company. By the turn of the nineteenth century, tea sales represented one-half of company-wide sales. During the period from March 1, 1800 to March 1, 1801, the Company recorded total sales of Company goods in the amount of £7.6 million, of which tea accounted for £3.5 million, or 46 percent. Sales of silks and nankeen cloth represented only 6 percent of the total, with the majority of the remainder consisting of sales of piece goods from Bengal and Surat. This situation was similar in the following year when tea accounted for 51 percent of total sales of Company goods, piece goods from Bengal and Surat accounted for 28 percent, and silks and nankeen cloth accounted for 9 percent.[13] But these overwhelming shares of tea sales did not fully reflect the profit contributions of tea to the operations of the Company. The end market for tea provided a receptive customer base that exhibited a consistently high demand for the commodity year after year, thereby generating healthy margins for the Company from its sales of tea.

Compared to Chinese tea, other products did not enjoy a similar reception. The woolens that the Hong merchants received from the Company at best could only generate modest margins for the Hong merchants, who would consider themselves lucky to be able to dispose of the imports without incurring heavy losses. In 1792, the Hong merchants complained that the swelling volume of imported British woolens had flooded the market and they were unable to dispose of the shipments. The Hong merchants then requested reductions in the standard prices for the woolens and advances from the British to alleviate their losses.[14] In 1794 the market for woolens worsened due to the flooding of the Yellow River. The Company had to renegotiate import prices with the Hong merchants so that they would share equally in the prospective losses from the woolens.[15] These products did not provide healthy returns to the trade partners, who were forced to accept these imports from the British who held a near-monopoly in the purchase of Chinese tea. For the Hong merchants, any losses from the woolens represented the cost of doing business with the EIC, akin to a licensing fee.

As a result, even though economic exchanges between the British East India Company and the Hong merchants entailed payments in the Chinese currency of silver taels, this exchange was far from a free flow of

of French, Swedish, Danish, Dutch, American, Genoan, and Tuscan traders, sent from Canton goods valued at close to 2 million taels, of which tea accounted for two-thirds. Morse, *The Chronicles of the East India Company*, 2:203–204.

[13] EIC IOR/l/F/5/1–53, Paper No. 64 of 1801, Paper No. 126 of 1801–1802.

[14] Morse, *The Chronicles of the East India Company*, 2:198.   [15] Ibid., 2:257.

goods lubricated by the use of a standard unit of account. In fact, it remained a system of barter, the terms of which the British managed to dictate to the Hong merchants because of their growing dominance as the main exporter of Chinese tea. The power of the British under this "truck" system was all the more palpable with the end of the Co-Hong and the waning influence of the continental European trading companies. The centrality of the allotments of the imported woolens and the associated quantities of tea to be contracted underscored the barter nature of this trade. In fact, the Hong merchants would discuss prices with the Company only after the two groups had settled on the percentage of the British business that each Hong merchant would take on during the following season.

The British East India Company made this its explicit policy, as plainly stated to the court in its final report of 1792: "Agreeably to our Plan of proportioning the Woollens to the Tea Contract 1/16 share of the former will be entitled to 540 chests of Bohea and about 6,000 chests of Congo." The Company divided its trade for that year into sixteen shares of its volume of imports and exports, with some merchants receiving multiple shares, whereas others each received a share of one-sixteenth (or 6.25 percent) of the Company's business for the year.[16] As the Select Committee stated repeatedly, with the exception of a special varietal which represented but a minor portion of the Company's tea purchases, the Company's tea contracts with the Hong merchants were "exactly regulated . . . by the division of our woollens [allotted]."[17]

By the Company's own admission, this system of barter persisted until at least 1820. Rejoicing over the pending arrival of specie from Bengal, the Company noted on May 20, 1820 that the sum that their Canton office was to receive would enable it to settle many of its liabilities "without bringing into calculation the Long Ells which remain[ed] unsold" and that it was "no longer under the anxiety of considering those Long Ells as forming a part of [the Company's] financial resources and therefore [were] relieved from the obnoxious measure of bartering" for tea.[18] The lack of liquid financial assets to pay for the purchases in Canton was a chronic problem for the EIC. The Company had to rely on a suboptimal solution that entailed the forced exchange of woolen goods for tea, causing much anxiety not only for the Hong merchants who had to

---

[16] In 1793, the Company allocated four-sixteenths, or 25 percent, of the total business to Puankhequa and Shy Kinqua; two-sixteenths, or 12.5 percent, to Geowqua, Mowqua, and Munqua; and one-sixteenth, or 6.25 percent, to Puiqua and Yanqua. See EIC G/12/103, 241; G/12/105, 6–7; G/12/110, 20–25; Morse, *The Chronicles of the East India Company*, 2:198.
[17] EIC G/12/122, 62.   [18] EIC G/12/220, 24.

accept an import not sufficiently welcomed in Chinese markets but also for the EIC officers in Canton who knew full well that the market could not digest the annual shipments forced into China.

Yet as long as the Chinese market (or more specifically, the Hong merchants) could tolerate the woolen imports, albeit at depressed prices, this bartering arrangement provided the trading partners with the advantage that each side could plan ahead for the following season according to the specified quantities and together these partners could establish a system of repeated exchange recalibrated on an annual basis. So precise was the Company's calculation in this system of bartering that at times the prescribed allotments posed practical challenges. In the report of 1792, the Company observed that although a one-sixteenth share of its business entitled each Hong merchant to supply 540 chests of Bohea, such allotments did not correspond to the usual packing arrangements. As a compromise, the EIC had to modify the arrangements so that a share of one-sixteenth would supply six hundred chests, whereas two shares would supply one thousand chests.[19]

Houqua's Family Enters the Stage

Genealogical documents do not provide much information about the origins of Houqua's immense business enterprise, but they do describe the many imperial honors his family received for his financial contributions to the imperial treasuries. In the section on merchants in the 1934 genealogy of the extended Wu clan in Guangdong, Houqua's name is listed first. A sixth-generation resident in Canton (including an ancestor who had been reinterred in the city) and the third of four sons of Guoying, Houqua served as the sole director of the Yihe Company (怡和行), "the nexus of all trade" between China and the West, with "tens of millions in turnover." According to this biography of Houqua, the Wu family was the richest in the Canton region and often contributed to the financial needs of the state. The family supplied 260,000 taels in 1841 for state military needs and donated an American ship worth over 18,000 taels.[20] For that Houqua received the honorary title of Provincial Administration Commissioner (buzhengshisi 布政使司). Similar honors

---

[19] Morse, *The Chronicles of the East India Company*, 2:198.

[20] Toward the end of the eighteenth century, a manual laborer could earn 200 *wen* per day, or some 70 taels per year. For basic subsistence, food expenditures cost some 13 taels per head per year (fish and vegetables, but no meat). I base my calculations on information compiled by Kishimoto Mio, *Shindai Chūgoku no bukka to keizai hendō* (Fluctuations in Prices and Economic Conditions in China During the Qing Dynasty) (Tōkyō: Kenbun Shuppan, 1997), 161.

were also bestowed on many of his seven sons.[21] Another Wu genealogy adds that Houqua began to accumulate such honorary titles by 1804.[22] Not unlike other Chinese genealogies, the Wu family documents tout the social distinction of its members. The documents make reference to business accomplishments largely in the context of how Houqua and his sons translated financial success into social capital within the cultural framework of official titles. For details on their business dealings, we need to examine the records of their trading partners.

The Western names of these Hong merchants differed from their names in the Chinese records because the Western versions did not include their surnames. Therefore, Houqua, who adopted the Chinese name of 伍浩官 (Wu Haoguan), came to be known among Westerners as Houqua, a rendition that included only the two characters of his Chinese given name and excluded his surname.[23] The Wu family is featured prominently in the records of the European trading companies operating in Canton, especially those of the British East India Company. However, Houqua does not figure in the arrangements of the woolen/tea exchange until 1792, even though he had already casually traded with the EIC for several years. In fact, even in 1792 his family's business was operating under the name of his brother, Puiqua, who had just obtained a formal license to be a Hong merchant.

As researchers have attempted to identify the roots of Houqua's family business, some have erroneously attributed the origins of Houqua's business to another Hong merchant (as these Chinese merchants dealing in Sino-Western trade were called) who traded under a similar name.[24] This earlier merchant called Howqua had no family relation with Houqua and the rise of Houqua owed nothing to this earlier Howqua. However, Geowqua, a Wu cousin of Houqua, did indeed predate Houqua

[21]   Wu Quancui, ed., *Lingnan Wushi hezu zongpu*, 4b.6a–7a.
[22]   Wu Ziwei, ed., *Wushi ru Yue zupu*, vol. "3rd branch."
[23]   Westerners refer to most of these Hong merchants with the suffix "qua," which corresponds to the Chinese reference to each individual merchant with *guan* as a suffix attached to the surname and the personal name of the merchant. Although *guan* also carries the meaning of "an official," the use of its transliterated form of *qua* does not connote any reference to an official capacity, but only conforms to the use of the Chinese character as a salutation, similar to the use of Mister or Esquire in English. See G. Lanning and S. Couling, *The History of Shanghai* (Shanghai: Shanghai Municipal Council, Kelly and Walsh, 1921; repr., London: School of Oriental and African Studies, n.d.), 132.
[24]   See, for example, Morse, *The Chronicles of the East India Company*, 3:35; Michael Greenberg, *British Trade and the Opening of China, 1800–42* (1951; rpt., Cambridge [UK]: University Press, 1969), 51; Louis Dermigny, *La Chine et l'Occident: Le commerce à Canton au 18e siècle, 1719–1833* (Paris: S.E.V.P.E.N., 1964), 2:914n6. Ch'en Kuo-tung was the first to note this erroneous attribution; see Ch'en, *The Insolvency of the Chinese Hong Merchants*, 279–283.

in his participation in the Canton trade.[25] As the following discussion will make clear, except for this cousin who failed in his business, the records reveal no evidence of earlier participation by Houqua's family in the trade. Instead, what would become Houqua's vast network of global trade began with Houqua's partnership with his brother Puiqua.[26]

[25] Ch'en Kuo-tung identifies Geowqua as the uncle of Puiqua and Houqua because the middle character of Geowqua's Chinese name was Guo, the character used in the formal appellation of members of the Wu family one generation ahead of Puiqua and Houqua (Ch'en, *The Insolvency of the Chinese Hong Merchants*, 154, 217, 312). However, my work on the genealogies indicates that the records rendered Geowqua's Chinese name either as Guozhao or simply as Zhao, suggesting perhaps that the optional middle character was an honor conferred on him as the only son of his father and the only grandson of his grandfather. In fact, the Wu genealogies clearly state that Geowqua was a second cousin to Puiqua and Houqua (i.e., they had the same great-grandparents, but not the same grandparents).

[26] The British East India Company traded with a certain Howqua (spelled with a "w" and not a "u") in the 1770s and 1780s. References to the company's business connections with this Howqua stretched from 1772 to 1792 when his business operations finally ended (EIC R/10/9; R/10/34; G/12/58–59, 62, 64–66, 70, 72–73, 76–89, 102). The EIC had stated that this Howqua served as the clerk or the purser for Puankhequa, another successful Hong merchant who accumulated a fortune in the decades leading up to the rise of Wu Bingjian, the later Houqua (EIC G/12/72, 76). There is indeed a record of this Howqua having arrived at the British factory in Canton to deliver a message from Puankhequa to the EIC (EIC G/12/72). The formal registration of this Howqua as a Hong merchant did not take place until 1783 and not until after some initial resistance on his part. In 1782, five new merchants received licenses (their "Chops"), but this Howqua was not one of them. The Governor General in charge of Guangdong and Guangxi was determined to put this Howqua in a position of responsibility, but he absconded, as observed by the EIC in June 1782. However, he could not escape for long and after six months of opposition, he was finally made a salt merchant. In 1783, he was released from his duties in the salt trade and became a Hong merchant (EIC G/12/76–7; Morse, *The Chronicles of the East India Company*, 2:82, 89). The economic fortunes afforded to Howqua by this office did not last. By 1788, he was encountering financial troubles and was reported to have fallen in arrears in his payment of duties to the Hoppo (EIC R/10/21; Morse, *The Chronicles of the East India Company*, 2:153).

That this Howqua was not related to Wu Bingjian, the later Houqua, is evident in the manner in which the EIC recorded the Qing state's conferral of official status on this Howqua in 1784, two years after the Wu-surnamed Geowqua received his license and became a Hong merchant. The EIC observed that Geowqua, who it claimed to have served as the purser of another Hong merchant Yngshaw, was a welcomed addition to the line-up of Hong merchants because of the esteem in which the Europeans and his fellow-countrymen held him and the solid credit he had developed for his business. As for the Howqua who finally succumbed to the Governor General's demand that he acquire an official license, the EIC thought that his joining the other Hong merchants would prove useful to the Company (EIC G/12/76–77). Despite the EIC's interest in discovering the background of the new Hong merchants, nowhere do the EIC records mention any relationship between Geowqua and this Howqua, a strong indication of the lack of any family connection between the two. And, as the Wu family records clearly indicate that Geowqua was related to the later Houqua, Wu Bingjian (see Figure 1.1), it can be confidently established that Houqua was not related to this earlier Howqua.

A comparison of the Chinese court records with the EIC documents provides further reassurance of the lack of any connection between Houqua and the earlier Howqua. A

Belying the erroneous attribution of Houqua's roots in an earlier business establishment is a desperate desire on the part of scholars to explain the sudden emergence of this Hong merchant who would quickly orchestrate a reconfiguration of global commerce and assume a pivotal position in the flow of goods and capital around the world. So then, how and when did Houqua arrive on the scene of the international trade centered in Canton?

Houqua did indeed begin his trade with the EIC early. By 1788, at the tender age of 19, he had started trading with the EIC and made it into the Company's records, which spelled his name as "Hooqua." He was already selling to the EIC various descriptions of teas – Congo, Congo Campoi, and Singlo.[27] Records of Houqua's business dealings with the EIC (registered as "Hooqua" throughout this period) populate the documents of the EIC from 1788 to 1792.[28] The paper trail of this promising young merchant under the early rendition of his name ended in 1793, however, when his second eldest brother, known to the European merchants as Puiqua, was named a Hong merchant.

Despite the genealogical seniority of Puiqua, his emergence on the scene of international trade as recorded by the British EIC was preceded by that of his younger brother, Houqua, the third son in this branch of the family and Puiqua's junior by two years.[29] The disappearance of

1786 memorial to the throne in which Emperor Qianlong issued his vermillion rescript lists nine Hong merchants who correspond to those listed in the records of the EIC (FHA 04–01–01–0418–038 QL51/3/20 [April 18, 1786]; EIC G/12/82 [entry for September 6, 1786]). As there was only one Hong merchant with the surname Wu listed in the Chinese court document and this merchant's Chinese name matches that of Geowqua in the genealogical records, one can be certain that no other relatives of Houqua served as a licensed Hong merchant at the time, discrediting any claims that Houqua inherited the seat of his father (thought to be the earlier Howqua) in the Hong business. Based on evidence gathered from multiple Wu genealogies as well as from Qing court documents and Western business records, my interpretation of the early days of the Wu family in the Canton trade differs from that of Eberhard, who relies solely on the 1934 Wu genealogy (Wu Quancui, ed., *Lingnan Wushi hezu zongpu*). See Eberhard, *Social Mobility in Traditional China*, 83–84.

I have opted not to delineate the different generational leaders of the Wu clan with Roman numerals (Houqua/Howqua I, II, III, etc.) because that was not the practice among the early China traders. Note that my account of the Wu family business in the eighteenth century differs from that of earlier works, particularly with regard to the founding of the Yihe firm and the involvement of Houqua's father. See, for example, Basu, "Asian Merchants and Western Trade," 356–358.

[27] EIC G/12/87. Records of Houqua's tea sales to the EIC were entered into the EIC records side by side those of Howqua, sometimes with an entry for each on the same page (EIC G/12/87 [February 14 and 15, 1788]), clearly indicating that they represented distinct accounts in the Company records. However, the EIC makes no mention of any relationship between them.

[28] EIC G/12/89, 94, 97–102.

[29] Wu Quancui, ed., *Lingnan Wushi hezu zongpu*, 2a:44a.

Houqua's name (or Hooqua as the EIC had called him) once Puiqua became a licensed trader with the EIC indicates that Houqua folded his operations under the rubric of his brother's business. The two brothers in this branch of the Wu family would maintain their foreign-trade operations as a collective endeavor. Before the brothers formed their own company, Puiqua had operated in the business of Geowqua.[30] Thus, in the closing decade of the eighteenth century, three members of the Wu family were actively involved in the China trade. From the perspective of the British East India Company, there were two business enterprises, one formed by an alliance between the brothers, Puiqua and Houqua, and the other represented by their cousin, Geowqua. This view of the EIC, which considered the two Wu teams to be distinct and separate, parallels the records of the Qing administration. In April 1792, local officials in Canton listed Geowqua and Puiqua separately in a memorial to the throne. Geowqua, whose name was recorded as Wu Guozhao 伍國釗 in official documents, ranked sixth out of a group of ten Hong merchants, whereas Puiqua, recorded as Wu Zhongcheng 伍忠誠 in court documents, ranked last on the list.[31] These official records of the British EIC and the Qing government suggest that there were two Wu business enterprises, even though it was common knowledge that the two were operated by Wu family relatives.

The British East India Company seemed not to have paid attention to the sudden appearance of this second eldest brother as his trading business had begun under the name Puiqua. It was not until a September 21, 1792, report by the EIC observed that a new Hong merchant had begun to stand surety for the Company's ships, thereby providing his guarantee over the business of the ships and the conduct of their crewmen while in Canton in exchange for a more important role in the ships' trading activities. In that year, several new Hong merchants were created. As the EIC had little knowledge about many of them, but understood that there were dubious characters among the newly admitted members, the Company proceeded cautiously in allowing these new merchants to provide securities for its ships. On the new Hong merchant Puiqua, the

---

[30] I thank Paul Van Dyke for alerting me to the early business relations between Geowqua and Puiqua. Based on his detailed examination of continental European sources, in addition to British records, Van Dyke provides an in-depth analysis of the trading accounts of these two Wu kinsmen of Houqua (Van Dyke, *Merchants of Canton and Macao: Success and Failure in Eighteenth-Century Chinese Trade*, ch. 5).

[31] Zhongguo di 1 lishi dang'an guan, *Qinggong Yue Gang Ao shangmao dang'an quanji*, 6:3126; Zhongguo di 1 lishi dang'an guan (Number One Historical Archives of China), *Qinggong Guangzhou shisanhang dang'an jingxuan* (Featured Archives on Thirteen Merchants in Guangzhou during the Qing) (Guangzhou: Guangdong jingji chubanshe, 2002), 158.

EIC report noted that he was "supposed to have some capital but hitherto we know little of him, except occasionally purchasing a few Chops of Tea." As the Company assessed its options of partners among the Hong merchants, the traders believed that "Puiqua . . . might safely be trusted with a ship but exclusive of his not being any desirous of it."[32]

Puiqua proved that the Select Committee's apprehension about his interest was unfounded. In fact, Puiqua was very desirous of increasing his business with the EIC, even in exchange for taking on more of woolens. In 1792, the EIC purchased from Puiqua 3,396 chests of Congo at 26 to 28 taels per picul.[33] Then, on February 9, 1793, as the Company was interviewing Hong merchants to negotiate contracts for the coming season, it received Puiqua after many established merchants had already paraded in front of the Company's Select Committee. This potential new partner expressed his willingness "to take any proportion of the business" the Company desired to send his way. In response, the Company informed him that it had allocated him one-sixteenth of a share of the woolens the Company expected to receive in Canton in the coming season. His acceptance of the woolens from the EIC admitted him into the quid pro quo with the EIC. In exchange for his agreement to accept this portion of the Company's imports, the Company was ready to contract with him for 600 chests of Bohea and 6,000 chests of Congo, nearly double the business he handled for them in the previous year.

Puiqua was not content with this doubling of the business volume that the EIC had allotted him. He "begged [that the Company] would permit him to add 4,000 chests more of Congo & 1,000 chests of Hyson," even if he had to take an additional quantity of woolens. As Puiqua was one of the later merchants to appear before the Company, he was told that the Company had already distributed all of the woolens and that it was too late to make any changes. But in appreciation of Puiqua's eagerness to work with the Company, the British traders assured him that the Company would consider him the next year. "[I]n reward for his willingness we agreed to allow him the 4,000 additional chests of Congo & 1,000 chests of Hyson," the report notes.[34] This additional allocation was no trifling increment to Puiqua's business. For Congo alone, from his original allocation of 5 percent of the East India Company's business, this additional allotment propelled him into a meaningful representation of some 10 percent of the Company's purchase of this single largest varietal of tea in 1793.[35]

---

[32] EIC G/12/103, 39.   [33] EIC G/12/103, 191.   [34] EIC G/12/103, 238–241.
[35] Assuming 74 to 78 pounds of tea per chest (Morse, *The Chronicles of the East India Company*, 1:185), Puiqua's total allocation was 740,000 to 780,000 pounds of Congo,

The eagerness of Houqua's brother to establish himself with the British
East India Company paid off. His readiness to work under the terms dictated by the Company and his enthusiasm to take on additional business
by receiving more than his allotted portion of the Company's imports
nearly doubled his share of business with the Company. This additional
allocation made him a significant contender in the Company's annual
procurement process, all without the expense of having to assume responsibility for selling more woolens on behalf of the Company. In the following years, Puiqua continued to maintain this aggressive posture as
he built his business with the EIC, at times assuring his dedication to
the EIC by providing quality tea that he claimed he was selling to the
Company at a loss.[36]

Puiqua's expanding role in the tea business of the British East India
Company could not have come at a more opportune time, as the British
trading concern was then experiencing a rapid increase in market share
at the expense of its rivals in continental Europe. As the rise of the
British East India Company became evident, Houqua's brother threw in
his lot with the leading contender from among the European purchasers
by agreeing to play the game according to the rules dictated by the
British. Selling British woolens was not a money-making proposition
for the Hong merchant, but the contract for tea he could earn from
the exchange guaranteed an escalating share of the British tea business,
which would be more than sufficient to compensate for the trouble of
having to dispense with the imported British woolens.

Losses over the woolens plagued the Chinese Hong merchants who
vied for a bigger portion of the British business.[37] Geowqua, the cousin
of Houqua and Puiqua, was a victim of this temptation to overextend.[38]
In February 1798, when the British learned of the financial difficulties of Geowqua, who was "almost constantly beset by the Persees and
Moormen," Puiqua quickly distanced himself from Geowqua, assuring
the Company that the interests of the Company were his first priority.
Expressing "every reason to be satisfied with Puiqua," the Company

out of the EIC's requirement of 8,600,000 pounds of Congo for that season (Morse,
The Chronicles of the East India Company, 2:257). This calculation is an approximation
as the exact size of the chests differed.

[36] EIC G/12/105.

[37] The closing decade of the eighteenth century saw varying fortunes and a changing cast
of characters. The former share leader, Shy Kinqua, encountered financial difficulties
due largely to his aggressive purchase of EIC woolens, and he lost his 35 percent of
the Company's tea contracts. A similar fate befell Munqua (Morse, *The Chronicles of the
East India Company*, 2:261–264).

[38] For a more detailed account of Geowqua's business with various European partners
and his eventual demise, see Van Dyke, *Merchants of Canton and Macao: Success and
Failure in Eighteenth-Century Chinese Trade*, ch. 5.

"did not hesitate to give him an explicit promise" of support. The Company did not object to Puiqua taking over the contracted portion that Geowqua had been unable to deliver, but only on the condition that Puiqua be responsible for Geowqua's liabilities. Puiqua negotiated a 20 percent abatement on Geowqua's debt to the Europeans and Moormen, totaling two hundred thousand dollars. For his part in this rescue plan to restore stability to the trade, Puiqua requested an advance from the British East India Company for relief "from the embarrassment his unfortunate connection & relationship with Geowqua exposed him to" and for assurance that he could depend on "the protection & favor of the English House as to that alone he could look for retrieving his present losses."[39]

The British offered support to Puiqua who thus averted the embarrassment that his financially troubled relative had brought upon him, turning it into an opportunity to further expand his partnership with the British. In 1798, Puiqua received a three-seventeenth (18 percent) allocation of the Company's business, second only to that of Puankhequa.[40] This allocation represented a threefold increase in Puiqua's portion of the Company's business over a five-year period. In 1799, the British East India Company again reassured Puiqua of his elevated position and awarded him 19 percent of the Company's contract. Accordingly, Puiqua's allocation of woolens and camlets also increased during the period, from 1/16 to 3/17, or from 6.25 percent to 17.6 percent, an eleven-percentage-point increase.[41]

Houqua Comes to the Fore

The increased allocation was a huge coup for the Yihe Company, the business concern headed by Puiqua.[42] Yihe was the Chinese name of the concern through which Puiqua and Houqua transacted their business. It was a family business in which specific branches of the Wu family could claim ownership shares. In this regard, the naming of the firm and the ownership configuration followed prevailing Chinese practices. From the standpoint of the EIC, the British company was transacting business with a merchant called Puiqua. As such, the officers of the EIC evaluated their business opportunities and risks associated with these transactions based on their assessment of Puiqua. The EIC regarded its business associate neither in the form of a family firm configured in the Chinese manner nor

---

[39] EIC G/12/119, 96–97, 120–121, 126–127.   [40] EIC G/12/122, 62.

[41] EIC G/12/103, 241; G/12/121, 62; G/12/122, 6.

[42] The earliest reference to the use of this name, Yihe, is found in Dutch records dated JQ1/2/6 or March 14, 1796. I am grateful to Paul Van Dyke for this reference.

as a chartered company licensed in the European fashion. This was the fluid yet ambiguous situation in early-nineteenth-century Canton when business entities were pragmatic in their search for profit opportunities and were not dogmatic in their definitions of corporate forms. Such loose arrangements required that the partners improvise strategies to ensure business continuity in the event of succession, as in the case of the demise of Puiqua and the succession by Houqua.[43]

Puiqua fell ill in 1800 and his brother Houqua, who had been operating behind the scenes in Puiqua's business, stepped forward to deal directly with the Western traders.[44] During this period, Houqua attended EIC meetings on Puiqua's behalf as the third of the three leading merchants of 1801, behind Puankhequa (now under the operation of Pan Zhencheng's son, Pan Youdu) and Mouqua. EIC records of these meetings explicitly spell his name and capacity as "Hooqua, Puiqua's brother,"[45] in keeping with the earlier spelling in EIC records of Houqua's name, confirming Houqua's business dealings with the EIC at an earlier stage than those of his brother Puiqua.[46]

In 1801, during the months leading up to Puiqua's death, Houqua was kept busy running the business: he made nine deliveries of Congo tea to the EIC, three of Bohea, two each of Souchon and Congo Campoi, and one each of Singlo, Twankay, and Hyson skins. In addition to these tea sales, he reimbursed the EIC for the subpar "Rubbish tea" that was returned to Canton. In addition to tea, he also made two deliveries to the EIC of nankeen cloth, an item for which Houqua was developing a niche market. As for purchases from the EIC, Houqua took deliveries of the contracted woolen products of broad cloth, long ells, camlets, and embossed cloth, as well as cotton, sandalwood, and lead.[47] All these transactions were completed under Puiqua's account, thus not only ensuring the continuity of the business concern but also preserving Puiqua's hard-earned shares in the EIC business.

In this emerging environment of international exchange, the succession of the family business did not simply follow the established rules of any given geographical area. Rather, it involved tricky negotiations across cultures and tactful maneuvers to ensure the continuity of its economic interests. Houqua had to safeguard the business that he and Puiqua

[43] I will elaborate on the implications of this fluid understanding of business configurations in a discussion of Houqua's succession plan and the lawsuit between Jardine Matheson and Houqua's family in Chapter 5.
[44] EIC G/12/128–133; for a specific reference to Puiqua's illness, see EIC G/12/131, 141.
[45] EIC G/12/133, 26, 33.
[46] The use of this spelling confirms Houqua's business dealings with the EIC concurrent with that of the earlier Howqua, with whom there was no family connection.
[47] EIC G/12/135.

had built. From the perspective of the EIC, the business relationship had been established under Puiqua's name. For the sake of commercial stability and continuity in its communications with the Company's court in London, the EIC desired no disruption and preferred to maintain the status quo. Thus, in its handling of such cases, the EIC continued to use the name of the deceased in the recording of the transactions, even after the successor was firmly in place.[48] In terms of the choice of successor between the partner's son and the partner's brother, the Company handled retirements and deaths in Canton on an ad-hoc basis. It would take several more years before the Company, under the direction of the court in London, began to articulate a policy on family succession based on precedent.[49] In this fluid frontier of international trade, neither Chinese family customs nor British corporate governance figured into the calculations of the EIC officers based in Canton.

To ensure that the Company registered reliable, stable profits from its operations in Canton, the officers on the ground did not care whether the son, the brother, or the brother-in-law of the deceased or the retired trader assumed the responsibilities, as long as the successor seemed creditworthy and capable of delivering the contracted quantities of goods. Houqua's ongoing involvement in his partnership with Puiqua helped to assure a seamless transition for their EIC partners and was instrumental to the Wu family's perpetuation of commercial dealings with the Company. That the Company insisted on calling him by his brother's name in its business dealings was a small price for Houqua to pay to preserve the family's interest in this network of international exchange.

Puiqua did not live to personally reap the benefits of his work with the EIC. On July 23, 1801, he succumbed to illness at the young age of thirty-four.[50] Houqua sent a note to the British merchants, in Chinese, informing them of the demise of Puiqua: "My second oldest brother, Puiqua, passed away on the thirteenth day of the sixth moon." Three days later, news of Puiqua's death reached the EIC factory, which had relocated to Macao for the off-season. Expressing no astonishment or concern about any impact on their business relations, the Company noted that Puiqua's family had prepared for this event, which apparently was anticipated by

---

[48] In 1790, Shy Kinqua died and was succeeded by his son Gonqua. But the EIC continued to record transactions under the name of Shy Kinqua (Morse, *The Chronicles of the East India Company*, 2:181). With another death in 1796, the EIC lost its partner Munqua. Initially, the Company allocated Munqua's share to his brother Seequa, but it then expressed concern about the surviving brother's credit (EIC G/12/113).

[49] EIC R/10/38.

[50] For a more detailed account of Puiqua's business with various European partners, see Van Dyke, *Merchants of Canton and Macao: Success and Failure in Eighteenth-Century Chinese Trade*, ch. 5.

all who knew Puiqua. Once the paper work and fee payment had been processed with the Qing authorities, Houqua would assume leadership of the firm, and the EIC assured its London headquarters. As Houqua had conducted the business "during a great part of the last season" and "from his regularity and talent," the EIC harbored "no doubt of his maintaining the credit of the House."[51]

Business between Houqua and the EIC continued without a hitch as the EIC continued to trade with Houqua and allotted him the shares that had been promised to Puiqua.[52] So smooth was the transition in the minds of the EIC officers that their records readily referred to Houqua as Puiqua, as evidenced in a report, dated December 3, 1801, in which they record the meeting with the top three Hong merchants, "Puankhequa, Mowqua, Hooqua (now called Puiqua)."[53] This ranking of the top three Hong merchants also matches the ranking presented to the throne by the Governor General of Guangdong and Guangxi in March 1801.[54] EIC's ease in the transition to Houqua, as well as the uneventful handover in the eyes of the Qing officials, stemmed not only from its dealings with Houqua during Puiqua's illness but also from its understanding that Houqua was the businessman behind Puiqua's concern long before Puiqua's death. "[I]t is well known that Hoequa [Houqua spelled yet another way], even during the lifetime of his brother, had the principal management of the concern of the house," observed the EIC as it commended Houqua in its report on the attentive service of his firm and noted that the officers "perceive[d] no just cause for withdrawing their confidence from [Houqua] on the present season."[55] The EIC records suggest that instead of Puiqua having taken Houqua under his wings when the elder brother obtained his license as a Hong merchant, Houqua had provided Puiqua with his business acumen that he had evinced during his earlier business and he remained the mastermind behind the business operating under the umbrella of Puiqua's name.

As he held on to the share of the EIC business that his firm had earned under Puiqua, Houqua further consolidated his relationship with the EIC. His efforts are most evident in his extending the Company's dependence on him in terms of nankeen cloth, his niche product. The EIC had been eager to build up its shares in the nankeen market, in which American buyers had already developed a formidable presence. Even before Puiqua's death, the Company had inquired into the possibility of sourcing nankeen cloth from Puiqua. Because the EIC was less

[51] EIC G/12/134, 108–109.   [52] EIC G/12/136, 9.   [53] EIC G/12/136, 105.
[54] Zhongguo di 1 lishi dang'an guan, *Qinggong Yue Gang Ao shangmao dang'an quanji*, 6:3519.
[55] EIC G/12/138, 124.

entrenched in this market, it was more willing to negotiate the prices in order to secure the desired quantity.[56] When the Company began to take shipments from Puiqua, Puiqua was already ill but Houqua had proved to be capable of stepping in for his ailing brother. He was effective in assuring the EIC, which was still learning about nankeen products, that the Company's concerns about the quality of the delivered products were unfounded and that his products met their specifications. To assuage the Company's anxieties, Houqua readily provided the EIC with indemnities against any defects.[57]

Not only did Houqua's sale of nankeen cloth consolidate his relationship with the EIC, it also provided him with a more aggressive platform than that of his brother to showcase his posture toward the EIC. After Puiqua's death, Houqua expanded his supply of nankeen cloth to the EIC, demanding from the EIC an upward revision in the prices due to the increased American demand for the product. He also required that the EIC give more advance notice lest he should fail to procure nankeen cloth in sufficient quantities for the Company.[58] When pressed in 1803 to renew his deliveries of nankeen cloth on the terms of the previous season, Houqua refused, revealing a determination to walk away from the business if the Company insisted on the last season's terms. This move by Houqua early on in his career of dealing with the EIC revealed a marked departure from his brother's acquiescence toward the EIC, as evidenced by Puiqua's persistent requests for unprofitable woolen allocations in exchange for a larger share of tea.

During the next several years, Houqua managed to keep the EIC dependent on him for these products. Houqua resisted the Company's demand to reject pieces it found to be deficient in either color or texture, stating that the selection "at the pleasure of the Committee... was never customary when similar purchases were made at Canton." For this additional quality assurance, the Company would have to pay extra. The Company relented. "Having no materials on which we can ground a calculation of the comparative value of the Company's nankeen, and that carried home in private trade, we are at a loss to decide," the Company admitted. Houqua had successfully led the EIC to explore a profitable business opportunity in which the Company had to rely on Houqua's expertise because of its lack of experience. Thus, the Company concluded, "under every circumstance and the difficulties we have to encounter we cannot but consider that by acceding to [Houqua's] proposal, greater benefit will be derived than by trusting to casual purchases

---

[56] EIC G/12/116, 249.   [57] EIC G/12/131, 235–237.
[58] EIC G/12/133, 172, 183; G/12/138, 123.

in the market." During the following years, Houqua continued to handle the Company's nankeen purchases, "very much to the satisfaction
of the Committee." By 1804, because the EIC's "supply of [this] article . . . had been so long entrusted to his management," Houqua successfully required repeated price increases and even prepayments in full.[59]
By involving the Company in markets different from those in which the
EIC customarily traded, Houqua prevailed in tilting the playing field
and seizing from the EIC power to dictate the terms of the trade. In his
handling of this niche commodity, we can already see Houqua's efforts
to present to the British not only his ability to supply them with choice
merchandise but also an alternative outlet of an American market for his
goods.

Thus, at the age of thirty-two, at the time of Puiqua's death in 1801,
Houqua reemerged from under his brother's business umbrella to strike
out on his own. He began to chart his own course in global business,
which over the next forty-two years he would weave into an intricate
network by situating himself in the nexus in Canton. Such an illustrious business record began humbly in 1801 when Houqua reassured the
British that his Hong would continue to conduct its various business
matters in the same manner that it had under his brother Puiqua. This
marked the beginning of the career of the signatory of Puiqua's death
notice to the British Company, "Wu Houqua of the Yihe Company."[60]

Configuring the Market to Deal with an
Overpowering Buyer

Foreign traders had been wary of any coordination among the Hong
merchants that would have reduced their competition, thereby controlling the supplies of tea and inflating the prices. The Qing government,
eager to maintain the Canton trade for its customs revenue, shared the
foreigners' concern. Therefore, after the abolition of the Co-Hong in
1771, there was no such formal guild organization of Hong merchants.[61]
Judging from the strategy with which Houqua and his fellow leading
Hong merchants handled the EIC, the EIC was confronted with what
was in essence an oligopolistic configuration of Hong merchants. The
EIC attempted to diversify its vendor base, but this was in vain due to

[59] EIC G/12/142, 215–217; G/12/145, 230–231.
[60] Xu Dishan, *Dazhongji: Yapian zhanzheng qian Zhong Ying jiaoshe shiliao* (*Dazhongji:* Sino-
British Historical Representations Before the Opium War) (1928; rpt., Hong Kong:
Longmen shudian, 1969), 171–172.
[61] Van Dyke, *Merchants of Canton and Macao: Politics and Strategies in Eighteenth-Century
Chinese Trade*, intro. and ch. 3.

a lack of merchants with sufficient capital and experience. The delicate maneuvering on the part of Houqua and his Hong merchant brethren in engineering their oligopoly kept in check the growing power of the EIC, in whose hands the purchase of Chinese tea came to be concentrated.

During the first decade of the nineteenth century, the ranks of the Hong merchants continued to swell as the British East India Company worked to diversify its base of suppliers and to nurture relations with new Hong merchants, just as it did with Puiqua in the 1790s. Houqua was content to steadily hold on to Puiqua's allotment of the Company's tea contracts and his share in the EIC business fluctuated little, hovering in the high teens, the same level as that at the time of Puiqua's death in 1801.[62] Houqua carried on the brothers' business with the British East India Company seamlessly, with the EIC continuing to record the business under the name "Puiqua" and paying no attention to Houqua's own trading name, with which he had signed the letter he had sent to the Company notifying it of Puiqua's death. Ranking among the top vendors for the EIC, Houqua enjoyed his sizable portion of the EIC's business without assuming the responsibility of the Senior Hong Merchant, who had to handle the administrative, financial, and diplomatic aspects of the EIC business. With this arrangement, Houqua remained content playing second fiddle to Puankhequa and the growing Mouqua.

Although dissatisfied with any concentration of power in any single Hong merchant, the EIC had to rely on the Senior Hong Merchant to serve as its interface in official dealings with the Qing state and as the coordinator in its interactions with the Hong merchants. Even though the Senior Hong Merchant (also referred to as the First Merchant) wielded much power in his capacity as the main interface between the Hong merchants and the EIC as well as with Chinese officials, he also had to answer to both the Westerners and the local officials whenever conflicts arose, be they as inconsequential as a minor skirmish or as serious as a diplomatic breakdown. Recognizing that such burdens were onerous, the EIC granted additional business to the Senior Hong Merchant in exchange for his service. Compared to Mouqua and Houqua, Senior Hong Merchant Puankhequa enjoyed but one additional share of the Company's business, which translated into some 5 percent of the Company's total business in Canton during this period,[63] a rather small compensation for the task of being the chief interface between the British and the Chinese

---

[62] The Hong merchants Exchin and Manhop joined the group in the middle of the decade. Poonequa and Lyqua were added in 1807 and Tinqua was added in 1808.

[63] EIC G/12/156, 252.

officials, especially during times of conflicts. As the additional business did not always promise sufficient profits to keep the Senior Hong Merchant in his post, the Hong merchants often made this an avenue to impress upon the EIC the indispensability of leading vendors with solid credentials.

Pan Youdu, the second-generation head of the house of Puankhequa, had long expressed to the British East India Company his intention to retire due to his ill health and the increasing demands of his position as Senior Hong Merchant. He had insisted that his intention be officially communicated to the Court of Directors of the East India Company, but the Select Committee remained dismissive of his retirement plan, considering it "almost impracticable for him to succeed in it" because the Committee thought it "by no means probable" that the Chinese officials would allow Puankhequa to retire.[64] For a Hong merchant, especially the Senior Hong Merchant, to retire from the trade, it was necessary not only to give notification to the EIC but also to secure permission from the Hoppo, the Qing customs official, and an application for such permission entailed the payment of a substantial sum. However, in 1807 Puankhequa re-presented his intention, articulating his determination to retire by citing "family considerations."

Puankhequa claimed that his obligation to the Company and the demands of the business had rendered him incapable of fulfilling his filial duties of providing a proper burial for his parents in their native Fujian, a duty he felt could no longer be delayed. He feared that in the event of his death, this and various other family arrangements to which he had not had the leisure to attend would cause innumerable difficulties for his children. Although the EIC had no rights to keep any merchant from exiting the business, in his capacity as the biggest trading partner with the EIC, Puankhequa's exit would greatly upset the balance in the allocation of the EIC's business. Out of courtesy rather than obligation, Puankhequa requested that the Company allow him to retire in order to "pass his latter days in tranquility," at the same time expressing his family's gratitude to the Company, in the service of which both he and his father had been employed for over fifty years.[65]

Only several years earlier, the EIC had had to handle the 1804 retirement of Yanqua on account of his declining health. Similar to the strategy it applied to Puankhequa's request, the EIC had delayed Yanqua's

---

[64] EIC G/12/153, 21–22. The community of foreign traders in Canton believed that Puankhequa paid "a large sum – (said to be $500,000) for the privilege of retiring from all commercial concerns" (PEM Tilden Box 1, Folder 1, 233, 1816).

[65] EIC G/12/156, 165–166.

retirement for a trading season.[66] Such discussions with the EIC about the retirement of Hong merchants were often protracted, but would conclude once the Chinese merchant secured the permission of the Qing authorities, undoubtedly after payment of a large sum of money. In Puankhequa's case, the Select Committee noted that it could not but accede to the Hong merchant's request as it "could not consider they had any right positively to object to his acting in the manner he appeared to think so necessary to the welfare of himself and family."[67]

It is noteworthy that the Pan family of Puankhequa, just like the Wu family of Houqua, had moved from Fujian to Canton to participate in the China trade. The Wu family had considered it necessary to reinter its ancestors in order to firmly establish the family in Canton as it began its engagement in trade. When the Pan family was ready to retreat from the business, it employed the strategy of reversing the process, claiming stronger ties to the native place from which the family had relocated more than half a century earlier. Perhaps as sojourners themselves in Canton, members of the Select Committee could empathize with Puankhequa and registered in its records no suspicion of any peculiarity, cultural or otherwise, of this claim by Puankhequa as he ultimately exited from the business.

In fact, although both the Pan family and the Wu family claimed to have hailed from Fujian, ongoing ties among their ancestral brethren in the tea-growing province of Fujian and their business location in Canton were tenuous at best for both families. Contrary to the impression that residents in the adopted home would maintain ties to the family in the ancestral homeland, the claims of ties as an excuse for business entries and exits may well have been fictive, as in the case of the Pan family of Puankhequa and the Wu family of Houqua. Both the Pan family and the Wu family had hailed from coastal Fujian before the establishment of a branch in Canton. However, there is not a single trace in the ancestral temple of the Wu family in Anhai, Fujian, of enduring linkages between the family in Canton and the family in Anhai.[68] A telling sign of the lack of a sustained business connection is an 1818 stone inscription found in the

---

[66] Van Dyke, *Merchants of Canton and Macao: Politics and Strategies in Eighteenth-Century Chinese Trade*, 195–196.

[67] EIC G/12/156, 165–166. Puankhequa's retirement and his return to Fujian are also registered in the records of the Qing government (NPM 11095 JQ13/I5/26).

[68] Even as early as the first compilation of the Wu genealogy by Houqua's eldest brother in 1824, the compilers had difficulties tracing their genealogical roots and had to resort to linking their lineage to another Wu family in Canton (Wu Ziwei, ed., *Wushi ru Yue zupu*, vol. 1). The extant Wu genealogies and local gazetteers from their ancestral town of Jinjiang in Fujian do not suggest any Wu family prominence prior to the establishment of the branch in Canton.

Pan ancestral temple in Baijiao. This stone inscription commemorated an isolated financial contribution from Puankhequa's branch in Canton of merely sixteen hundred dollars, a not-so-significant amount given the size of the tea trade. On the stone inscription was written a regulation precisely governing management of this amount. Such fanfare and celebration accompanying a single contribution implied the isolated nature of the event and the lack of any serious ongoing business dealings among the Pan branches in the 1810s. The absence of any hint of links between Houqua's branch in Canton and the family in Anhai indicates a business model in which the migrants did not necessarily continue ties with relatives in the ancestral town. The Pan family and the Wu family certainly had business dealings in Fujian, from where they sourced their tea for the China trade, but they did not necessarily rely on kinsmen in their ancestral homes for procurement. Nonetheless, explanations pertaining to ties to ancestral roots resonated among the sojourning merchants in this community of global traders. Geographic mobility was a prerequisite for participation in global trade as the various states imposed restrictions on the locations where the merchants could interact.[69]

The issue of Puankhequa's imminent retirement was complicated by Mouqua's rumbling about a similar intention. In April 1807, Mouqua promised the Company that he would stay on for another season for he thought it improper to execute "in the hasty manner he proposed to relinquish his extensive concerns with the Company."[70] Regardless of Mouqua's reasons, the Select Committee took delight in his desire to remain, for the simultaneous retirement of two merchants, who had "in the most satisfactory and creditable manner transacted so large a portion" of the Company's business, would be a "serious inconvenience" to the Company. Mouqua was adamant, however, that the postponement of

---

[69] Although his ties to his ancestral home might not have been as strong as he would have liked the EIC to believe, Puankhequa's explanation for his retirement plan rested on a cultural feeling that nonetheless resonated with the EIC officers in Canton. Cultural expressions of ties to different places provided the means by which merchant families could justify their entry and exit from their businesses. The Pan family of Puankhequa had proven to be adroit in articulating its business repositioning in cultural terms. It remained to be seen how the British East India Company and the Wu family of Houqua would be repositioned in the evolving world of international commerce.

[70] Instead of the "impropriety of his conduct," Mouqua noted apologetically to the Select Committee that his decision to postpone his retirement for a year stemmed from his financial troubles arising out of the *Neptune* affair, a skirmish between sailors on a British ship and local Chinese that resulted in the death of one Chinese. Mouqua was believed to have made financial "contributions" to the local officials to settle the case, thus requiring that he remain in the trade (Morse, *The Chronicles of the East India Company*, 3:40–49).

his retirement plan was only temporary due to his advanced age and his reluctance to continue to be exposed to serious liabilities.

Houqua declared to the Select Committee that he was incapable of undertaking "the labourious and responsible situation of first merchant [Senior Merchant]" due to his "delicate health."[71] Poor health was often an excuse to retire and escape the continuing responsibilities, but Houqua employed the same reasoning to evade assuming responsibility in the first place. Houqua's slight frame, as depicted in his many portraits, would not lead one to question his claim of "delicate health," but he could well have also been economically motivated in his reluctance to take on the leading position of Senior Hong Merchant.

Together with Mouqua, Houqua requested that the Select Committee restore Puankhequa's share of the Company's business taken from him in December 1806 as an enticement to retain Puankhequa.[72] Puankhequa was insistent, however, stating that he would not "under any circumstances forgo his resolution of retiring from business with a view to the adjustment to his family concerns" and he declined to renew his contracts with the Company for the following season, formally or otherwise.[73] The Company could not but proceed without Puankhequa. Considering it fortunate that Mouqua had to postpone his retirement, the Select Committee appointed Mouqua to succeed Puankhequa as Senior Merchant, thus entitling him to an increased share in the Company's business "to the extent enjoyed by his predecessor, as a compensation for the additional labour and anxiety to which he will be unavoidably exposed by that office."[74] Judging from the anxiety among the EIC officers to install a solid partner in the leadership position, Houqua and his leading Hong brethren had clearly impressed upon the EIC their indispensability.

The Select Committee was concerned about Mouqua's advanced age and the impossibility of counting on him beyond the immediate future. Although the Committee dismissed Houqua as a possible successor because of his "indifferent health" and his "unwillingness to take the lead in [the Company's] affairs with the [Chinese] Government . . . in former occasions," it retained Houqua as its key partner second only to Mouqua while also nurturing new partners from among the rising commercial talents in Canton. Accordingly, the Select Committee awarded an additional share to one merchant and recognized four new Hong entrants by adding them to its list of partners.[75] In this manner, Houqua

---

71 EIC G/12/156, 252.   72 Ibid.   73 EIC G/12/157, 44.   74 Ibid.
75 Chunqua received an additional share (one seventeenth, or 6 percent) of the Company's business. Exchin, Manhop, Poonequa, and Lyqua also joined the Company's list of partners (EIC G/12/157, 44–45).

and Mouqua once again reconstituted the oligopoly, despite the exit of Puankhequa from their partnership.

Before any of these newly admitted merchants were ready, however, the succession issue again emerged in 1809. When Mouqua once again requested retirement, the EIC informed Houqua that "it would shortly be necessary for him to take upon himself the duties of Senior Merchant." Houqua reiterated his long-expressed fears of his "inability to discharge the troublesome duties" of the office and he threatened to retire along with Mouqua. The concerns of the EIC at this juncture were telling: the Company's fear of two principal merchants quitting at the same time stemmed from its fears over the structural integrity of the entire trade. The EIC was less concerned about the sourcing of the tea, which the EIC thought could be "obtained without difficulty." Its greater fear lay in the sale of their imports of woolens and other products which "would then be in the hands of men whose circumstances will not permit their keeping them however unfavorable the markets may be at the moment." The leading merchants had to provide financing and warehousing for the EIC's imports into China, even though the sale of the woolens and other British imports was far more difficult and unprofitable than the sale of Chinese tea in Western markets. At stake for the EIC at this juncture was not only its ability to set the rules of the game but also the liquidity and stability of the overall structure of its trade in Canton. Houqua and Mouqua had once again demonstrated that they were crucial to the overall structure of Sino-Western exchanges.

Figure 2.3 illustrates EIC's strategy to create a stable but diversified vendor base. As the figure shows, throughout this period the EIC allocated its shares primarily to a handful of vendors, including Puankhequa, Mouqua, Puiqua/Houqua, Chunqua, and, for a while, Conseequa. Even among these main vendors, only Puiqua/Houqua persistently worked with the EIC from the turn of the century to the conclusion of the EIC's business in Canton in 1834. Some had failed during this period, whereas others had intermittently retired from the trade. At any time, however, at least three of these vendors worked with the EIC, accounting for a large share of the Company's business. In addition to these key partners, the EIC also allocated shares to a group that I have aggregated in my calculation as "Others." During certain years, these partners could account for a substantial share of the EIC's business, reflecting the Company's intention to diversify away from the key vendors. Equally noteworthy, however, is that this category included twenty such Chinese merchants during the period under analysis, even though in any given year only one to eight of them received any share of the Company's business. In other words, the drop-out rate was high and there were many cases of

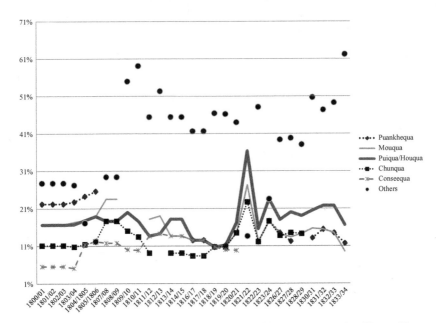

Figure 2.3. The EIC's Allocation of Shares among the Hong Merchants, 1800–1833.
Note that the involvement of Mouqua lingered and that of the house of Puankhequa reemerged, albeit on a reduced scale. Puankhequa was compelled by the Qing government to return from retirement; it is ironic that the motive of the Qing state to secure a larger group of qualified traders coincided with the interests of the EIC and conflicted with the interests of the Chinese merchants. Sources: EIC G/12; R/10; Hosea Ballou Morse, *The Chronicles of the East India Company, Trading to China, 1635–1834* (Oxford: Clarendon Press, 1926–1929), *passim*.

failed vendors. Nonetheless, the EIC insisted on cultivating new Hong merchants.

The EIC had devised this system to ensure the stability of its business in Canton and to avoid an overconcentration of power in any of its vendors. The allotted shares, communicated to the merchants at the conclusion of the previous season, allowed them to procure for the Company the appropriate amount of tea and to prepare for the British imports of woolens and other merchandise that would arrive in Canton in the coming season. This system allowed the EIC to take comfort in the predictability of the export and import markets, the rules of which it had come to dictate. The merchants would supply the exact quantity of tea in the varietals prescribed, making it necessary for the EIC only to adjust for market deviations during the season. The system also assured the Company of a reliable outlet for its imports to China, which the Company coerced its trading partners to accept.

Despite the EIC's insistence on diversifying its vendor base, the critical role played by Houqua and his fellow leading merchants was clear. Insolvency was a recurring problem plaguing the new entrants that the EIC had nurtured. The unreliability of the new entrants can be seen from the broken record of the category "Others." The cautious officers of the EIC had attempted to cultivate new relations with Chinese merchants so as to avoid what it deemed to be an excessive concentration of business in the hands of the leading merchants. However, in the end, it had to rely on certain select vendors, and Houqua proved to be the only partner who worked with the EIC year in and year out in all of its thirty-four years of operations in Canton.

After both Puankhequa and Mouqua had served in the capacity of Senior Hong Merchant, Houqua finally had to take his turn in heading the oligopoly. By the end of the first decade of the century, the EIC put Houqua's name first among the merchants, in exchange for which Houqua ended up with an extra share of the Company's business. During this period, this extra share could generate an annual profit of some thirty thousand dollars.[76] Despite this 2 percent increase in the Company's business, Houqua managed to pull in Chunqua to share his responsibilities, and the EIC called the pair "really efficient merchants." Even Mouqua was recruited to continue his assistance to the EIC officers, who continued to be waited upon by "[t]he senior merchants Mowqua, Puiqua [Houqua] & Chunqua" in December 1810.[77] Mouqua still served as the intermediary between the merchants and the EIC and Houqua avoided official engagements in 1811 due to the death of his mother.[78] In this manner, Houqua managed to reconstitute an oligopolistic team of merchants, consisting primarily of Mouqua and himself, and during the earlier period also Chunqua, to service the EIC without assuming all the responsibilities that total leadership would have entailed.

By 1812, the EIC could sense the threat of this concentration of power among the Chinese merchants. As reported in the Secret Consultation of the EIC, "there are but two merchants at present of established credit[,] . . . Mowqua & Puiqua . . . it is therefore extremely desirable that some of the other Hong's should be sufficiently established to admit

---

[76] Ch'en, *The Insolvency of the Chinese Hong Merchants*, 48.

[77] EIC G/12/171, 26; G/12/174, 184.

[78] EIC R/10/26, 24. The EIC's record of the death of Houqua's mother matches the entry in the Wu genealogy. According to Wu Ziwei, ed., *Wushi ru Yue zupu*, vol. 1, Houqua's mother died on March 21, 1811.

of their taking a share in the general trade. Otherwise the effects of a
monopoly in the hands of the two Senior Merchants may be severely
felt." As the survivor among the European trading monopolies, the EIC
knew all too well how a concentration of trading power could allow the
dominant player to flex its muscles. Nonetheless, the Company simply could not groom sufficient trading partners who were competent to
check the powerful duo of Mouqua and Houqua. Whereas the Company believed that Mouqua was "little inclined to take advantage of his
situation," it was "not altogether so confident of the views" of Houqua.

The delicate balance of these conflicting interests hinged upon
Mouqua, who shielded Houqua from some responsibilities as the Senior
Hong Merchant and in whom the EIC placed more trust. Mouqua's
advanced age was a source of concern for the EIC, and these fears were
confirmed with his death in 1813. "The liberal manner in which he
had long conducted a large proportion of the foreign trade at Canton will cause his loss to be severely felt," the Company lamented.
His death forced the family business to devolve to his three sons who,
according to the EIC's assessment, were "young, inexperienced and
unacquainted with Europeans."[79] Mouqua's death thus crystallized the
inevitable ascension of Houqua as the primary partner of the EIC in Canton, upon whom "the situation of head Hong Merchant [had] fallen."[80]

The timing of Houqua's assumption of the position of head Hong merchant in the EIC's books matches the record of his ascension in the documents of the Qing administration. In a memorial to the throne dated January 3, 1814, the Governor General of Guangdong and Guangxi and the
Hoppo listed Houqua's name at the top of the list of Hong merchants.[81]
The Qing court summoned Puankhequa back to service as a Hong merchant in 1814 and requested that he serve alongside Houqua.[82] The Qing
court shared with the EIC the objective of maintaining several financially
sound merchants in the upper echelons of the Hong merchants. However,
Puankhequa did not maintain a high profile after he returned from retirement and he took his lead from Houqua. Although the court's summons
nominally reintroduced competition among the leading Hong merchants,

---

[79] EIC R/10/26, 93–94, 10.   [80] EIC R/10/26, 10, 26.

[81] Zhongguo di 1 lishi dang'an guan, *Qinggong Yue Gang Ao shangmao dang'an quanji*,
7:3924. Other Qing court documents also reveal that Houqua assumed the title of the
head Hong merchant by 1814 (see, for example, NPM 16712 JQ19/10/27).

[82] Zhongguo di 1 lishi dang'an guan, *Qinggong Yue Gang Ao shangmao dang'an quanji*,
7:3949. The community of foreign traders in Canton also paid attention to the Qing
court's summons of Puankhequa back to the trade, despite his having paid a large sum
to Qing officials for his retirement just several years earlier (PEM Tilden Box 1, Folder
1, 233, 1816).

this revolving cast of characters continued to involve the previous rounds of oligopolistic partners.

In contrast with the strategy of his brother, Puiqua, who aggressively built the family business with the EIC, Houqua allowed his portion of the business with the Company to remain steady to satisfy the desire of the EIC to avoid an excessive concentration of market share in any single merchant. However, Houqua's alliance with Mouqua, as well as with Puankhequa and others, during the thirty-four years of EIC operations in Canton allowed him to consolidate his trading business and to build his capital base, turning him into a stable and indispensable partner for the EIC. Despite the EIC's impression of having groomed competitors to counterbalance Houqua's rising power, Houqua, along with his fellow leading Hong merchants, maintained an oligopolistic configuration in Canton sufficient to offset the EIC's command over the trade when the Company's continental rivals were all but eliminated.

Taming an Important but Difficult Trading Partner

Houqua did not end with his efforts, together with the other leading Hong merchants, to counterbalance the ascendancy of the EIC. Far from stagnating in a defense-only posture, Houqua managed to extract profits from the EIC through channels outside of the formal exchange of tea and woolens, all the while eschewing a direct confrontation with the EIC. For that, Houqua leveraged the capital base he had amassed.

From 1813 until the conclusion of the EIC monopoly, Houqua remained the Company's most important partner. Houqua's allocation would fluctuate, at times spiking to extraordinary levels when other merchants failed to supply an appropriate level of tea to the EIC. However, the EIC was vigilant in guarding against any sustained expansion of Houqua's representation in their trading volume. Basing my calculations on the average piculs per chest of tea for the various varietals and the price levels during those years, in 1813 Houqua transacted about 600,000 taels in tea sales with the EIC. Such a scale of business transactions year after year cemented the relationship between the two parties. However, the tea trade did not accrue equal profits to the two sides; the significantly higher margins for the EIC required that Houqua seek additional profits outside of the tea transactions to redress the imbalance.

The EIC recorded the sale price of Chinese tea in the London market. For example, from March 1817 to March 1818 the Company sold 10.6 million pounds of Congo in four auctions, with average sales prices in each auction ranging from 2s. 4.4d. to 2s. 6.9d. Weighted by the sales volume of each auction, in that year Congo commanded an average price of £0.153 per pound. This average sales price translated into £20.35, or 61 taels, per picul. At a cost of about 28 taels per picul in Canton, the tea trade yielded for the EIC 33 taels per picul, or a margin of 54 percent, before accounting for the costs of shipment and other expenses.[83] This margin is comparable to that generated by the sale of other varietals of tea during the year, which varied from 55 to 69 percent.[84] Of course, from these profit margins one must deduct freight, customs, and other charges. Of such charges, "Freight & Demorage" represented the largest cost item, averaging about 20 percent of sales. According to the figures recorded on the books of the Company, from 1801 through 1806, sales of all articles from China yielded a profit of 22 percent of sales.[85]

Profit margins for the Chinese Hong merchants, however, paled in comparison. No extant record allows us to calculate precisely the margins on Houqua's sales of tea to the EIC, but we can estimate the profits based on the occasional revelations in the EIC records of the profitability of the business for certain merchants. In cases of defunct or dysfunctional merchants, the Company often allowed the more solid merchants to take over their shares and repay their debt obligations to the EIC on behalf of the failed merchants with the profits generated from the assumed business.

In April 1823, Houqua assumed Exchin's allotment when the latter encountered financial difficulties. For a chop of 390 piculs of Congo tea, the Company offered a contract price of 26 taels per picul. The cost of the tea, along with the duties to the Emperor, shipping expenses, and allocated expenses, such as the proportion of the debt repayment for bankrupt merchants which totaled 3 taels, totaled 20.9 taels per picul. This would have produced a respectable gross margin of 19.6 percent; however, it did not include the losses from the allocation of woolen imports that the British company had bundled with this tea contract.

For this chop of Congo, the EIC forced upon the seller 350 pieces of Long Ells at 6.7 taels per piece. Along with the charge for duties and other expenses, the Company had calculated the prime cost to the merchant to be 8.2 taels per piece. The sale of this product in the Chinese market only yielded 7.5 taels for the Hong merchants. As a result, the merchant incurred a loss of 0.7 tael per piece, or 245 taels for the entire batch. This translated into a loss of 0.628 tael per picul of tea (the loss over Long Ells of 245 taels divided by the associated 390 piculs of Congo for this chop). Taking into account the losses over the coerced acceptance of the Long Ells, the profit margin decreased from 19.6 percent to 17.2 percent. But this level of profitability was at the high end among the bailout situations

---

[83] EIC R/10/49, 33–ab.   [84] EIC R/10/52, 40.   [85] EIC H/72, 187.

in which Houqua rescued his troubled brethrens. In one of these cases, after accounting for the loss over the associated purchase of woolens, the margin ran as low as 9.4 percent.[86]

Such losses over the sale of Long Ells were hardly surprising; as early as 1803 the Company had reported to London that "these goods were almost unsaleable" and acceptance of this article continued to be weak.[87] Merchants with fewer financial resources at their disposal were known to have exchanged the woolens with tea suppliers, who then dumped the British imports in the market: "When the Long ells are received, everyone will be striving to sell first, and perhaps lose by each piece, from five to six, or from seven to eight mace."[88] In the two intervening decades since this latter case, losses over woolens deepened as a result of the cumulative stuffing of this unwelcomed product into the Chinese marketplace and the predictability of more unwanted products in the ensuing seasons. For the lack of an alternative, the British insisted on shipping more woolens to China and managed to overstock the Chinese market only because of its overwhelming share in the purchase of Chinese tea.

After subtracting the losses on woolens, the Hong merchants should have had profit margins in the high single digits or in the teens. However, these calculations still do not take into account the usual costs of capital on the advances to the tea merchants which, for Houqua's loans to junior merchants arranged by the EIC in 1817 (more on this later), ran anywhere between 10 percent per annum to 1 percent per month.[89] From these cases, one can conclude that the contracted sale of tea to the Company was only marginally profitable, with gross margins in the single digits for the more successful cases after deduction of interest charges!

This was the risk/return tradeoff that the average Hong merchant faced. Net profit margins in the single digits should have been respectable; however, taking into consideration the risks involved, the returns were only modest. Prices specified by the EIC for the various types of tea that the Company contracted provided the Hong merchants with some measure of stability in this international exchange. However, the Hong merchants operated in an environment that was far from secure. They had to come up with the substantial advances that the tea suppliers demanded, a difficult situation aggravated by the dearth of willing and able leaders and thus leading to the high cost of capital. In addition, they had to withstand the capriciousness of the market for woolens, which

---

[86] EIC R/10/28, 175–177; see also Ch'en, *The Insolvency of the Chinese Hong Merchants*, 67.
[87] EIC G/12/142, 211–213; G/12/189, 116.   [88] EIC G/12/220, 22–23.
[89] EIC G/12/206, 19.

was not favorable to the seller in the first place. On top of these business factors, the Hong merchants also had to contend with the exactions that the Qing state levied on them on an ad-hoc basis.[90] These challenges explain the numerous instances of insolvency among the Hong merchants and the rarity of successful cases among the players in the Canton-based international trade.[91]

Comparing the profit margins of the EIC in excess of 20 percent and those of the Hong merchants in the low single digits (if they managed to withstand the business fluctuations), it is evident that the playing field for Sino-Western trade in Canton was tilted in favor of the British EIC and against the Chinese Hong merchants. However, the many aspiring Hong merchants who were eager to cater to the needs of the EIC are indicative that the low profitability of this business was not transparent to new entrants. Lured by the high margins for the sale of tea, the new Hong merchants were probably inexperienced and not fully cognizant of the undesirability of the woolen contracts. Nor did they fully appreciate the capital-intensive nature of the tea business that required advance investments to the tea growers.

How then did Houqua manage to capture a respectable share of the profits from the business in Canton? To respond to the challenge of the ascending British trading power that was all too happy to flex its muscles, Houqua could not rely solely on his niche in nankeen cloth and other products that did not fall under the auspices of the EIC-created scheme. Such products, although effective in helping him to avoid the limits the Company had placed on the exchange of goods, were but a small fraction of the size of the tea market and they did not generate a sufficient trading volume. The secret to Houqua's success lies in his ability to redefine the playing field as he expanded his business beyond commercial tea transactions to the financial arena of lending.

Through his long involvement in the tea trade, Houqua had built up a formidable capital base. In addition to providing his business with financial power to withstand market variability in woolens and other products, his capital afforded him leverage with the EIC, which faced a perennial cash-shortage problem as the profits from the Canton trade rarely remained in its treasury there. To ensure a balanced base of tea

---

[90] Kuo-tung Anthony Ch'en estimates that government exactions on the Hong merchants totaled over five million taels between 1773 and 1835 (*The Insolvency of the Chinese Hong Merchants*, Table 2.6). Frederic D. Grant Jr. points to the escalation of government demands in the early nineteenth century, which from time to time precipitated liquidity crises for the Hong merchants (*The Chinese Cornerstone of Modern Banking*).

[91] For an elaborate analysis of their failures, see Ch'en, *The Insolvency of the Chinese Hong Merchants*.

suppliers, the Company made a strategic decision to groom junior merchants. This strategy required that the Company finance these upstarts, thus presenting an opening for Houqua to deploy his capital to finance the Company's efforts and to generate from this arrangement handsome profits. Observing this opportunity, Houqua stepped in with his capital and became the linchpin in implementation of the EIC's agenda.

The opportunity afforded to Houqua by extending credit to junior merchants through the Company resulted from the requirements of inland tea merchants for an advance in exchange for their promise of tea to the Hong merchants. The leading merchants, Houqua, Puankhequa, and Mouqua, had no problem in producing such advances from their own coffers and their financial muscles even allowed them to extract a discount from the tea suppliers. In 1817, the three leading merchants settled their contracts with the suppliers for 16.8 taels per picul, with an advance of 4,200 taels per chop of tea. With the ability to offer an advance of only 3,000 taels, the junior merchants were forced to agree to a price of 17.5 taels per picul. The EIC calculated that at 12 percent interest the junior merchants' total cost was 18.25 taels per picul, versus the senior merchants' total cost of 17.85 taels per picul.

This cost disadvantage for the junior merchants, versus the advantage of their capital-rich seniors, formed a high barrier for them to establish themselves in the trade. The EIC desired to rectify the problem and to demonstrate its "determination to uphold" the junior merchants by financing their advances to the tea suppliers. However, the Company's treasury did not have sufficient resources to support such a measure.[92] Despite its stated intention, the EIC lacked the financial power to execute its plans.

The capital requirements proved too arduous for the junior merchants, but the EIC was not in a position to offer help from its own coffers.[93] To solve its capital-shortage problem, the EIC turned to Houqua. By the end of the 1810s, the EIC, acknowledging its own lack of funds to aid the junior merchants, had come to regard Houqua as a source of capital for his lesser brethren in times of financial difficulties.[94] By 1819, all active merchants, with the exception of Mouqua, owed Houqua money, with the total amounting to about half a million taels.[95]

This structure became so ingrained in the Canton network that the Company repeatedly begged Houqua to aid the junior merchants, and

[92] EIC G/12/207, 85–86.
[93] The occasional requirements to present "gifts" to the Emperor, in addition to the demands of advances by the tea suppliers, added to the financial burdens of these up-and-coming merchants.
[94] EIC G/12/216, 35.   [95] EIC G/12/214, 110.

Houqua proved to be capable of coming up with sizable amounts of money on short order. One such cash requirement of the EIC occurred on May 18, 1821, when the Company requested a loan of one hundred thousand dollars from Houqua. This amount would put the EIC in a position of being able to assist the junior merchants even if the money for its Bengal bills did not arrive on time to supplement the holdings of the treasury, which did "not contain enough to supply [the Company's] wants." The day after Houqua received the Company's letter, he responded favorably, promising "in a few days make ready the amt that [the Company] may have it whenever" it pleased, upon sending a letter informing Houqua of the requirement.[96] Houqua's financial resources allowed him to serve as a standby line of credit for the EIC, and by its arrangement, for the junior merchants. He deployed his unparalleled capital base, which he had accumulated over decades by selling tea to the EIC, to generate a separate income stream for his business enterprise. Unlike the tea trade in which Houqua's prominence was circumscribed by many, albeit smaller, merchants, the terms of his money-lending business, specified by the EIC but predicated on his being the only capable provider, were highly favorable to Houqua.

As the EIC played an active role in arranging these loans, the Company also designated the interest rates and facilitated the repayment to Houqua. These loans often carried an interest rate of 1 percent per month and the EIC assumed the role of the borrower in securing the money from Houqua. "We this morning received your letter," wrote the Company to Houqua, "telling us you could *lend us the money* which we requested for which we return you our thanks" [italics added]. The principal and interest were therefore guaranteed by the EIC. "For this money," the EIC added, "we can pay you an interest of 1 p cent p month commencing on the 25th day of the 5th moon."[97] This letter from the EIC to Houqua, dated May 28, 1821, regarding the sums to be advanced to the junior merchants underscores how deep the Company's capital dependence on Houqua had become by this early date. Houqua had not only taken advantage of the retirement of Puankhequa and Mouqua from their successive leadership positions of the Hong merchants to capture the extra share of the EIC's business allotted to the lead merchant, he had also redefined the role of the lead merchant so as to make him the

---

[96] EIC G/12/223, 32–33, 39.
[97] EIC G/12/223, 40–42. Kuo-tung Anthony Ch'en also refers to this arrangement whereby Houqua lent money to the junior merchants through the intermediary of the EIC. See Ch'en, *The Insolvency of the Chinese Hong Merchants*, 169–170. I differ from Ch'en in my interpretation of these figures in that I see Houqua as being a frequent lender in large quantities to the junior merchants, as evidenced by the aggregate amount indicated earlier. This was a lucrative investment for Houqua, with the guaranty of repayment by the EIC.

EIC's banker in Canton and, as such, the sole beneficiary of the interest accrued on the loans that the EIC took out both for itself and for the junior merchants.

Compared to the sale of tea to the EIC, which, when adjusted for the woolen losses and the cost of capital, generated a profit margin only in the high single digits (as noted earlier), the interest rate offered and guaranteed by the Company presented to Houqua a lower risk yet a more lucrative business endeavor. The EIC court in London objected to it as the Company was "only allowed eight percent per annum for the large sum remaining due to [the Company] from Conseequa," below the 10 percent per annum the Company had allowed Houqua for 1822–23.[98] However, the operations in Canton must have continued to find it difficult to come up with sufficient capital as the Company remained dependent on Houqua for financing, requesting in 1826 not only tea advances for the other merchants but also money to pay for the Company's own incoming shipments. Again, the officers in Canton offered Houqua interest at 1 percent per month.[99] Time and again, the court in London complained of the Company's financial arrangements with Houqua. In 1828, a letter from London admonished the officers in Canton for allowing the Company to be held responsible for an advance of 60,000 taels from Houqua to Goqua, his fellow Hong merchant, stating the court's wish that there be "no occasion to enter into any similar engagement on account of [the Company's] purchase of Canton Bohea."[100] Yet, the same issue resurfaced in a letter dated March 31, 1830, in which the court in London took issue with another 140,000 dollars borrowed from Houqua for advances for Bohea, again at an interest rate of 1 percent per month.[101] This chronic shortage of capital for EIC operations in Canton persisted to the end of the monopoly as the Company remained dependent on Houqua for financing. On February 29, 1832, the Company's accountant recorded a credit to Houqua consisting of 477,758.751 taels in principal and 24,791.549 taels in interest.[102]

In essence, Houqua bankrolled the upstarts that the EIC had nurtured to fulfill the Company's hopes of neutralizing Houqua's growing influence over the tea trade.[103] The EIC might have succeeded in cultivating a new crop of junior Hong merchants to keep in check Houqua's share in the Company's business, as indicated by the upsurge in the representation

---

[98] EIC R/10/52, 107a.   [99] EIC G/12/236, 44.   [100] EIC R/10/56, 145a.
[101] EIC R/10/58, 24a.   [102] EIC G/12/251.
[103] As the reliance of the Company on Houqua increased, there came a change in the EIC's view of him. The Company's officers in Canton stated in 1821 that "in . . . our commercial transaction . . . he is so liberal, his capital is so essential, and his services as a negotiator with the government so important" (EIC G/12/223, 95). Of course, the Company's attitude toward Houqua shifted during the period of their interactions depending on the circumstances, but its reliance on Houqua's capital was indisputable.

of "Others" in Figure 2.2. The effectiveness of this arrangement for the EIC, however, was illusory because the economic benefits from the participation of these newcomers accrued largely to Houqua in the form of interest payments on the loans that Houqua extended to them through the EIC. Not only did this arrangement transform the EIC's perception of Houqua, but it also set Houqua apart from the Company's other trading partners in Canton, conferring on Houqua a leadership role that allowed him to represent the group of Hong merchants as an oligopolistic entity. In the end, Houqua transformed what began as the Company's effort to foster competition among the Hong merchants and to contain Houqua's power into a profitable tool for enhancing his own criticality in the Company's operations and in the entire trade system.

By the time Houqua assumed leadership of his family's business in 1800, Canton was not only the port where the New Worlds of China and the West converged. At this port that handled a tremendous volume of global exchange, the rise of a British hegemon among the Western powers was already exerting great influence on the mechanics of trade among Sino-Western trading partners. Houqua took over a family business that was but one of many contenders for the Canton trade. Although careful in catering to the desire for continuity on the part of his important British partner, Houqua also adroitly explored alternative business opportunities presented by the evolving system of trade. From his supplies of nankeen cloth to his role as the provider of financing, Houqua was transformed into an indispensable partner to the British East India Company, deepening the Company's dependence on him at a more critical level every step of the way. He proved as capable in playing defense as in playing offense. While maintaining his share of the EIC business at a level with which the Company could feel comfortable, along with the other leading Hong merchants Houqua constituted the upper echelon of EIC partners and together they were able to keep in check the power of the growing monopolistic influence of the EIC.

Houqua did not directly confront the monolithic EIC. Instead, he took advantage of the inconsistencies in the EIC's grand plan. The EIC had endeavored to broaden its supplier base in spite of its inability to provide them with sufficient operating capital. Houqua spotted this opportunity and diversified his business from the trading of goods to the facilitation of capital. As the primary capital supplier, Houqua appropriated some of the EIC's commanding power in the trading network. Houqua's formidable capital base made him not only an essential partner for the EIC but also the perennial lender for the Hong merchants (with loans secured by the EIC) and a linchpin in the entire Canton system.

Impressive as Houqua's accomplishments were during this period, it would be erroneous to attribute his success to any orchestrated game plan that he set out to execute from the outset. Luck and historical contingencies certainly played a role in the unfolding of events. For instance, had the EIC allocated more of the Company's capital to operations in Canton, Houqua would have found it difficult to deploy his liquid assets and capture an additional portion of the profits from the Canton trade. In addition, not all Hong merchants conformed to the oligopolistic framework to counteract the growing hegemony of the EIC; fortunately for Houqua, with Puankhequa and Mouqua he established a triumvirate that underwrote the stability of Sino-Western trade in the early nineteenth century, each shouldering for a period the burdens of the leadership of the Hong merchants. It would be equally wrong, however, to assert that Houqua owed his success to sheer luck. In his dealings with the EIC that spanned nearly four decades, Houqua demonstrated patience in building his business at a calculated pace, thereby avoiding the liquidity crises that often befell the more aggressive and not well-funded Hong merchants. At the same time, he showcased his ability to identify the lacunae in the EIC's business framework, be it the Company's desire to expand its presence in the nankeen cloth market, in which it lacked substantial experience, or its insistence on nurturing Hong startups, despite the paucity of capital under its command. With these astute observations, Houqua not only became an entrenched partner with the British company but also leveraged the business initiatives of the established monolith to further his own financial and commercial interests.

By the 1820s, the Canton system had evolved into a partnership between the EIC monopoly and the oligopolistic configuration under Houqua's leadership. To expand beyond his role in this arrangement, which was already generating lucrative profits, Houqua would extend beyond Europe, which did not present him with a viable alternative to Britain, and would avail himself of the growing presence of American merchants in Canton in order to bypass the configuration of global trade centered around the British hegemon.

3   Weaving a Trading Network
Breaking Free with the Eagle

In a confidential report dated February 10, 1812, the EIC accused Houqua of being "neither so attached or [*sic*] interested in the welfare of foreign commerce" and complained about "his extreme disinclination to dispute the wishes of the government." How could Houqua, a leading Hong merchant deriving a steady income stream from the trade, be not "so attached or interested"? This "lack of attachment" reflected Houqua's tactics time and again of threatening to withdraw from the trade, which proved to be an effective leverage against the EIC. As for the complaint about Houqua's "disinclination" to oppose his own government, it did not represent the Company's impression of Houqua's personality as much as it underscored the EIC's growing desire to have the Senior Merchant do its bidding in front of the Qing government and Houqua's insistence on some measure of autonomy from the EIC. Belying the "timid disposition" that he projected to the EIC were Houqua's daring maneuvers that allowed him to diversify his commercial activities and fashion a sophisticated portfolio of business interests.[1]

Just as the EIC nurtured new Hong merchants to foster competition among its trading partners in Canton, Houqua also actively cultivated trading relationships with other Westerners arriving at the port to offset the overwhelming share of the British business. Most prominent among Houqua's new trading partners were the Americans. "The first vessel which sailed from the U.S. for China was the ship *Empress of China*, Captain Green, she left New York 22d February 1784," recorded *The Register of Pennsylvania*.[2] In time, these newly arriving American traders would provide Houqua with the needed leverage to break free from the British hegemon. However, it was many decades before Houqua was able to structure a tight alliance with the American traders. He had to ascertain that the American traders would form a sustainable presence in Canton

---

[1] EIC R/10/26, 93–94.
[2] Samuel Hazard, *The Register of Pennsylvania, Devoted to the Preservation of Facts and Documents, and Every Other Kind of Useful Information Respecting the State of Pennsylvania* (Philadelphia: W.F. Geddes, 1828), 1: 284.

so as to provide him with a reliable alternative to the British. More importantly, Houqua had to handpick a trusted ally with whom he could chart a new course of trade to faraway lands. With his handpicked American allies, Houqua cautiously began expanding his trading network to link partners with shared economic interests in the worldwide flow of goods and capital. In the process of constructing this network, Houqua not only had to overcome language barriers and identify the desired goods of exchange, but he also had to assess the risks and evaluate the channels for recourse within the new framework of transnational business operations. As he transformed the pattern of global interactions, Houqua had to negotiate new rules for a reconfigured network of interconnectedness with his American partners and maneuver into positions that best served their needs.

Finding a Common Language for Capitalistic Exchange

The arrival of the first American traders in Canton coincided with Houqua's appearance on the stage of foreign commerce. Since his early days in commerce, Houqua had always dealt with partners from different countries. However, before the beginning of the nineteenth century, Houqua and his brother had busied themselves with positioning themselves strategically with the growing power of the British traders. Their business connections with the continental Europeans were disintegrating and, as indicated in the previous chapter, Puiqua quickly ingratiated himself with the British EIC, and Houqua, after assuming leadership of the family business, focused on consolidating its position with the British.

This is not to say that the Wu brothers shunned American businesses. In fact, Houqua was consigning tea for sale in the American market as early as 1799 under the Hong name "Puiqua," in keeping with the brothers' practice with the EIC. The use of this Hong name continued until 1801, shortly after the death of Puiqua.[3] During the next several years, Houqua traded with American shippers who recorded his business by various spellings of his name.[4] In general, Houqua adopted a cautious approach in expanding his business with the Americans during the first decade of America's trade with China. In keeping with the measured maneuvers that Houqua employed in his dealings with the British EIC, his forays into partnerships with American merchants were equally prudent. That he was building his business with the Americans slowly and cautiously did not preclude him from taking advantage of the American

---

[3] JCB Brown Box 499, Folder 6; Box 655, Folder 7; Box 655, Folder 10.
[4] JCB Brown Box 493, Folder 11; Box 494, Folder 3.

presence in the market or from extracting concessions from the British. Nor were the Americans meant to displace the British. As British tea buyers continued to procure more expensive and higher-quality tea from Houqua, the American market provided an outlet for lower-priced products. An American trader recounted an 1815 exchange with Houqua's tea purser, who was said to have remarked, "Ayah! . . . you amelica mans – no pay so much plice for so fashion Bohea as dat inglis man pay for he Bohea – He tea hab all same same as first chop Congo tea!!" [Aiya! You American men do not pay as high a price for fashionable Bohea as those Englishmen. The Englishmen all have first-rate Congo tea.][5]

In addition to this early segmentation of the tea market for the different clientele, Houqua commanded a niche market for nankeen cloth, actively procuring it for both British and American buyers, as we have seen in the previous chapter. By playing the British buyers against the American buyers in that market, Houqua derived substantial leverage in his dealings with the British EIC. As early as 1802, he exacted a price increase from the British due to the "enhanced prices" of nankeen cloth as a result of the "very extensive demands of the Americans."[6] Long before he consolidated a partnership with select American traders to make them into a formidable alternative to the British as an outlet for tea from Canton, Houqua had succeeded in conjuring up in the minds of his British customers an image of a competitive marketplace from which Houqua was due a fair share of the profits.

Houqua was equally careful to establish a reputation among the American traders. It was reported by one American that in 1805 only five or six Hong merchants were trading with the Americans. The big Hong of Mouqua declined any American business, whereas Houqua was channeling his business through Perkins & Co. To this American, Houqua was "very rich" and he was "to be depended on." "A very hard & very cautious [man] but when you have contracted with him, he will execute his contracts honourably & punctually." Another American arriving in Canton later in the decade noted that Houqua "is very rich, sends good cargoes & just in all his dealings, in short is a man of honour and veracity; has more business than any other man in the Hong and securing 12 or 14 American ships this year."[7]

Forging trade ties with the new partners from America entailed many obstacles. One of the major obstacles was the linguistic barrier between Houqua and the newly arriving business prospects from America. Although their communication was far from seamless, Houqua's experience in his dealings with the British paved the way for him to

---

[5] PEM Tilden Box 1, Folder 2, 96, September 3, 1835.   [6] EIC G/12/138, 126.
[7] PEM Shreve Box 10, Folder 4.

deal with the Americans linguistically. Of course, the common language between the Americans and their former colonizers enabled them to easily work with each other in international commerce. From the perspective of Houqua, the language shared by the ascending British powers and the budding American interests lowered the barriers for him to diversify his commercial outlets. This shared linguistic background was also connected to a broader institutional framework that had been established by the British and in which the Americans could participate. Before long, Houqua would be tapping into the financial networks of the expanding British Empire through his American partners, directing the flow of goods and capital not only in U.S. markets but also along the British imperial sinews that linked London to Bombay and other British imperial outposts. In short, the relatively easy linguistic transition contributed to a trading structure that privileged Anglophonic participants during the early part of the nineteenth century.

Unlike the British East India Company that had nurtured linguistic skills among some of its staff members to conduct business with the Chinese, the Americans lacked the infrastructure to consistently interpret the offers and demands of the Chinese traders in Canton. Nor could Houqua, who attempted to bypass British interests by admitting the Americans into his trading network, rely on the assistance of the British interpreters to translate his ideas for his American partners. But Houqua did have a modicum of English proficiency. To be more precise, Houqua was fluent in the fusion language of "pidgin" English,[8] allowing him to converse freely with his English-speaking partners. The following is a representative dialogue in pidgin English, as constructed by William Hunter, a long-time resident in Canton:

"Well, Houqua," you would say on some visit, "hav got news to-day?" "Hav got too muchee bad news," he would reply; "Hwang Ho [the Yellow River] hav spilum too muchee." That sounded ominously. "Man-ta-le [Mandarin] hav come see you?" "He no come see my, he sendee come one piece 'chop.' He come to-mollo, He wantchee my two-lac [hundred thousand] dollar." It was the old complaint, a "squeeze," and this time a formidable one. "You pay he how mutchee?" "My pay he fitty, sikky tousand so." "But s'pose he no contentee?" "S'pose he, No. 1, no contentee, my pay he one lac."[9]

This dialogue, as remembered by an American trader who worked with Houqua for many years, indicates that Houqua's pidgin English sufficed to communicate information, especially business information. It

---

[8] "Pidgin" is a rendition of the English word "business"; therefore, in early-nineteenth-century Canton "pidgin" English referred to "business English." For further details, see the discussion in the following chapter.

[9] Hunter, The "Fan Kwae" at Canton, 36–37.

is also clear that his American friends were accustomed to the peculiar inflections in his pronunciation of certain English words (e.g., the added articulation of final syllables and the replacement of those consonant sounds that were difficult for Houqua and other Cantonese speakers to pronounce) and together they adopted some non-Chinese, non-English numeric references, such as "lac" which they must have borrowed from the Indian traders to represent one hundred thousand. Such accepted usages, however, existed primarily in verbal form. Thus, Houqua could communicate orally in pidgin English with his American partners, but such exchanges could not be rendered into written pidgin. Nor could the partners rely on business documents written in Chinese because the Chinese-language proficiency of the American traders was far from sufficient for it to be an effective business language. Therefore, Houqua depended on his business partners to prepare on his behalf documents in English which he then executed in his distinguished signature in cursive English, "*Houqua.*"

Robert Bennet Forbes, an American partner who worked with Houqua for many years, noted that Houqua "did not read English nor write it beyond his signature." The confidential nature of his work in commerce as well as in political dealings with foreigners required that he have some trusted friends among his foreign partners. "It resulted from this state of things that his foreign correspondence and his political negotiations were laid before some American friend, who read, explained, and under his direction, answered all his letters."[10] However, before he could be reassured of a secure relationship, Houqua had to traverse the multilingual world by improvising notation techniques to suit his own purposes.

On November 29, 1801, Thomas Thompson, representing Brown & Ives in Rhode Island, took cargo onboard the ship *Ann & Hope* from Houqua, Mouqua, and Ponqua in the amounts of $28,657, $26,236.28, and $2,974, respectively. The notes Thompson wrote to the three merchants specified similar terms, except that the note to Ponqua did not include any provision for interest. On the back of all three notes were notations in Chinese. Ponqua's was the simplest, with the equivalent of the date on the Chinese calendar (the twenty-fourth day of the tenth month in the sixth year of Jiaqing), the name of the debtor, and the amount in Spanish dollars. The Chinese notation on Mouqua's note offered the additional detail that the amount represented the value of the goods taken, as well as a term of twenty months and an interest rate of 12 percent per annum. Houqua's note was the most detailed, specifying in

---

[10] Robert B. Forbes, *Personal Reminiscences*, 2nd rev. ed. (Boston: Little, Brown, 1882), 370.

Chinese the date according to both the Western and Chinese calendars, information about the vessel (including its security merchant), that the cargo was tea exported from Houqua's Hong, as well as the expiration month of the twenty-month note. The Chinese parties did not sign these notes.[11] But from this set of notes, it is obvious that language was a common barrier for the Hong merchants, but practices varied slightly from merchant to merchant in terms of their bilingual abilities.[12]

Another early transaction involved only Houqua among the Chinese merchants. A business entry by Benjamin Carter noted the 1805 purchase from Houqua by the Rhode Island merchant of fifty chests of Souchong for 1,533.12 dollars, with partial payment of 383.12 dollars in cash and the remainder rendered in a note of 1,150 dollars. Carter soon paid the balance and received a receipt for payment in full. All these proceedings were recorded in notes and the receipts were written in both English and Chinese. The Chinese version addressed Carter as "doctor" and transliterated his name according to the Cantonese pronunciation, while referring to Houqua by "Yihe," the name of his Hong in Chinese.[13] Unlike his transactions with the EIC that followed an established protocol, Houqua proceeded cautiously with his early American trading partners, retaining bilingual accounts of his financial dealings in order to minimize conflicts.

On yet another set of receipts involving multiple Hong merchants, the Chinese notations revealed the differences between Houqua's practices compared to those of his Hong peers. On January 19, 1807, Brown & Ives repaid both Houqua and Conseequa the notes that they had taken out in 1807. In this set of receipts, both Hong merchants signed their names in cursive English. Both also recorded Chinese notations. Conseequa wrote his Chinese Hong name and his last name in Chinese next to his English signature. In contrast, Houqua made a functional notation, indicating in Chinese, "This is a record only; no repayment necessary" ("此係記數單不用繳回" cixi jishudan buyong jiaohui).[14]

Business records indicate Houqua's consistent use of functional notations in Chinese along with his English signature. He made similar notations on a receipt dated December 29, 1806, acknowledging another repayment from Brown & Ives.[15] Similarly, on February 9, 1809, both on

[11] JCB Brown Box 494, Folder 3.

[12] During earlier decades, Puankhequa had earned a prominent role in the Canton trade partly due to his proficiency in Spanish (Van Dyke, *Merchants of Canton and Macao: Success and Failure in Eighteenth-Century Chinese Trade*, ch. 3). By 1800, however, the changing fortunes of the European trading powers in Canton posed a different set of linguistic challenges to the Hong merchants.

[13] RIHS Carter-Danforth, Series I: Benjamin B. Carter, 1781–1831, Box 1.

[14] JCB Brown Box 497, Folder 3.   [15] JCB Brown Box 685, Folder 9.

the receipt and against the original note dated March 27, 1807, Houqua noted in Chinese that payment was made for the balance of the note in his favor ("兩訖" *liangqi*).[16] This practice, not followed by the other Hong merchants, continued in 1813 and 1814 as Houqua acknowledged payments of both the principal and the interest from his debtors.[17]

These were not isolated records in which the entries were made in both Chinese and English. But it should be noted that the Chinese entries were not necessarily mere translations of the English content. For example, among the papers of Oliver Wolcott Jr., a New England businessman with whom Houqua had business transactions as early as 1807, there are many business records written in English, with nothing but a simple notation in Chinese indicating the type of document. In an 1810 letter to Wolcott, Houqua went into detail about the geopolitical situation at the time and the commercial ramifications thereof. He communicated this information entirely in English, written by the hand of an interpreter: "Very sorry to hear that the differences between your country & the bellingerento still continued. I had hopes from the former aspect of affairs that the continent would have been open'd for foreign produce & that the markets in America would have been proportionally benefited by so desirable an event." Not only did Houqua make observations in the letter on general conditions, but he also proceeded to elaborate on specific business arrangements: "Your agents here have paid me all the demands I had against you & closed the concerns of the *Trident* entirely to my satisfaction & altho' they did not think it necessary to obtain any credit for you this year, I shall be happy at all times to facilitate your business as much as lays in my power. I should not have charged an interest upon the notes taken up by your agents had it not been that others who owe me large sums might have expected the same allowance & that in such cases I should want a plea of refusal." The content, presented in English, included information of substance and was relevant to the calculation of the business profits and losses between the parties. "I am obliged by your advice respecting shipments to Europe," continued Houqua in the letter, "& shall certainly follow it while the present disturbances exist." It was clear from the letter that even during this early period when Houqua was proceeding cautiously with his American allies that they were plotting business strategies to circumvent the commercial power of the British, who enjoyed the backing of a strong military force. On this English letter, which conveyed strategic and material information, Houqua signed his

[16] JCB Brown Box 497, Folders 8 and 10.
[17] JCB Brown Box 276, Folders 10 and 11.

name in English and next to his signature was a notation in Chinese "此係信" (*cixixin*).[18]

This simple Chinese notation indicated for the record and for the comfort of Houqua, the signatory, that "this is a letter," not an invoice or a receipt. The Chinese notation obviously had no legal significance, but the legal implications were not Houqua's primary concern. That it had to be marked "this is a letter" underscores Houqua's lack of written proficiency in English, so much so that he was not able to readily recognize the category of the document from its format. However, he was comfortable signing such a lengthy document without complete comprehension of the content, suggesting that he placed sufficient trust in his amanuensis or that he considered the business opportunity to be worth the risk of any legal proceedings that might be launched against him based on his signature, easily recognizable in its English form. The format of this letter in English, as well as that of the business records prepared in English at the time, contrasts sharply with Chinese business documents on which the names of the people and the business concerns, along with numeric information on the quantity of goods and the amount of money involved, were stamped in red with the appropriate chops and seals as a safeguard against forgery or tampering. Such differences notwithstanding, Houqua became comfortable in executing these documents largely due to the guarded pace with which he expanded his business and his careful plans for risk management. That Houqua was as confident in signing English documents as he was in executing Chinese documents, be they correspondence with the Qing state, other Chinese, or the British EIC, indicates the ease with which he traversed the multilingual, multicultural world of international commerce as well as his fortitude in exposure to different legal regimes.

Calculated Risks

In expanding Canton's trade with America, Houqua was blazing new trails. In addition to adding to his potential legal exposure by executing documents in a language in which he was not proficient, Houqua's expansion into America also entailed an escalation of his business risks. As he became more comfortable in assessing the risks, Houqua proceeded cautiously. Puankhequa, a successful Hong merchant who began

---

[18] CHS Oliver Wolcott Jr., Folder XLIX.9 "Trident" 1807, letter, 1810. In the folder, one can decipher the different notations in the letter. In another letter, this one dated November 5, 1810, Houqua requested an update on market conditions. Similarly, he closed the letter with his signature brush stroke in English, but he marked this letter "問候信" (*wenhouxin*) – "a letter of greetings."

his involvement in the Canton trade before Houqua, "never had . . . done any American business" and he refused to secure his ship from America, complained Rhode Island merchant Sullivan Dorr as he reported to his brothers from Canton in 1801.[19] Even at the turn of the century, business prospects in America were not deemed to be sufficiently significant for this established leader among the Chinese Hongs to devote his time cultivating relations with the Americans. Houqua assessed the situation differently, but he too followed this business opportunity in a guarded manner.

Houqua's ventures into the new market deviated from the established structure of trade with the British EIC that had assured him recurring profits. Unlike the EIC, which specified annual tea contracts in the prior season that enabled Houqua to procure the appropriate quantity and mix of tea and to forecast his profits from the annual transactions, his business with the Americans offered no such predictability or advance notice. Without a long institutional trading history and lacking the financial prowess and systematic framework of the EIC, American buyers purchased tea from Houqua on a batch-by-batch basis without any detailed forecast of demand and distribution. As his 1805 transaction with Carter indicates, Houqua's initial forays into the American market took the form of one-off transactions conducted on an ad-hoc basis. Such an arrangement made it difficult for him to scale up his American involvement and also confined his dealings with the Americans to the residual odd-lot teas. To further his presence in the U.S. market, Houqua soon began to sell tea not only to the Americans in Canton but also on consignment through his American partners who would carry his tea back to the United States on returning vessels.

This new arrangement was a riskier proposition: Houqua had to entrust his cargo to the care of his partners, sending his tea to destinations half a world away without receiving any advance payment and trusting that his partners would sell his tea in America on terms that best suited his needs. Not only did he have to postpone receipt of the proceeds from the tea sales until the transactions were complete in the end market overseas and the funds were remitted back to Canton, but he also had to assume business uncertainties regarding the price of the tea, which was negotiated by his agents in America and not by him. Compared to the profits from his trade with the EIC that largely were predetermined, this new arrangement magnified the risks of the tea trade. He had to retain title on the teas as the cargo traveled across the oceans to destinations where he exercised no direct control and return of the proceeds from

[19] RIHS Dorr, Letter dated Canton, July 4, 1801.

the sales could be no quicker than that allowed by a round-trip voyage around the world.

Houqua's consignments of tea on board ships bound for America began no later than 1807, about the same time that he was making repeated threats to the British about retiring from the business. On board the ship the *Trident,* Curtiss Blakeman master, traveling from Canton to New York in late 1807, Houqua consigned to Oliver Wolcott, "for sale, on account & risk of the shipper, a native of the Empire of China," close to forty-eight thousand dollars of tea, along with some four thousand dollars of chinaware and nearly twenty thousand dollars of other merchandise. The shipping records of the *Trident,* bearing the signature of Houqua in English, marked the beginning of a new business venture that reoriented the global flow of goods from Canton and recalibrated the risk-sharing mechanism for partners in the Canton trade. Putting his own capital at risk as he sent his goods to America, Houqua sidestepped the Americans' perennial problem of a shortage of capital for the purchase of goods in Canton.[20] With his substantial capital, Houqua replaced the Americans as the principal in these transactions, engaging his U.S. partners as agents for the transportation and the sale of his goods abroad. Extending the shipment of his tea to America, Houqua challenged Britain's supremacy at sea not by confronting the military might of the British Navy, but by charting new trade routes and transforming the cast of global traders to the detriment of British commercial profitability.

Such challenges to British power did not consistently yield high profits. In 1811, in a letter marked "信書/信付" ("[this is] a letter"), Houqua wrote to his American partner: "I am sorry to hear of the discouraging state of your market but feel every confidence that you will do the best you can with my goods." Houqua was now encountering a capricious market that was very different from the established channels of selling tea to the British. As for the consigned tea, Houqua recommended that it "be sold if the prices are not such as will make a loss upon the shipment, in preference to holding them much after the receipt of this, as they were old when shipped & teas arriving with you in 1812 must tend to depress their value." Had he not risked his goods by shipping them to America, he could well have offloaded this surplus with any of the willing participants

---

[20] As indicated in Chapter 2, the EIC faced a similar capital-shortage problem. However, with their extensive trading experience in Canton and an established mechanism for annual transactions, the British enterprise could boast higher creditworthiness, as compared to their relatively inexperienced American competitors. From Houqua's perspective, an important difference was that he was merely the lender to the EIC, which remained the owner of record for the shipment from Canton, whereas in his trade with America Houqua retained title of ownership of the goods as they were shipped overseas, a much riskier business proposition.

among the many buyers in Canton. Now, with the goods docked half a world away, Houqua was at the mercy of his partners. Therefore, in such a case, he could only offer advice: "You will have the goodness therefore to consider whether it will not be better to dispose of them at such price as may offer at auction or private sale before 1812 even should it be a losing one."[21]

From Houqua's perspective in Canton, the situation would deteriorate in the coming months. In a letter to Oliver Wolcott dated November 15, 1811 (also marked "此係付信," or "This is a letter"), Houqua noted: "I have had the pleasure to receive your letter by the *Tea Plant*, but the *Hannibal* has not yet made her appearance & I begin to fear some accident has happened to her." Houqua might have been able to outsmart his British partners, but he could not out-gun them. The British forces proved to be too powerful in the War of 1812 for the American merchants charged with the shipment and sale of Houqua's goods. Fortunately for Houqua, he had apportioned his American investments cautiously and British reliance on him for tea in Canton remained the bedrock of his business. Also, with the timely market intelligence he commanded in Canton, he proved to be sufficiently agile to alter course. "Owing to the state of the American market," Houqua informed Wolcott, "I am deterred from making shipments this season, particularly as I see no prospect of an opening for teas in Europe."[22] Houqua was well aware that much of the America-bound tea was earmarked for reexport to Europe to circumvent the British sea blockade of French-controlled continental Europe. Not an arms supplier who then could have altered the course of the conflict, Houqua was nonetheless a tea supplier to all the parties. Confident that his major customer, the British EIC, could not function without his tea supplies, Houqua teamed up with the adversaries of the British and shipped his tea via America, directly against the interests of Britain at war. Sensing the prospects of American reexports dimming, Houqua nimbly redirected his resources away from the partners that were losing militarily. In order to accomplish such intricate maneuvers, Houqua had to surmount significant linguistic challenges in order to maintain secrecy. That he managed to execute this plan without antagonizing the British underscores Houqua's agility in balancing the interests of his warring trade partners.

Houqua also moved quickly to recover his losses. Writing to Wolcott a month later, on December 14, 1811, Houqua expressed his concerns

[21] CHS Oliver Wolcott Jr., Folder XLIX.9 "Trident" 1807, letter dated Canton, March 11, 1811.

[22] CHS Oliver Wolcott Jr., Folder XLIX.9 "Trident" 1807, letter dated Canton, November 15, 1811.

about a missing ship, the *Hannibal*. "I now begin to fear some accident has happened to her," wrote Houqua, "in which case please do what may be necessary to recover my insurance." Having availed himself of the insurance policies of the West, Houqua requested that Wolcott make good on the policy and compensate him for his losses. Fearing that "the present bad markets will continue for a long time," Houqua decided to "ship as little as possible" until the situation improved. Although he conveyed his hope "at some future period to renew business" with Wolcott, he had "only to request . . . attention to closing my sales in America."[23]

Houqua's fear of the loss of the *Hannibal* proved to be unfounded for the ship soon brought him Wolcott's response to his various inquiries, along with the bill of lading for the ten thousand dollars' worth of goods that Houqua had consigned onboard. Despite his claim in his March 17, 1812, reply to Wolcott that he was "unwilling to adventure further till better times,"[24] Houqua was anxious to again test the waters. He wrote to Wolcott in November, "Altho' the Embargo in America has deprived me of the pleasure of hearing from you, I embrace this opportunity to assure you of the pleasure I shall feel in receiving business with you whenever the times become better."[25]

When he resumed shipments to America, Houqua again demonstrated that he was keenly aware of the possibility of seeking protection for his shipments with insurance and making claims against the policies that he had purchased. For his 1814 shipments on board the *Hunter*, the *America*, and the *San José Almas*, Houqua expressed to his American partners his wish to secure insurance coverage. In Boston, Providence, and New York, where Perkins & Co. sought to purchase policies on Houqua's behalf, he was told of the "increasing hazards of underwriting," which had almost induced the insurance companies to cease "subscribing to any policy," and they "refused to write or even name a premium" for the shipments that Houqua had wanted to be covered. The stipulated protection against losses was also questionable: "[W]e were informed no Insurance could be effected on which any reliance could be placed – that if there were any of the offices willing to write it was unsafe to trust them – that we should be bound to pay good money for the premium in case of safe arrival and, probably, in case of loss, be unable to recover anything." Houqua's

---

[23] CHS Oliver Wolcott Jr., Folder XLIX.9 "Trident" 1807, letter dated Canton, December 14, 1811.

[24] CHS Oliver Wolcott Jr., Folder XLIX.9 "Trident" 1807, letter dated Canton, March 17, 1812.

[25] CHS Oliver Wolcott Jr., Folder XLIX.9 "Trident" 1807, letter dated Canton, November 1, 1812.

pragmatic team would spend its precious capital only on an insurance policy that truly provided protection against losses.

Houqua was very conscious of the geopolitical situation and the ramifications regarding the collectability of insurance coverage should there occur any unfortunate losses. During the troubled period of the 1810s, political divisions mattered in terms of commerce. An insurance policy would be condemned and all claims would be voided on grounds of a violation of the blockade. Apprised of such provisions in the Western marketplace, in his instructions Houqua warned Perkins & Co. against providing warranty on the subject of the ownership of the goods "which should operate as a bar to [Houqua's] claims, in case of loss." Unfortunately for Houqua, no matter how careful he was in structuring the insurance policy, the insurers had become too risk-averse in the world of military conflicts. With a blockade along the American coast, even shipments along the coast commanded a premium of "75 & 80 pr ct," and for requests such as Houqua's, respectable insurers did not care to assume the risks and "would not write even at 95 pr ct."[26] The escalated global volatility had increased the risks of conducting business. The promises of financial institutions, usually enforced under Western legal regimes, had ceased to provide any reassurance. It would be up to Houqua to assess the opportunities and the associated risks.

So alluring was the American bypass to the British stranglehold on international commerce that Houqua could not resist, even though he was fully aware of the involved military risks and political uncertainties. He would, however, proceed with caution. At times, he would suspend his exposure in American consignments, but he never abandoned this precious opportunity to open another outlet for his tea and to broaden the range of his investment options.

Choosing Strategic Partners and Sanitizing Opium Exposure

Business records show that Houqua continued to test the waters with his smattering of dealings with American traders in a manner similar to his previous trade with continental Europeans. By the mid-1810s, he had developed a very good reputation among American traders along different parts of the U.S. eastern coast. Nonetheless, Houqua's deep involvement in the trade with the Americans developed even further as he forged a partnership with John Perkins Cushing.

---

[26] MHS Samuel Cabot Box 1, Folder 11.

The same promises of trading profits that had swept Houqua's Wu family ashore to Canton a century earlier propelled Cushing's uncle, Thomas Handasyd Perkins, to set up shop in Canton. Orphaned at an early age, Cushing came under the tutelage of T.H. Perkins. At the age of 16, Cushing was dispatched from the home base of Perkins & Co. in Boston to Canton. Young Cushing was to serve as a clerk to Ephraim Bumstead, who, soon after his arrival in Canton, became indisposed and had to return home. Without a ready replacement, Perkins & Co. had no choice but to put young Cushing in charge of Canton operations, a responsibility "such as few young men ever met with." Although they expressed in their letter dated March 20, 1805 their "confidence that [Cushing would] conduct with all the propriety and caution," the untimely disposition of the designated head of the Canton shop upset the plans of Perkins & Co. and they could not but feel apprehensive about putting a young boy in charge of an overseas venture. "We shall calculate upon your throwing off all juvenile pursuits and acting up to the situation in wh. circumstance[s] have place[d] you," wrote Perkins & Co. to Cushing. "Let the sage councils of y'r good Grandmother still vibrate on your ear, and let them sink deep into your heart," cautioned Cushing's anxious uncle. When the lengthy voyages delayed letter deliveries, the uncle was quick to express displeasure to Cushing "that you have not written us since y'r arrival in Canton; should you be so silent on the subject of business as you have been as to y'r situation, etc., we shall have much reason for pain and mortification." At stake was not only Cushing's budding commercial career; rather, as Perkins & Co. noted, "our reputation is deeply involved in y'r good conduct."

The concerns of Perkins & Co. soon proved unfounded as they finally received Cushing's December 10 letter on May 6, obliging them to apologize to Cushing "as we find you have not as we perhaps hastily concluded left us to conjecture what was the state of our business." The business update that Cushing had prepared must have impressed his uncle in Boston because the uncle noted in his reply that "it gives us pleasure to see by y'r style of writing that you have no apology for being silent." The uncle in Boston was quick to reverse course, reassuring Cushing: "Believe us always inclined to duly estimate y'r exertions." By June 19, not even three months after their initial exchange, Perkins & Co. told Cushing, "you will consider y'rself as the principal agent of an important Establishment."[27] This was an unanticipated promotion that Cushing

27 Baker Perkins, "Letters to Jno. P. Cushing." See also Mira Wilkins, "The Impacts of
    American Multinational Enterprise on American-Chinese Economic Relations, 1786–
    1949," in *America's China Trade in Historical Perspective: The Chinese and American*

received after the turbulent waves first carried him to Canton where, except for a brief home visit in 1807, he would remain for the next twenty-four years.

To assuage any concerns about the risk of a new venture, especially in the absence of total transparency in the language, nothing worked better for Houqua than the continuous presence of a business partner at his side in Canton. During his long sojourn in China, Cushing earned his fortune and forged with Houqua a partnership that lasted for generations. Beginning with his friendship and alliance with Cushing, Houqua "had long maintained the closest intercourse" with the Americans, largely to fulfill his "policy of allying himself with the enterprising Americans as an equipoise to the somewhat overbearing and pugnacious English East India Company," noted one of Cushing's cousins and successors in Canton, Robert "Bennet" Forbes.[28]

For almost a quarter of a century, Cushing stayed away from his native Boston and secluded himself in Canton, as "almost a hermit." There, young Cushing devoted his early adulthood to "studying commerce in its broadest sense, as well as its minutest details," wrote Bennet. This shared passion for the exciting and lucrative world of global commerce explains why Cushing, although "hardly known outside of his factory, except by the chosen few who enjoyed his intimacy," formed such a strong bond with "his good friend Houqua."[29] According to Bennet, Houqua always spoke of Cushing as his "schoolmaster." Cushing "studied the East India Companies trade & taught Houqua how to avail himself of the same & how to manage exchanges – hence the title of schoolmaster."[30] This special personal and professional bond between Cushing and Houqua would continue even after Cushing had returned home to Boston. On a return visit to Canton, an American trader noted how "Houqua always inquires about his old American friends, particularly the Messrs Perkins, and John P. Cushing Esqr which latter gentlemen he talks of and seems to love as a son."[31] This duo of global traders guided America's burgeoning trade in Canton. An American trader who first arrived in Canton in 1815 wrote in his journal, "I am greatly indebted to Mr. Cushing and Houqua for good advice and many personal attentions [sic]." As this trader noticed, Cushing and Houqua had "great confidence in each other" and conducted "much business together."[32]

Performance, ed. Ernest R. May and John K. Fairbank (Cambridge, MA: Committee on American–East Asian Relations, Department of History, Harvard University, 1986), 260.

[28] Forbes, *Personal Reminiscences*, 370.   [29] Ibid., 338.

[30] MHS Forbes Reel 5, No. 26, Letters from Robert Bennet Forbes.

[31] PEM Tilden Box 1, Folder 2, 117, September 15, 1835.

[32] PEM Tilden Box 1, Folder 1, 151, November 20, 1815.

The tight personal and business relations between the two masters of international trade notwithstanding, they differed in a significant approach to the principles of trade. Cushing, like most American traders in Canton at the time, had found a lucrative alternative to ginseng and fur products as a means of deriving capital from his imports to Canton. After trial attempts with ginseng and fur, which proved not to have sufficient appeal in Canton, the American traders found an answer in Turkish opium, which they shipped to Canton as a competitive alternative to the variety imported by the British from India. Although Houqua was fully aware of the source of their capital, records of his American associates indicate that Houqua stayed clear of the opium trade and his overseas partners structured their business to avoid implicating Houqua in the opium business.

Smuggling opium into China was illegal both for Houqua as well as for his foreign trading partners; however, the ramifications were unequal for the two sides should Qing officials decide to prosecute the offenders. As the direct interface with Qing officials, Houqua was immediately answerable to the Chinese state for any opium trafficking and was thus more vulnerable to the vagaries of government actions and the associated penalties. At stake was his license to conduct the tea business and his tremendous wealth which attracted the attention of Qing officials eager to find an excuse to expropriate his assets to respond to the demands of the state or to line their own pockets. The greater onus placed on Houqua to avoid being incriminated in the opium trade made it even more difficult for him to structure a consistent two-way trade of commodities from his base in Canton. His American partners had finally found the winning recipe for exporting tea from Canton by recycling the proceeds from their opium imports. Nonetheless, they had to be careful in their blatant violation of Chinese law against opium smuggling so as not to allow Qing officials to inculpate Houqua.

Houqua's eagerness to stay clear of the opium business probably intensified after his troubles with the state in 1821 when his official privileges were revoked for "his failure in enforcing vigorously the ban on opium and his mismanagement of the foreigners." He was deprived of his titular Third Rank and his official cap, honors that had been previously bestowed on him for his various contributions to the imperial treasuries.[33] It should come as no surprise that in the mid-1820s Cushing regrouped his business dealings in order to end what in Houqua's eyes was an evil venture. In this reorganization, Cushing placed management of the opium business of Perkins & Co., as well as that of Bryant & Sturgis, in the house of Samuel Russell, forming the joint entity of Russell & Company. Several

---

[33] FHA 04–01–30–0367–001 DG1/10/14.

years later, when John Murray Forbes succeeded Cushing and became Houqua's trusted American partner, he managed Houqua's business as an operation distinctly separate from that of his brother Bennet who openly admitted to have profited from smuggling opium into Canton. As Bennet recalled, "I am aware that Houqua . . . never liked the flavor of opium. One day when I was gossiping with Houqua, he said referring to the three Forbes – Tho' [eldest brother Thomas Tunno Forbes who drowned in 1829 shortly after taking over from Cushing], John & myself . . . 'Inside three brothers have got only one bad man.' This was an allusion to me as having had the opium ship."[34]

One cannot be certain if Houqua's dislike of the opium business reflected his disapprobation because the selling of opium offended his sense of morality or because it underscored his anxieties about the opium trade due to the repeated official condemnation of his inability to suppress the trade, costing him not only financially but also socially in the form of public humiliation. Either way, Houqua appeared to have adopted a pragmatic approach to managing his position with respect to the opium trade, which was all but impossible for him to eradicate. As Bennet noted, Houqua had desired to "whip the devil round the stump" as he "always knew" of the dealings in opium of Perkins & Co. as agents of American businesses and Houqua was just "willing to shuttee eye" to his partners becoming involved, at least indirectly, in the illegal trade.[35] Merchants far less astute than Houqua would have had no problem understanding the source of the capital for these partners exporting tea from Canton. As a British trader noted, "Opium is the only ready money article sold in China."[36] Then again, what choice did Houqua have but to distance himself from this illegal trade which was indispensable to funding the legal export of tea from Canton? Just as the British and the Americans had to search for goods with lasting appeal to offer in Canton, Houqua had to search for a viable channel in the global marketplace of goods to redeploy the proceeds from the sale of tea.

Completing Circulation in the Network: What to Do with the Money?

The illegality of the opium business not only exposed Houqua to repeated political and financial troubles, it also limited his commercial opportunities in the one-way trade of exporting tea and other products from Canton, depriving him of gains from the import of merchandise to Canton. This one-sided trading pattern of Houqua's business explains his

---

[34] MHS Forbes Reel 5, No. 26, Letters from Robert Bennet Forbes.
[35] Ibid.   [36] JM C4/6.

accumulation of capital, for which he eagerly sought profitable outlets of money-making opportunities. Houqua had to redeploy the profits he made from the sale of tea to foreign merchants, but he lacked any reinvestment options. In addition to his extensive investments in land and properties in and around Canton, the loans he extended to the British EIC and through the EIC to other Hong merchants answered his needs, at least in part. However, as much as the British and American traders encountered difficulties in identifying a product that appealed to the Chinese market, Houqua faced the issue of not having a viable product he could purchase from his partners and resell in China at a profit. As a result, he amassed vast sums of money, mostly in the form of silver. As much as it was a store of value and a unit of account, in Houqua's hands silver functioned as a product that generated healthy returns to the enterprising merchant.

Before the widespread addiction of opium took hold in China and opium supplanted silver as the source of capital for foreign traders in Canton, the balance of trade was largely in China's favor and Canton came to be a reservoir for the global circulation of specie. At the turn of the nineteenth century, Canton was still benefiting from "[t]he vast influx of specie... from various quarters," noted an American observer residing in Canton.[37] By one calculation, during the period of 250 years ending in 1821, Manila received some 400 million silver dollars from the Spanish New World. Half of this silver inflow is believed to have reached China.[38] A single Spanish vessel from Manila that perished in 1802 near Pedro Blanco (85 km to the east of present-day Hong Kong) was said to be carrying 1.2 million dollars.[39] Even as the influx of silver from other parts of the world abated, American inflows remained strong. From 1805 through 1812, American exports to China totaled 31 million dollars, over 70 percent of which came in the form of specie. As American activities intensified in the 1820s, specie continued to represent the greater portion of American exports to China. From 1816 through 1827 when Bills on England began to supplement specie, silver accounted for over 70 percent of the total American exports in all but three years (see Figure 3.1).[40]

[37] Howard Corning and Sullivan Dorr, "Letters of Sullivan Dorr," *Proceedings of the Massachusetts Historical Society*, third series (October 1941–May 1944), 67: 220.
[38] James R. Gibson, *Otter Skins, Boston Ships, and China Goods: The Maritime Fur Trade of the Northwest Coast, 1785–1841* (Seattle: University of Washington Press, 1992), 102, citing Lo-shu Fu, comp., *A Documentary Chronicle of Sino-Western Relations (1644–1820)* (Tuscon: University of Arizona Press, 1966), 2: 613.
[39] Corning and Dorr, "Letters of Sullivan Dorr," 67: 328.
[40] Timothy Pitkin, *A Statistical View of the Commerce of the United States of America, Including also an Account of Banks, Manufactures and Internal Trade and Improvements: Together with that of the Revenues and Expenditures of the General Government: Accompanied with Numerous Tables* (New Haven, CT: Durrie & Peck, 1835), 303.

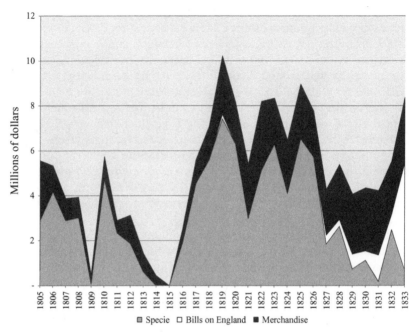

□ Specie □ Bills on England ■ Merchandise

Figure 3.1. Amount of Specie, Bills, and Merchandise Exported to Canton on the American Accounts, 1805–1833. *Sources:* Timothy Pitkin, *A Statistical View of the Commerce of the United States of America, Including Also an Account of Banks, Manufactures and Internal Trade and Improvements: Together with that of the Revenues and Expenditures of the General Government: Accompanied with Numerous Tables* (New Haven, CT: Durrie & Peck, 1835), 303. See also Yen-p'ing Hao, "Chinese Teas to America—a Synopsis," in *America's China Trade in Historical Perspective: The Chinese and American Performance,* ed. Ernest R. May and John K. Fairbank (Cambridge, MA: Committee on American–East Asian Relations, Department of History, Harvard University, 1986), 23.

Lighter than the Chinese silver ingots and capable of having more value than the Chinese copper cash, the silver dollars circulating in Canton and in the Southeast Asian ports that traders frequented served as a medium of exchange.[41] Not only were these "Old Heads," as the Carlos IV silver dollars from New Spain were called, a more convenient factor for carriage than the Chinese silver ingots, their distinct purity and quality, as perceived by the traders, conferred on them a value different from that

---

[41] Gibson, *Otter Skins, Boston Ships, and China Goods,* 102.

of the other silver dollars imported into Canton. An American trader in Canton, writing to his correspondents in the United States, took care to report that there was "a loss of 10 Per Cent on American Dollars" in Canton.[42]

A Rhode Island trader delivering copper to Houqua in 1817 reported the propensity of the Chinese to discount the "new impression of dollars" which, although "equal to the old dollars as to quality," would not be taken by the Chinese without a considerable discount.[43] Such "brand" recognition of silver coins, such as the "Old Heads," allowed them to command a premium, indicating a clear differentiation in what would otherwise be considered a commodity market for silver. The traders in Canton also watched out for counterfeits. In 1816, an American trader credited Houqua's account for forty-seven dollars of counterfeit.[44] As a result of such discrepancies in the quality of the different factors made with silver, the metal was more than merely a standard of value or a medium of exchange. Noted for their silver content and appreciated for the ease with which one could transport wealth with it, specie became a merchandise in and of itself and was a commodity in high demand, the trading thereof providing profit opportunities for both buyer and seller, much like the trading of tea, sugar, and other popular goods at the time.

Houqua generated from his tea trade tremendous financial assets in the form of various metals and bills. At home in Canton as well as abroad, Houqua traded these assets. In 1812, his partners in Rhode Island were informed of Houqua's inability to dispose of their bills because "[t]he demand for bills this season has been extremely limited & none have [sic] been sold (except English Govt Bills) but at a very considerable sacrifice." For these partners, Houqua would hold the bills to their order, "provided he is not able to dispose of them upon reasonable terms."[45] In 1815, from these same partners Houqua bought bills on Bombay in the amount of 115,555. At an exchange rate of 248/100 dollars, Houqua paid 46,595.65. These bills were sold to Houqua at such an unfavorable rate because of "the low price of bullion," which had rendered it "impracticable to dispose of the bills upon better terms."[46]

Houqua's network of American connections were keenly aware of the premium or discount at which each of the different monies traded, and Houqua availed himself of the opportunities these connections presented and partook of this premodern world of "foreign-exchange" transactions. His relations with Cushing provided him access to overseas brokers, with

[42] Corning and Dorr, "Letters of Sullivan Dorr," 67: 245.
[43] JCB Brown Box 50, Folder 17.   [44] PEM Shreve Box 8, Folder 2, 9.
[45] JCB Brown Box 276, Folder 10.   [46] JCB Brown Box 276, Folder 12.

Cushing serving as his intermediary. Cushing's correspondence with traders in Boston mention some of these transactions. For example, Cushing wrote to Perkins & Co. in 1820: "We have sold some of the Doubloons [gold coins minted in Spain and Latin America] for Houqua at 15 ½ dolls & hope to get rid of the whole at the same rate, we have before written you particularly on the subject of gold bar, silver & silver coin of all sorts."[47]

To make sure that he generated healthy investment returns on these assets, Houqua and his partners tapped into the active trading networks both inside and outside of Canton that were all too aware of the different types of money, in addition to the Chinese copper cash and silver ingots. The American connections enabled Houqua to deploy his capital and to remit his liquid holdings around the world in the most productive of ways, alongside the remittances of his American partners. Houqua's partners moved assets around global markets in a calculated manner. "[W]e think it ought to be a standing rule not to send other than Spanish dollars when they are not more than 3 to 5 per cent higher than other silver coin or gold," wrote Cushing from Canton in the same 1820 letter in which he articulated to his Boston partners the strategy he had developed based on market conditions in Canton and beyond.[48]

For his part, Houqua served as the linchpin in Canton capital markets for the Americans. By the opening in the 1810s, Houqua had built his paramount position in tea credit markets in Canton since he proved to be more resilient than the other Hong merchants in weathering the financial difficulties during a period when the Americans were once again becoming embroiled in conflicts with the British. As the level of commercial activities flagged in Canton, in August 1811 Cushing noted to his contact in Providence that "the credit of almost all of them except Houqua & Mouqua is totally destroyed both with their own country & also with foreigners & many of them do not even pretend to make a show of doing business." In the following year, Houqua further consolidated his status as the sole partner of the Americans in Canton.[49]

From this privileged position, Houqua commanded the market in Canton. By the middle of the decade, he was "very popular as a merchant, particularly among Americans," who believed his business to be so great that he had "more than three hundred coolies...in daily employ [during peak seasons]...besides a great many additional

---

[47] Baker Perkins, vols. 19–20, Perkins & Co., Canton, to J. and T.H. Perkins, Boston.
[48] Ibid.
[49] RIHS Edward Carrington, SGI/Series 1/subseries 1, Boxes 11–13.

clerks."[50] Houqua's reputation also extended down the eastern seaboard. In 1816, China trader Stephen Girard of Philadelphia referred his super-cargoes to Houqua, whom he called "my respectable friend" and "a correct and intelligent merchant."[51] In 1817, Rhode Island shipper John L. Bower observed, "Mr Houqua appears truly the Man of business – uses few words, is prompt and I believe correct in his dealings."[52] To the American traders, Houqua was tough but honest. "Houqua we found to be formal in his manners and by many thought to be haughty," noted an American trader during the 1819–20 trading season. "He knows more of trade and in my opinion is the best merchant in the Co-Hong – he does not solicit business and will engage in no speculation without a prospect of profit to himself. You seldom sell as high or purchase as low from him as from others but he is very punctual and strictly conforms with his engagements and will not deceive you in the goods he furnishes you. He has I believe given universal satisfaction in his teas. They have been esteemed the best in Europe & America of those imported by our flag."[53]

Just as he was an important source of capital for the operations of the British EIC, Houqua was also the creditor of choice for the Americans. He was the one to whom American traders wrote to negotiate credit for new arrivals in Canton from America. As an American trader said to his Canton-bound captain in 1815, "[o]n Mr. Houqua & [Cushing's] Perkins & Co. you must principally rely [for credit]."[54] Leveraging his formidable capital, Houqua broadened his dealings with the American traders. However, even as his portfolio expanded, Houqua remained guarded in his credit exposure. For instance, in his dealings with his Rhode Island trading partners, he collected a portion of the value of the goods he sold to American buyers, taking a note for the balance payable shortly after the conclusion of the sale (usually 15 months and only extending to 20 months in exceptional situations), specifying an interest rate of 1 percent per month on the amount outstanding.[55] Nor did he easily provide a discount on the interest payments stipulated in the

[50] PEM Tilden Box 1, Folder 1, 55, September 2, 1815; Box 1, Folder 1, 119, November 1, 1815.
[51] Jonathan Goldstein, *Stephen Girard's Trade with China, 1787–1824: The Norms Versus the Profits of Trade* (Portland, ME: MerwinAsia, 2011), 68; Jonathan Goldstein, *Philadelphia and the China Trade, 1682–1846: Commercial, Cultural, and Attitudinal Effects* (University Park: Pennsylvania State University Press, 1978), 69.
[52] JCB Brown Box 50, Folder 11.
[53] PEM Log 148, Journal of the U.S. frigate *Congress*.
[54] RIHS Edward Carrington, SGI/Series 2/subseries 2, vol. 2, Letterbook A, 10/1815–10/1817.
[55] JCB Brown Box 50, Folder 10.

agreements.[56] "[T]he truth is," reported one shipper to the partners in Rhode Island in 1817, "Houqua is very rich and so fond of his capital's being in a situation of accumulating by interest, that he is averse to receiving payment of a good note on interest before it becomes due, then he wishes to have it punctually paid." American traders in Canton could not but adhere to Houqua's strict practice of financial discipline. "I am endeavouring to get along with him in this business as well as I can for your interest," the shipper continued. "He is the only man here that can give any extensive credit, and he takes care to be well paid for it."[57]

The Use of the Law, or Not

Houqua's American partners would look back at early-nineteenth-century Canton trade and sing its praises. John Murray Forbes, who worked alongside Houqua for almost a decade, reminisced half a century after his stay in Canton that "I never saw in this country [the United States] such a high average of fair dealing as there [in China]." Forbes's predecessor, John Perkins Cushing, also called Canton "a place of business where he had had more facilities and less disputes than any other he was acquainted with." Of his extensive interactions in Canton, Cushing claimed, "I can only say that the Americans never had much difficulty in business there; they have always gone on very regularly, and without any embarrassment [indebtedness], except on one or two occasions."[58] Such recollections by Forbes and Cushing possibly provide us with an overly romantic image of the Canton system, which certainly had its fair share of undesirable participants. Their positive views of their experience in Canton, however, might have been directed more appropriately to their dealings with Houqua, their partner and patron in Canton. As John's brother, Bennet, said of Houqua, "One point in his habitual dealings will always be remembered by those who knew him. His word was his bond, and in many of his largest transactions was the only one which ever passed between the parties."[59] Even then, however, in his extensive interactions with generations of American traders who arrived in Canton to make a quick profit by partaking in the volatile market of international commerce, Houqua was not completely free from legal entanglements.

Houqua did not expect to always be able to resort to legal recourse in Canton as he executed financial documents with his partners. Certainly, the documents written in English did not form much of a basis for any

[56] JCB Brown Box 50, Folder 14.   [57] JCB Brown Box 50, Folder 16.
[58] Gibson, *Otter Skins, Boston Ships, and China Goods,* 191, citing Great Britain, *Sessional Papers,* 5: 377–378.
[59] Forbes, *Personal Reminiscences,* 371.

claims in the eyes of Qing officials. From the perspective of the Hong merchants, the Qing state was more protective of the foreign merchants, ensuring that the Chinese merchants collectively shoulder responsibility for any financially troubled Hong.[60] The converse was not true, however, as failed foreign merchants were not held to the same standards of responsibility. In fact, the laws of the Qing Empire held the foreign traders responsible not for obligations arising out of financial disputes but more often for criminal wrongdoings, for which the Hong merchants were also liable in their capacity as the guarantors of these visitors from overseas. For Houqua, this was the unfortunate asymmetry in the obligations levied upon the Hong merchants and the foreign traders in Canton. In the world outside of China where Houqua extended his business and deployed his capital, could he (and did he) demand fair dealings by resorting to legal channels in overseas jurisdictions?

Houqua's December 14, 1811, request that Wolcott initiate a claim against the insurance policy he had taken out in the event of the loss of the *Hannibal* revealed that he was fully aware of his rights in international markets for financial instruments and that he was ready to exercise such rights. At the nexus in Canton, Houqua's world of global commerce was far more complex than the notes that "bore simply the endorsement of sum and date with the names of the drawers," as described by Hunter,[61] and Houqua could pursue legal action through his American agents, if he so chose, to recoup any capital through the courts of law domiciled outside of China.

The earliest legal proceeding in the United States to which Houqua was party was Master Houqua v. James Perkins et al., 3 Rec. Pt. 1, P. 226 (U.S.C.C.D. Mass., May 1812). The origin of this lawsuit went back to March 12, 1804, when Thomas Thompson of Providence issued in Canton a note to Houqua for $44,000, which he promised to pay within twenty months' time as compensation for the tea he was shipping to America on the *Patterson*. "[I]f not then paid Interest... at the rate of twelve per cent per year." According to Thompson's deposition, he had signed this note "for and in behalf of John Innes Clark Esqr, Messrs James & Thos H. Perkins, Munro, Snow & Munro, merchants of America."[62] One of the parties, Messrs James & Tho. H. Perkins, was none other than the Boston firm that John P. Cushing was representing in Canton. When the note came due, Cushing paid Houqua $22,500, half of the

[60] Ch'en, *The Insolvency of the Chinese Hong Merchants*, ch. 5.

[61] Hunter, *The "Fan Kwae" at Canton*, 43–44.

[62] Master Houqua v. James Perkins et al., 3 Rec. Pt. 1, P. 226 (U.S.C.C.D. Mass., May 1812). Minute Book References, October 1811 Term, N–23, and May 1812 Term, C–163. I thank Frederic D. Grant Jr. for providing me with copies of these legal documents.

outstanding principal, for which Houqua issued a receipt, signed with his name in English. Another $11,250, again half of the outstanding balance, was returned to Houqua on January 30 1806, along with "Two hundred ninety two dollars fifty cents / $292.50 / on account of the interest of the within note."[63] Again Houqua acknowledged this payment by appending the original receipt and signing his name in English. The third and last entry on the document recorded a payment on December 22, 1807 from Perkins & Co. in the amount of $2,906.20, without specifying any division between the principal and the interest. Then, in 1811, Harrison G. Otis and George Sullivan filed a suit on behalf of Houqua in Massachusetts, seeking repayment on the note.

Before the lawsuit was filed, Munro, Snow, & Munro had declared bankruptcy in 1807. The court deposed Thompson, who testified to the veracity of the payment record, but highlighted the role of Cushing in the transaction. The court then received an accounting record for the homebound cargo on the *Patterson* in 1804, and what was alleged to be a copy of the letter of instructions, issued jointly by Munro, Snow, & Munro, James & Thos H. Perkins, and John Innes Clark, S. Dexter and Charles Jackson, attorneys for James & Thos H. Perkins, argued that they "did not promise the Plaintiff in manner and form as he has within thereof declared against them."[64] The jury concluded otherwise and found "the said James Perkins and Thomas H. Perkins with the said John Innes Clark, James Munro Samuel Snow, Benjamin Munro did promise in manner and form as the plaintiff has alleged and assess damages in the sum of [$14,645.65] for the breach thereof."[65] However, the sum would not come from all the parties listed as defendants: "It is therefore considered by the court that the said Master Houqua recover against the said James Perkins and Thomas H. Perkins the sum of [$14,645.65] debt or damage, and costs of suit taxed at [$49.04]. It is also further considered by the court that the said Master Houqua the Plaintiff aforesaid / as to the said John Innes Clark, James Munro, Samuel Snow and Benjamin Munro / shall take nothing by his writ there having been no service upon them."[66]

In the end, the amount the jury awarded Houqua helped him to recoup the outstanding principal, but it did not provide for the full payment of the interest for the intervening years, calculated at the agreed upon simple interest rate of 12 percent per year. What is interesting, however, is that Houqua allowed his representation in a foreign court at such an early date and that he was recognized as "Mr. Houqua of Canton in the Empire of China, Hong Merchant so called," or even more formally as "Master

[63] Ibid.   [64] Ibid.   [65] Ibid.   [66] Ibid.

Houqua of the City of Canton in the Empire of China merchant and an alien to each and every of the United States" in an official notice issued in conjunction with this case in the name of the President of the United States of America to "the Marshall of our district of Massachusetts, or his Deputy."[67] Houqua's representation by American attorneys in a U.S. court not only recovered assets to which he was entitled but also served to leverage a foreign legal infrastructure to mediate a dispute among his American debtors over their individual responsibilities.

Between the two possible explanations for the 1811 lawsuit, namely, simple recovery of Houqua's assets or mediation of the distribution of responsibilities among the American defenders, the latter is more likely. A chain of debt collections in the United States that Houqua launched in 1814 indicates that between Houqua and Perkins & Co. there was no animosity that would have necessitated the involvement of a U.S. court for Houqua to collect some fifteen thousand dollars. By the mid-1810s, the conflict between Britain and the United States had upset the plan of Houqua and his American partners to bypass the British in their shipments. "In consequence of the situation of Great Britain & America & the consequent stoppage of the accustomed intercourse between this Country & the United States," Houqua began collection proceedings on his outstanding loans from his American partners. On January 28, 1814 Houqua sent a letter from Canton to Richard Gardner in Salem, enclosing therewith Gardner's note in his favor. The agents whom Houqua named in this collection effort were none other than James and Thomas H. Perkins of Boston, one of the defendants in the lawsuit launched in Houqua's name in 1811. A copy of Gardner's note was certified to be "[a] true copy of the original...duly compared" by none other than John P. Cushing, the representative of Perkins & Co. in Canton and Houqua's confidant.[68] Thus, the 1811 lawsuit most likely represented not a temporary rift between Houqua and Cushing (along with Perkins & Co.), but their collective ploy to leverage U.S. law to induce the co-defendants, Clark, Munro, Snow & Munro, to contribute to the repayment to Houqua.

If Houqua was merely a passive party to the legal maneuvers in the 1811 Massachusetts lawsuit, he was more direct and active in his efforts to reduce his American exposure during the difficult decade of the 1810s and more pragmatic in his collection instructions despite the availability of legal recourse overseas. The notes he forwarded to Perkins & Co. for collection clearly specified the terms of the loans. For instance, Gardner's note, dated "Canton 7th November 1809," stated, "Value received of

[67] Ibid.   [68] MHS Samuel Cabot Box 1, Folder 11.

Mr Houqua, security merchant at Canton. I promise to pay to his order at the expiration of eighteen months from date, ten thousand, four hundred & thirty two dollars & forty seven cents with interest afterwards at one pr. cent pr month," and it was signed "Charles Pearson, attorney to Richard Gardner."[69] Along with Gardner's note, Houqua forwarded to Perkins & Co. in Boston similar notes for collection, including the note of Thomas Bryant of Philadelphia, dated February 11, 1812, for 5,882.46 dollars, the note of H. Tingley of Providence, dated February 1, 1812, for 2,966 dollars, and the note, dated November 20, 1812, for 22,080.96 dollars that Captain Richard M. Field had signed for Messrs P. Armidon & Co., the owners of the ship *Sally*. These, combined with other notes referred to the correspondence between Houqua and Perkins & Co., involved total claims of about one hundred thousand dollars from debtors residing in cities up and down the American seaboard, stretching from Salem to Baltimore.

These claims, which only included Houqua's financial assets invested among his American partners and did not include any physical goods that he might have had circulating in North America, underscore his early determination to penetrate this market and the diversity that he had achieved among his customer base. Upon receiving the notes that Houqua had sent Perkins & Co., Perkins & Co. first applied to Houqua's debtors in the vicinity of Boston and "immediately afterwards, our THP sat off for Providence, New York, Philadelphia & Baltimore on the same business" to recover Houqua's debts in those areas.[70] Reporting the results on November 16, 1814, barely nine months after Houqua had sent his requests from Canton, Perkins & Co. explained that for some who "could not make it convenient, at present, to discharge the whole amount of the notes," they extended the payment terms and subsequently received some repayments.[71] For others whom they "found unable to meet this call & in great distress," Perkins & Co. obtained as much as they could procure in money and obtained from the debtors security for the balance. Thus, 3,158 dollars and property from the ship the *Rapid*, valued at 2,842 dollars, was collected from Henry Dorr for Houqua. These collected repayments "were immediately invested in the following Exchange on London & remitted to Sam'l Williams Esq, London with orders to place the same to your credit and apply the proceeds in such Exchange on Bombay, Calcutta or Canton as should, in his opinion, promise to be most for your interest & forward the same to you at Canton to care of Perkins & Co." The remittances totaled "£14850 stg [or] $57224.44."[72]

[69] Ibid.   [70] Ibid.   [71] Ibid.   [72] Ibid.

As impressive and diverse as Houqua's American exposure was, the dissolution of these holdings, enabled by his network of overseas agents, was implemented swiftly and the proceeds were redistributed on a global scale.

Some delinquent loans would always end up being uncollectible and bad debts were an inevitable cost of doing business. Gardner had fled to Brazil, leaving behind no visible property. Perkins & Co. believed that the loss of a ship during the war had precipitated his bankruptcy. As for the other debtors, "H. Tingley promises to pay his note in the course of a short time. We hope he will comply with this engagement. Bery D. Jones cannot pay at present but assures us that he will make arrangements as soon as possible to discharge his obligations," reported Perkins & Co. There were other outstanding claims regarding which Thomas H. Perkins could not bring "any one to a settlement." In his treatment of financial losses stemming from bad debts, Houqua proved to be no stickler for legal enforcement of the contractual terms. He knew his rights under the law, but these rights would not do him any good unless the debtors had the financial wherewithal to live up to their end of the bargain. In such cases, as in 1821, Houqua showcased his pragmatic approach to business. In the later episode, he instructed Perkins & Co. to collect from his debtors, provided that they could "ascertain that the Drawer had property," but not to pursue the debtor "if it should appear that he is destitute." He requested that Perkins & Co. "make such settlement as you may deem adviseable [sic], but by no means insist on the payment of the whole or a part if should appear that it would distress [the debtor]."[73] In collection from his debtors, Houqua was realistic about his chances of recovery and human in his dealings with his partners.

Houqua's difficulties in collecting on his notes in the 1810s stemmed from a larger issue that affected his financial interests in the international marketplace. Houqua's debtors were not alone in their financial troubles "owing to the universal embarrassment occasioned in New York, Phila & Baltimore by *the suspension of all specie payments in those places* (by the banks as well as individuals)." In Houqua's interest, Perkins & Co. endeavored to delay demands from those who might be able to repay in specie thereafter, and avoided being compelled to receive depreciated bank notes. Upon "taking the best legal & private opinions on this subject," Thomas H. Perkins would decide for Houqua whether he would "suffer more from receiving & making the most of the current money there, or suspending the claim under a hope that specie payments may be revived whenever the causes which have led to the suspension shall

---

[73] Baker Perkins, vols. 19–20, Perkins & Co., Canton, to J. and T.H. Perkins, Boston.

cease to prevail." From Boston, Perkins & Co. planned to decide on the
form of remittance of the proceeds to Houqua depending on the price.
"Bills on London at Philadelphia & Baltimore are at par & varying daily;
as their Bank paper rises or falls."[74] In the early-nineteenth-century world
of finance, Houqua and his partners made business decisions based not
only on investment conditions in any one home base, but they were also
guided by an understanding of macroeconomic forces around the world.

In Houqua's world of economic exchange that featured a vast array of
financial arrangements, legal recourse did not provide equal protection to
all forms of transactions. In their communications with Houqua, Perkins
& Co. was careful to make the distinction between notes and consignments: in notes, Houqua, the debt-holder, had "an *equitable* right, which
cannot be disputed, to demand specie, & when the laws of the Union can
be promptly enforced, this right may be *legally* established." As for the
proceeds of consignments, consignees could complain that they received
from the banks "no other payment than thin notes, redeemable at a future
day in effective money – & therefore can make thin payments in this paper
only." Houqua and other consignors would then have to decide if it was
"most expedient to receive this paper & submit to all the loss which might
arise, rather than risk the issue & delay of a litigation, which might be
prolonged, by legal process, until the parties should be no longer able
to pay, or until the Government might be wicked enough to make bank
bills, or their own paper, a legal tender."[75] The letter of the law provided
Houqua with recourse in the event of a delinquent loan or delinquent
remittance of proceeds from consignment. Even if this recourse enabled
him to collect from his debtor or consignee, the value of the payment
could prove to be less than what the stipulated payment was supposed
to be worth because of fluctuations and manipulations of the exchange
rates. Houqua's real defense in such cases rested not in the courts of law,
but in his global network of partners whom he could trust to promote
his interests. Settlement in courts of law offered at best stop-gap reme-
dies; his partners, however, connected with him not only as one-time
debt collection agents but also allies in repeated business dealings, who
understood what would serve Houqua's interests in the ever-changing
arena of global trade and finance.

Houqua was pragmatic and generous in his legal maneuverings overseas, but some of his trading partners in America were artful in their
use of U.S. law against Houqua. In 1820, Edward Thomson brought a
lawsuit against Houqua in the Supreme Court for the Eastern District of
Pennsylvania for non-delivery of stipulated goods. The suit alleged that

[74] MHS Samuel Cabot Box 1, Folder 11.   [75] MHS Samuel Cabot Box 1, Folder 11.

"on the seventeenth day of August in the year one thousand eight hundred and eighteen at Canton . . . the said Edward at the special instance and request of the said Houqua would buy of him the said Houqua certain goods, wares and merchandises called crapes and sewing silks at and for a certain price or sum of money to wit for the sum of eighty thousand dollars lawful money of the United States." Houqua had promised, Thomson claimed, to deliver "goods first quality merchantable articles, of eighteen tales weight per piece, under the said sewing silk also were of the first quality." What was delivered, however, was of "inferior quality not merchantable and less than eighteen tales weight per piece."[76]

At stake in this lawsuit was assignment of responsibility for the quality of the goods as they traveled around the world. Even after Houqua had sold the products to this American buyer in Canton, the buyer held Houqua responsible for the quality of the goods, judged by inspection upon arrival at their destination. This arrangement would have been fair to Houqua had he sent the products to America on consignment, as he would have retained ownership title of the goods until their final sale overseas. However, the demand of quality assurance after arrival in America not only burdened Houqua with responsibility for loss or damage at sea but also put him at risk for questionable overseas inspection standards, over which he had no control. That this lawsuit surfaced in America reveals the developing standards of America's trade in Canton and the fluidity over the definition of the terms of trade. In the absence of any defined standards, the plaintiff in this case was probably attempting to impose the more stringent standards that the British EIC had enforced for its tea trade in Canton. On the insistence of the EIC, upon reaching London Houqua and the other Hong merchants were held accountable for products classified as "bad teas." As much as Houqua was leveraging the American presence in Canton to break free from control by the British, certain Americans were eager for treatment based on the same stringent standards that were demanded by the British.

The trial that ensued called into question the appropriate legal jurisdiction for this lawsuit, that "the contract on which this Plaintiff, founded

---

[76] Thomson v. Houqua, Interrogatories, Case no. 34, December term 1820, Records of the Supreme Court (Eastern District), Division of Archives and Manuscripts, Pennsylvania Historical and Museum Commission; Continuance Docket, 1818 (July term)–1825 (December term), 197, Records of the Supreme Court (Eastern District), Division of Archives and Manuscripts, Pennsylvania Historical and Museum Commission; Appearance Docket, 1817 (December term)–1823 (December term), 303, Records of the Supreme Court (Eastern District), Division of Archives and Manuscripts, Pennsylvania Historical and Museum Commission. I thank Frederic D. Grant Jr. for providing me with copies of these legal documents.

himself, was made in Canton, there to be executed and was to be construed and governed by the Law of China." The court also read reports of interrogations of "witnesses to be produced, sworn or affirmed and examined on the part and behalf of the defendant, under a commission to Canton" who testified to such things as "the usual course of trade and business at Canton." Particularly contentious was the issue of inspection: "Is it or is it not the usual course of trade and business at Canton upon the delivery of any and what kind of goods contracted for in China, for the Supercargoes to make such examination as to satisfy themselves as to the quality of the goods and their Conformity to the terms of the Contract and is not the neglect to make such examination always considered as satisfactory of the approbation of such Supercargo?" In the end, a special jury favored the plaintiff and assessed damages in the amount of $15,377.01. The defendant pleaded "non ass.[77] + payt with lease." In short, Houqua did not contest the findings and paid to settle the dispute. Satisfaction was acknowledged by Thomson on April 18, 1826.

Despite this settlement, Houqua, together with his allies in Canton, did not admit that "contriving and fraudulently intending to injure the said Edward did not perform or regard his said promise and undertaking so by him made as aforesaid but thereby craftily and subtilly [sic] deceived and defrauded the said Edward," as the suit alleged.[78] In his correspondence with Perkins & Co. in Boston, dated June 25, 1821, Cushing lamented: "It is unfortunate for H[ouqua] that Mr. Rush has gone from here, as his evidence would have been conclusive in Houqua's favor." His American partners promised to "exert ourselves to procure full & satisfactory evidence for our friend." Houqua and his partners insisted that Houqua had been wrongfully accused of providing products of subpar quality. "We do not mean to implicate the old Gent personally in any way whatev, as we

---

[77] "*NON ASSUMPSIT*, pleading. . . . 2. Under this plea almost every matter may be given in evidence, on the ground, it is said, that as the action is founded on the contract, and the injury is the non performance of it, evidence which disaffirms the obligation of the contract, at the time when the action was commenced, goes to the gist of the action. Gilb. C. P. 6 5; Salk. 27 9; 2 Str. 738; 1 B. & P. 481. Vide 12 Vin. Ab. 189; Com Dig. Pleader, 2 G 1," John Bouvier, *A Law Dictionary Adapted to the Constitution and Laws of the United States of America*, 5th rev. ed. (Philadelphia, 1855), 2:233. I thank Humphrey Ko for his assistance in interpreting these legal terms.

[78] Thomson v. Houqua, Interrogatories, Case no. 34, 1820 (December term), Records of the Supreme Court (Eastern District), Division of Archives and Manuscripts, Pennsylvania Historical and Museum Commission; Continuance Docket, 1818 (July term)–1825 (December term), 197, Records of the Supreme Court (Eastern District), Division of Archives and Manuscripts, Pennsylvania Historical and Museum Commission; Appearance Docket, 1817 (December term) –1823 (December term), 303, Records of the Supreme Court (Eastern District), Division of Archives and Manuscripts, Pennsylvania Historical and Museum Commission.

believe him as . . . honorable as any man upon Earth, but he has probably reposed too much confidence on those he employed & has after he
imposed on by them," his partners maintained. Yet they were practical
in their thinking, allowing that it would be beneficial if Houqua had to
"pay a few thousand Dollars" to put the lawsuit behind him. The settlement notwithstanding, Cushing was adamant in his support for Houqua:
"[W]e know positively that he always pays . . . more than any other . . . in
the place in order that the goods they furnish may be better than others.
He always pays 2/3 or 3/4 of the money in advance which if he was dealt
fairly by, ought & would give him a decided advantage in the quality of his
goods, over any other merchant in the place."[79] Cushing's remarks were
more than a simple endorsement of the quality of Houqua's goods. It was
a statement about the integrity with which Houqua always conducted his
business.

Extending one's commercial and financial reach to new pastures was
not easy. Based on his years of interaction with the British and the Americans, Houqua had built his linguistic confidence in the use of English. But
more difficult was the sporadic occurrence of legal issues, the management of which required an acute business sense and pragmatic assertion
of one's rights. Applying the same principles as he did in his continuous
assessments of business risks and opportunities, Houqua instructed his
American allies to be practical and non-dogmatic in representing him in
the courts of law.[80]

Through his persistent efforts, Houqua fashioned a trading network that
allowed his American partners to establish a firm footing in Canton in the
1810s. In this network, Houqua occupied a pivotal position, as Cushing
reported to his China trade brethren in 1811 – "Houqua of course has
almost all the America business."[81] Houqua had overcome the linguistic
challenges of operating with his American allies, but the struggles continued with the search for commodities of lasting appeal to ensure the
continuity of the bilateral trade. Just like the British, Houqua's American partners found the answer in opium, but Houqua faced a serious
obstacle because of the huge potential costs if he were to be discovered
involved in the import of opium. This asymmetry of business opportunities necessitated the deployment of his capital by extending loans and

[79] Baker Perkins, vols. 19–20, Perkins & Co., Canton, to J. and T.H. Perkins, Boston.
[80] For other cases of U.S. debtors who defaulted on loans extended to them by Chinese
merchants, see Frederic D. Grant Jr., "Hong Merchants Litigation in the American
Courts," *Proceedings of the Massachusetts Historical Society* 99 (1987): 44–62.
[81] RIHS Edward Carrington, SGI/Series 1/subseries 1, Boxes 11–13 (Incoming correspondence 1799 [11 December 1798]–1805, 1806–1809, 1810–1811).

consigning boatloads of merchandise overseas. This new business model represented a drastic departure from the stability of annual contractual arrangements that he had put in place with the British EIC. At risk were vast amounts of capital, which he floated to the land of opportunities on the other side of the Pacific.

To manage his risks, Houqua proceeded in a calculated manner, relying on his close-knit crew of trading partners. Over time, he cultivated a group of confidants, despite the linguistic difficulties. Forged through hardships brought about by geopolitical conflicts and economic depressions, in a pragmatic manner Houqua's alliances with his American partners handled issues that cropped up in the emerging world of global commerce. With the assistance of his American agents, Houqua demonstrated that he was aware and capable of leveraging different jurisdictions in seeking financial returns in courts of law. Yet he considered legal proceedings one of only many business options and he asserted his legal rights with a practical view regarding the possible outcomes.

Houqua's business enterprise began with his masterful handling of the EIC at home; however, as the landscape of international commerce began to undergo a rapid transformation, he could ill-afford to be content only with his dominance in Canton. From the nexus in Canton, Houqua worked together with his partners to fashion a network that altered the routes of global trade and rivaled, although not always successfully, the ascending power of the British. Unlike his predecessors who balanced the international powers primarily from their home base in Canton, Houqua expanded beyond the Chinese city and extended his influence to overseas markets. To function effectively in this new global configuration, which he had participated in engineering, Houqua projected his presence strategically and cultivated trust in his trading network.

4   Sustaining Trust
Overcoming Business Uncertainties through Time and Space

It is easier to maintain a business connection when the partners are located in the same place and business exchanges are transacted instantaneously. Hence, Houqua's business with the EIC involved few complications. The EIC had representatives stationed in Canton and Houqua did not have to wait before he received payment for his delivery of tea. In contrast, the consignment of tea shipped to America, as noted in the previous chapter, escalated Houqua's risk profile. His business in America entailed the risk of sending his goods half a world away, and for the return of the proceeds to reach Canton, Houqua had to wait until completion of the sale, which could take months, if not years.

In his study of the trading mechanism among eleventh-century Mediterranean traders, Avner Greif examines a similar situation.[1] The long-distance traders Greif studies faced issues that would have been familiar to Houqua: information asymmetries, insufficient communication technologies, and limitations to contract specifications and legal enforceability. So how did these traders manage to structure their exchange relations over long distances? In response to the challenges, the Mediterranean traders that Greif examines formed coalitions that functioned to police their members through a reputational mechanism, such that "[b]y establishing ex ante a linkage between past conduct and a future utility stream, an agent could acquire a reputation as honest, that is, he could credibly commit himself ex ante not to breach a contract ex post."[2] In essence, because the expected reduction in future profits resulting from dishonest behavior outweighed short-term gains through deception, traders would resist any temptations to cheat. Such

---

[1] Avner Greif, "Reputation and Coalitions in Medieval Trade: Evidence on the Maghribi Traders," *Journal of Economic History* 49, no. 4 (December 1989): 857–882; Avner Greif, "The Organization of Long-Distance Trade: Reputation and Coalitions in the Geniza Documents and Genoa During the Eleventh and Twelfth Centuries," *Journal of Economic History* 51, no. 2 (June 1991): 459–462; Avner Greif, *Institutions and the Path to the Modern Economy: Lessons from Medieval Trade* (Cambridge: Cambridge University Press, 2006).

[2] Greif, "Reputation and Coalitions in Medieval Trade," 858–859.

calculated maneuvers were predicated on good information flows among the traders. In his analysis, Greif privileges economic motivations, as opposed to social-control systems or ethics, in the regulation of such trade linkages. According to Greif, their social configuration was instrumental, but only in the transmission of information which underwrote the operation of the economic institution.[3]

Similar economic motivations certainly played an important role in facilitating continued exchanges between Houqua and his trading partners. However, the parties with whom Houqua traded, most notably his partners in America, were separated from Canton by voyages across the vast seas, whose length and duration aggravated the already imperfect information flows. The intractable American debtors named in Houqua's debt collection attempt in the 1810s demonstrated their willingness to sever ties with Canton and to forswear future trading in China. In such a situation, purely economic factors explicated by game theory cannot fully explain the enduring trust between Houqua and his selected partners.

In Houqua's world of business, profits over the long run overwhelmed considerations of the collectability of accounts gone bad. Houqua demonstrated that, in his pragmatic approach to business, he considered legal recourse only as a last resort. Instead, he relied on the bonds of personal trust that he cultivated with his partners in his exclusive network. To cultivate these bonds of trust required the presence of the partners in Canton for continuous interactions with Houqua, as well as concerted efforts by Houqua to sustain these interactions, even after the partners left Canton. The dislocation of trading patterns caused by political and military turmoil would test their connections, but these trials only tempered the bonds that Houqua had so painstakingly nurtured with his selected partners.

The Continuing Chain of Delegates to Canton

To develop the initial confidence in shipping goods overseas on consignment, nothing worked better than the reassuring presence of the selected business partner by one's side. Houqua could intensify his involvement in American business with comfort because for a long time he had by his side in Canton his handpicked American ally, John Perkins Cushing. Not only was Cushing Houqua's scribe in his English correspondences and an important source of information on the world of commerce, but he was also the one whom Houqua held accountable for the shipment of his goods to destinations around the world.

---

[3] Ibid., 859, 882.

This situation changed when Cushing decided to retire after two decades of transacting his global business activities from Canton. Cushing had groomed his cousin Thomas Tunno Forbes to be his successor in Canton after his return to Boston. But Thomas's drowning at sea in 1829 necessitated the dispatch to Canton of Thomas's younger brother, John, to whom Houqua readily entrusted his American business as a continuation of his partnership with Cushing. John served as Houqua's confidant in Canton for most of the 1830s, not returning to Boston until 1837. A third Forbes brother, Bennet, arrived in Canton in 1839 to take John's place, assuming leadership of Russell & Company, the enterprise through which Houqua continued to funnel business to the Forbes family. Therefore, Bennet continued the long-rooted partnership between Houqua and the Cushing/Forbes family, following the unbroken tradition of the family's presence in Canton to work alongside Houqua. Cushing and his Forbes cousins served as the bedrock of Houqua's American confidants and his access to the world that operated in written English.[4]

This continuous flow of Cushing and then the Forbes provided Houqua with constant company in Canton of a representative from the American team. This continuous presence of a member of the American team argues for the economic significance of the exchange to both sides and was no doubt a key contributing factor to their enduring ties. However, this continuous flow of partners through Canton was more than a stable channel of exchange. The return of his partners from Canton also dispersed his allies to various commercial and financial centers in the West. On the one hand, this dispersal added to Houqua potential risks. On the other hand, the distributive effect of these partners also allowed Houqua to extend his network in America through these secure allies. In addition to Cushing and the Forbes, many of Houqua's other business partners traveled to and from Canton from America and Britain. With these partners, albeit partners of varying degrees of business affiliation, Houqua extended his global reach. For the purpose of securing continuing connections with his partners overseas, Houqua presented to them his portraits, which would serve as a constant reminder of their ties to the Chinese merchant in the faraway port of Canton. Leveraging the presence of a community of artists in Canton, Houqua cast a commanding image of himself as an authoritative business figure and projected this image on his partners and prospective associates around the world.

---

[4] See Yen-p'ing Hao, "Chinese Teas to America – a Synopsis," in *America's China Trade in Historical Perspective: The Chinese and American Performance*, ed. Ernest R. May and John K. Fairbank (Cambridge, MA: Committee on American–East Asian Relations, Department of History, Harvard University, 1986), 19.

The Express Use of Portraits and the Prototype of a Global Iconic Image

In the nineteenth century, as products came to be produced in large quantities and advances in transportation and communications increasingly facilitated long-distance distribution, it became important for global traders to craft a respectable image of reliability that would allow them to set themselves apart in the midst of the sea of commodities and to assume a position of trust in their networks of trade.[5] This was especially significant for Houqua, the man who, by the 1810s, had funneled the lion's share of Chinese tea to the rest of the world. From Canton, tea was exported in vast volumes across the oceans to markets in Europe and America. To engender trust among his business partners and to impress upon them that he stood behind the quality of his products, Houqua depended on the distribution of a visual representation of himself that would convey his message non-verbally in this multilingual world.

Houqua intended that his portraits would serve an instrumental function in reminding his trading partners who had returned to America from Canton of their enduring ties to their Chinese patron half a world away. A portrait of a young Houqua is believed to have been sent to China trader Stephen Girard in Philadelphia. Historian Jonathan Goldstein, who has identified this Houqua image, calls it a "calling card" portrait.[6] For his more intimate partners, the function of Houqua's portraits extended well beyond such a "calling card" purpose: these portraits served to cement the bonds that he maintained with his select partners.[7] To John Murray Forbes, who had just returned to Boston, Houqua wrote on March 4, 1837: "My young friend, . . . Before you receive this you will probably have been at home more than six months. I count on seeing you again, probably before another year is ended, and shall be most glad to welcome you back." John was Houqua's trusted confidante in the world of commerce and had just left Canton after having served by Houqua's side for eight years. Houqua was eager to have John back in Canton but, short of fulfillment of that wish, Houqua would be content with entrusting his business in America to John. "You must recollect that I have given you authority to manage my business," continued Houqua, "and I do not wish you to delegate it to anyone

---

[5] Kevin Lane Keller, *Strategic Brand Management: Building, Measuring, and Managing Brand Equity*, 2nd ed. (Upper Saddle River, NJ: Prentice Hall, 2003), 52–53.

[6] Goldstein, *Stephen Girard's Trade with China, 1787–1824*, 62.

[7] Elsewhere, Goldstein places greater emphasis on Houqua's portraits as a symbol of the bond between the Chinese merchant and his partners (*Philadelphia and the China Trade, 1682–1846*, 69–70).

unless you should come back to China." The maintenance of that relationship would entail many written exchanges and for that Houqua beseeched John not to neglect to write to him. More effective than a steady stream of exchange of letters, a portrait of Houqua staring at his American partner in Boston would serve as a constant reminder of their mutual obligations. "I promised to sit for my portrait for you," pledged Houqua.[8] In fact, the portrait that Houqua gave to John was not the first of such portraits; John's copy was the product of an exploratory process by which Houqua and the artists in Canton developed and refined a pictorial representation of the Chinese business partner.

By this time, many Chinese artists were living in Canton, which had appealed to foreign merchants long before Canton became China's sole legal port of call for Western traders in 1757. These artists had developed techniques for producing oil paintings for export. By the early 1820s, they were already producing "stock paintings" of Admiral Nelson, Washington, Jefferson, and Madison for the export market. Among these paintings, one could also find likenesses of Houqua for purchase in the export shops in Canton.[9]

The arrival of Western painters in Canton fueled this development. George Chinnery, a British artist who left Britain at the age of 28 and spent twenty-three years of his life in India, arrived in Macao on September 29, 1825. In the Pearl River Delta area, Chinnery would spend the remaining twenty-seven years of his life, often venturing to the international port of Canton where the juxtaposition of Chinese elements and a Western presence offered many fascinating objects for depiction, as well as willing patrons for his paintings. It did not take long for the local community to embrace Chinnery. No more than two years after his arrival in Macao, Chinnery received a commission to paint a portrait of Houqua.[10] On a pen-and-ink sketch of the Hong merchant, the painter inscribed, in shorthand, "December 26th [18]27. Canton."[11]

In the associated oil portrait of Houqua, still housed in the HSBC collection in Hong Kong (Figure 4.1),[12] Chinnery details many Chinese

[8] Sarah Forbes Hughes, ed., *Letters and Recollections of John Murray Forbes in Two Volumes* (Boston: Houghton, Mifflin, 1899), 1:98.
[9] "Extract from the Port Folio of a Canton Supra-Cargo, Painters of Canton," *National Gazette and Literary Register* (Philadelphia) 4, no. 381 (August 5, 1823). I thank Patrick Conner for pointing out this reference to the early Houqua portraits.
[10] We cannot be certain whether Chinnery modeled his portrait of Houqua after the earlier paintings because the earlier portraits are no longer extant.
[11] Patrick Conner, *George Chinnery 1774–1852: Artist of India and the China Coast* (Woodbridge [Suffolk, UK]: Antique Collectors' Club, 1993), 172.
[12] Houqua also holds court across the street from the HSBC headquarters in Hong Kong where a copy of this portrait by Chinnery occupies center stage at a bar called "The Chinnery," in the Hong Kong Mandarin Oriental Hotel.

Figure 4.1. George Chinnery's Portrait of Houqua. Oil on canvas, 28 × 18 in., in HSBC. Reproduced with the permission of HSBC Holdings plc.

features of his subject, but the portrait is drawn in a style that, according to art historian Patrick Conner, is "wholly at odds with traditional Chinese notions of portraiture." Houqua assumes a pose that is decidedly non-Chinese.[13] As opposed to the traditional Chinese

---

[13] For a detailed description of the "iconic pose" in Chinese ancestral portraits, see Jan Stuart and Evelyn S. Rawski, *Worshiping the Ancestors: Chinese Commemorative Portraits*

full-frontal portrayal of the subjects, this image of Houqua only offers the viewer a three-quarter face. Sitting upright, Houqua is crossing his left leg over his right, affording the viewer an almost ninety-degree frame formed by his head and torso at the one end and his lower body at the other.[14] This cross-legged pose, in which Chinnery chose to portray Houqua, would have been considered "casual to the point of rudeness" when measured against Chinese conventions. It reflects, however, the "elegant ease" commonly displayed by European portrait sitters, a posture Chinnery often adopted with his subjects.[15]

Chinnery employs dramatic chiaroscuro to highlight Houqua's face and upper body. The subject, depicted serene and sagacious, rests on a Chinese chair next to a heavy column with an ornate base. A romanticized Chinese home and garden, along with a decorative lantern, form the backdrop.[16] Notwithstanding the Chinese subject and the oriental (or orientalized) surroundings, in his portrait of Houqua Chinnery showcases styles and techniques that are conspicuously European, in keeping with similar paintings produced in Canton at the time that were destined for export markets in Europe and North America.

In addition to the fine Chinese furniture and the hanging lantern, next to Houqua Chinnery displays a fine porcelain cup and saucer, perhaps a reminder of tea, the market of which Houqua commanded. The cup and saucer, along with the depicted spittoon, also connote the lifestyle that Houqua's wealth and status afforded him. However, nothing suggests his status more than the Mandarin cap on the Chinese stand and the Mandarin gown draping Houqua's thin frame. Despite the clear suggestion of Houqua's position in Qing officialdom, the cap and gown, even in the theatrical spotlight, would not have provided sufficient details even to an informed Chinese viewer to discern the exact rank of Houqua's title, which would otherwise have been distinguishable by the type of bird embroidered on his gown and the precise arrangement of his cap.[17] This

---

(Washington, DC and Stanford, CA: Freer Gallery of Art and the Arthur M. Sackler Gallery, in association with Stanford University Press, 2001), 83–90. It should be noted that there are several extant examples of informal Chinese portraits painted during the lifetime of the sitter (Ibid., 65–72).

[14] Conner, *George Chinnery 1774–1852*, 10, 165, 175.

[15] G. H. R. (Giles Henry Rupert) Tillotson, *Fan Kwae Pictures: Paintings and Drawings by George Chinnery and other Artists in the Collection of the Hongkong and Shanghai Banking Corporation* (London: Spink & Son for the Hongkong and Shanghai Banking Corporation, 1987), 17.

[16] Conner, *George Chinnery 1774–1852*, 175.

[17] *Qinding Da Qing huidian tu (Jiaqing chao)* (Pictorial Section of the Collected Statutes of the Qing Compiled during the Reign of Jiaqing [1796–1820]) (Taipei: Wenhai chubanshe, 1992), *juan* 45–46, for the official caps and gowns. See Stuart and Rawski, *Worshiping the Ancestors*, 111–114, for a discussion of the conformity of costumes depicted in Chinese portraits to sumptuary codes.

lack of specificity on a feature that would have been meaningful to a Chinese viewership provides further evidence that the intended audience of this portrait resided in the West. The Western viewer would not have been able to interpret the exact rank of the title the Qing court had conferred on Houqua, even if the portrait had provided more specific clues. What truly mattered in the message of the painting was that Houqua's material wealth was inseparable from his ability to provide Western traders an interface with Chinese officialdom. That Houqua donned Mandarin garb would have sufficed in conveying to this Western audience the authority he commanded in the Chinese port of Canton.

Deviating from the approach of traditional Chinese portraits that emphasize specific features at the expense of emotional suggestions, Chinnery imbues Houqua's facial depiction with hints of his mindset. Houqua does not bear the jovial look becoming of the material prosperity represented by his surroundings. Instead, he is wearing the guarded expression of an astute businessman, which Conner associates with the description of Houqua by British emissaries in 1818: His "person and looks bespoke that his great wealth had not been accumulated without proportionate anxiety."[18] This betrayal of the sitter's inner feelings is nothing less than a direct contradiction of the principles of Chinese portraiture in which the subject seldom wears his heart on his sleeve. Had Houqua chosen to be painted in traditional Chinese style, he would have had a stoic expression on his face and he would have offered a full frontal view, presenting his Mandarin cap with elaborate details to signify his rank.

Chinnery's portrait of Houqua therefore was not intended for the typical Chinese viewer. His was not to be a portrait to be kept in the Wu family compound, but rather it was a representation of the thoughtful businessman prepared with Western artistic techniques drawn to impress Western eyes. Despite its Western touches, Chinnery's portrait of Houqua captures many Chinese elements to help the viewer place Houqua in Qing China. The Western painting style combined with the exotic Chinese features in the portrait parallels the role of Canton as the interface between China and its Western trading partners and the function of Houqua as the fulcrum in this interface. Rendered thus, the portrait of Houqua, the vanguard merchant in the Chinese port of Canton with whom Western traders interacted, could find a comfortable place in a Western home.

This Chinnery portrait of Houqua is believed to have sailed to England with W.H. Chicheley Plowden, president of the Committee of the East

---

[18] Ellis, *Journal of the Proceedings of the Late Embassy to China*, 305.

India Company in Canton in 1830.[19] Plowden's portrait of Houqua was one of four portraits by Chinnery that appeared in the Royal Academy exhibit in 1831.[20] On June 15, 1831, *The Morning Post* in London reported on this painting, numbered 248 among the exhibits: "*Portrait of Howqua, Senior* Hong *Merchant at Canton, China.* G. CHINNERY. Mr. C had some clever portraits in the same style in the last Exhibition of the Academy. There is an *air Chinois* about them, and an elevated tone of colouring, which is no doubt quite in character with the objects and the scene of action."[21] This was years before the outbreak of the Opium War and the appearance of the Houqua portrait in London inspired a fantastical notion of the international world in Canton. The Chinese merchant in Canton appeared exotic and foreign to the world in Britain, yet he was also responsible for their tea, an important staple for the British consumer. His connections to the Western traders who traveled to Canton bridged the two worlds and brought to the markets in Britain and beyond a critical commodity that fueled the daily lives of Western consumers. For the traders who carried home paintings of the celebrated merchant, the images of Houqua reassured them of their trusted partnership with the pivotal figure who was instrumental to their trading with the far-flung Qing Empire.

Replicating the Image

Chinnery's depiction of Houqua, an exotic subject in a style familiar to European viewers, must have struck a chord in Western markets beyond the audience at the Royal Academy exhibition in London. Without generating as much fanfare as the display of the original Houqua portrait, similar paintings, attributed either to Chinnery or portraying Houqua in a similar manner in a comparable setting, began to proliferate. An early portrait of Houqua had found its way to America with John Perkins Cushing. When Cushing left Canton in 1827 to return to Boston, he held in his possession a portrait of Houqua that he then contributed to the exhibition at the Boston Athenæum in 1829. The catalog for the exhibition lists the portrait of "Houqua, Chief of the Hong Merchants, Canton," attributed to "Chenery" (most likely Chinnery) and exhibited by "I. [John] P. Cushing."[22] This record of the display of the portrait in a respected institution in Boston as early as 1829 attests to the iconic status

[19] Conner, *George Chinnery 1774–1852*, 177.   [20] Tillotson, *Fan Kwae Pictures*, 17.
[21] *The Morning Post* (London), June 15, 1831.
[22] *Catalogue of Pictures, in the Athenæum Gallery, 1829* (Boston: s.n., 1829), 10. There is no further information about this portrait, which could well have made it into one of the collections listed later. It is not easy to ascertain which one, if any, of the following

of Houqua's visual representation on both sides of the Atlantic, thanks largely to the transmission of his image through his trading partners.

Comparable to the original that is known to have come from Chinnery's hand are four other extant oil-on-canvas portraits, all housed in the United States.[23] These four portraits, which are almost identical, feature most of the same paraphernalia as the original, save the Roman column. They set Houqua against a similar background, but one that is more brightly lit than that in the original.[24] In addition, the Peabody Essex Museum houses the same portrait of Houqua, but produced in a different medium, i.e., mezzotint engraving (Figures 4.2a and 4.2b). This piece is the work of John Sartain.

Sartain's engraving represents a faithful rendition of the four oil-on-canvas portraits. According to PEM records, this piece is "identified in the plate as being after a portrait by George Chinnery in the collection of Benjamin Chew Wilcocks (1776–1845) of Philadelphia." Sartain's home in Philadelphia and the work's present location in Salem span the eastern seaboard in the United States from which Houqua's U.S. partners set sail to trade with him in Canton. The Chinese characters written below the engraving are of particular interest. The two Chinese characters represent an attempt to transliterate the name "Houqua" into Chinese, evidently oblivious to the fact that the name "Houqua," rendered in various spellings in English, is itself a transliteration of the Chinese merchant's trading name. Whoever wrote these Chinese characters with a Chinese brush paid no attention to the identity of the sitter as represented

portraits was the one originally held by Cushing because the records of the collections do not provide sufficient details regarding provenance.

[23] One of these portraits was located by Zhuang Su'e in a private collection ("Shijiu shiji Guangdong waixiaohua de zanzhuzhe: Guangdong shisanhang hangshang" [The Sponsors of Export Paintings from Nineteenth-century Guangdong: The Merchants of the Canton Trade], in *Quyu yu wangluo: Jinqian-nianlai Zhongguo meishushi yanjiu guoji xueshu yantaohui lunwenji* [Regions and Networks: A Collection of Essays Presented at the Academic Conference on Chinese Art History of the Last One Thousand Years] [Taipei: Guoli Taiwan daxue yishushi yanjiusuo, 2001], 533–578). Another one of the portraits resides in the India Club House in New York City. A third is held at the Metropolitan Museum of Art in New York, and the last is housed in the Peabody Essex Museum. Philip Chadwick Foster Smith also identifies one in a private collection. See Jean Gordon Lee, *Philadelphians and the China Trade, 1784–1844* (Philadelphia: Philadelphia Museum of Art, 1984), 36–37. This copy was reportedly painted for Benjamin Chew Wilcocks, a China trader from Philadelphia. It might be the same copy that was located by Zhuang Su'e.

[24] Instead of seating the cross-legged Houqua against an axis to the viewers' right, these three portraits rest Houqua on the left side of the paintings. This lateral transposition of the subject parallels the different portrayals of another Chinese Hong merchant, Mouqua, in two portraits in the HSBC collection. Interestingly, in the latter case, Chinnery paints Mouqua on the right, whereas the portrait drawn by the native Chinese artist puts Mouqua on the left.

(a)

(b)

Figures 4.2a and 4.2b. John Sartain's Portrait of Houqua, circa. 1830. Mezzotint engraving, 24 × 18.7 in. Courtesy of the Peabody Essex Museum, Salem, Massachusetts.

by the Chinese trading name that he had long adopted in his business correspondence. Instead, the inscriber of the Chinese label had come to associate this portrait with the articulation of the name "Houqua" by Western tongues, attesting to the iconic status of Houqua's likeness not among Chinese, but among Western traders in Canton during the first half of the nineteenth century.

A variation of this set of paintings, considered to have been brought from China in about 1840 by Edward King, who was actively involved in Russell & Company and who was in Canton during Houqua's time, shows Houqua resting his arm and weight to the viewers' right.[25] A notable difference in this portrait is the Chinese calligraphy scroll, which clearly reveals the last several characters, *woshi*, namely, "my teacher." This detail stands in sharp contrast to Chinnery's works in which the English painter scribbled outlines of Chinese characters but did not engage the service of native writers to produce faithful renditions of the Chinese script. This painting with Chinese characters, which is not considered to be a work by Chinnery, firmly confirms the shift in the painting of Houqua's portraits into the hands of native Chinese artists in Canton.

Distilling the Image and Achieving Mass Dissemination

The portraits thus far discussed in this chapter, be they works by Chinnery or copies thereof, preserve many of the elements of the original Houqua portrait that Plowden carried home to England. They situate a cross-legged Houqua casting a knowing glance at his viewer from the exotic setting of his Chinese home and garden appointed with exquisite oriental furniture and lantern. The fascinating oriental details would have captivated the traders among the British audience. However, as Houqua broadened his reach to America and beyond, his portraits came to represent a different setting, a setting streamlined for economic reproductions. More importantly, these streamlined portraits were optimized to highlight Houqua's persona, the perspicacious trading partner in Canton.

A small oil painting in the Peabody Essex Museum presents just such a streamlined portrait (Figure 4.3) and accentuates the facial features of the sitter. In particular, the portrait features Houqua's distinctive "domed forehead, hollow cheeks, wispy beard" that Conner believes to have reached "an almost iconic status, the acceptable face, as it were,

---

[25] Henry and Sidney Berry-Hill, *Chinnery and China Coast Paintings* (Leigh-on-Sea, UK: F. Lewis, 1963), Plate 39.

Figure 4.3. Lamqua's Portrait of Houqua. Oil on canvas, 18¼ × 16½ in.
Courtesy of the Peabody Essex Museum, Salem, Massachusetts.

of the China trade."[26] As the iconic representation of Houqua was reproduced, the portrait lost some of its less important features. The full-body
portrait by Chinnery was truncated to waist-length, producing a sharper

[26] Patrick Conner, "Lamqua, Western and Chinese Painter," *Arts of Asia* 29, no. 2 (March–
    April 1999): 54.

focus on his facial features, which came to occupy a larger area of the painting. The only reminder of Houqua's location in the faraway Qing Empire is his official cap (partially visible on the right) and his gown. Gone is the orientalized rendition of his home and garden, as are the lantern and the spittoon. What is left of the backdrop of the romantic landscape is reduced to half a window frame, relegated to the side of the picture.[27] In the development of Houqua's iconic image, later rounds of his portraits shed the superfluous elements and draw the viewers' attention to Houqua, the man behind this image of trust.

To widen the distribution of his trademark image among his partners in America and beyond, Houqua leveraged the studios of Cantonese artists, who by the nineteenth century had gained tremendous experience in painting in a Western style for the export markets in Europe and North America. In fact, so adept were native Chinese artists in producing or reproducing portraits for Western viewers that it is difficult to distinguish Chinnery's portraits of Houqua from those painted by native Chinese artists. Most of the extant Houqua portraits in America are the handiwork of the Cantonese artist Lamqua, whose Chinese name is believed to have been Guan Qiaochang. Some of his contemporaries believed that he had studied with Chinnery. Whether or not this is true, Lamqua soon proved to be a serious rival to Chinnery as he produced paintings of sufficient quality to the Western eye and undercut Chinnery by charging substantially lower prices.

Lamqua's likeness of his subject is as convincing as that of Chinnery, but his pricing made his offerings all the more appealing. Whereas Chinnery was charging in the range of $150 to $250,[28] Lamqua rendered a likeness of his sitter in Canton for merely $15.[29] So good was Lamqua's work that *The Canton Register* quipped that he "be *ordered* home by the ladies of the land in the U.K. for we can assure them . . . that they will never *again* look so beautiful unless under the *vivida vis* of the sparkling and magic touch of CHINNERY." The Western residents in Canton were evidently so impressed with the works by this Chinese painter that they drew a direct comparison between Lamqua and Chinnery. So persuasive

---

[27] There is a similar painting included in the illustrations in *Journey to the Far East – George Chinnery and the Art of Canton, Macao and Hong Kong in the 19th Century* (Tokyo: Tokyo Metropolitan Teien Art Museum, 1997), Plate 111.

[28] JM, Accounts Current A4/19, 88 (October 31, 1840) and 89 (January 31, 1841), cited in Conner, *George Chinnery*, 265.

[29] "Chinese Painters," *The Canton Register* 8, no. 49 (December 8, 1835): 195. Another source quotes portraits by Chinnery costing 50 to 100 piastres, whereas comparable portraits by Lamqua fetched 15 to 20 piastres. See Robin Hutcheon, *Chinnery: The Man and the Legend* (Hong Kong: South China Morning Post, 1974), 77.

were Lamqua's portraits that the paper proceeded to wittily remark about this celebrated Chinese artist: "The knighthood would then follow as a matter of course, as having been mostly deservedly earned and richly merited."[30] More importantly, however, the Chinese master's works cost less than one-tenth that of those by the British artist.

Houqua might not have requested that Lamqua render a beautified impression of him as much as Western sitters might have requested "a more *handsome* or acceptable memorial . . . than their sweet countenances." In fact, Chinnery's three-quarter presentation of Houqua's facial features probably concealed his protruding tooth, a disfiguration that supposedly earned him the nickname of "Wu, the pierced cheek."[31] Lamqua would have had to follow Chinnery's representation in his own portrait of Houqua to achieve similar results. Additionally, Houqua would not have agonized over the difference in the cost of a single portrait. After all, several hundred dollars for a painting would hardly be a significant outlay in Houqua's account book. Of greater importance was the ability of Lamqua to produce numerous copies. The low costs and the streamlined production in Lamqua's studio allowed Westerners in Canton to dream of sending their likeness to their "mothers, sisters, their fair ladye's loves."[32] For Houqua, Lamqua's low costs and swift reproductions served a different purpose. Houqua's courtship with these portraits was commercial, not romantic, in nature. Through these portraits, Houqua sought to cultivate business opportunities and consolidate relationships with his existing trading partners.

Many of Houqua's portraits found their way to America via Houqua's partners who were returning home after sojourns in Canton. Figure 4.4 is one such portrait. This portrait, housed in the Ipswich Library, comes from the estate of Augustine Heard, Houqua's close business associate who returned home from Canton to Ipswich, Massachusetts. The painting, believed to have been executed by Lamqua, was exhibited at the Boston Athenæum in 1850.[33] Note the blurry lines of the embroidery on Houqua official robe, which are less distinct than those on Chinnery's original. Also, the entire garden and villa setting has dissolved into a dark background against which Houqua's trademark face stands out. Not only

[30] "Chinese Painters," *The Canton Register* 8, no. 49 (December 8, 1835): 195.
[31] Liang Jiabin, *Guangdong shisanhang kao*, 12.
[32] "Chinese Painters," *The Canton Register* 8, no. 49 (December 8, 1835): 195.
[33] Listed as the first of four Hong merchants who, along with Commissioner Keying, were the subjects of "Five Portraits of Eminent Chinese Personages, by Lamqua, a Chinese Artist," in the *Catalogue of the Twenty-Third Exhibition of Paintings in the Gallery of the Boston Athenæum* (Boston: Eastburn, 1850), 12.

Figure 4.4. Lamqua's Portrait of Houqua. Oil on canvas, 32¾ × 25¼ in.
Courtesy of the Ipswich Public Library, Massachusetts.

was the native Chinese artist skilled at rapidly copying Western paintings less expensively, but he was also adroit in distilling the essential features of Houqua's likeness to produce an efficient replication for distribution far and wide.[34]

[34] In this respect, one should bear in mind the analogy that Winnie Wong draws between the paintings of early-nineteenth–century native Chinese artists to present-day workshops in the Dafen Oil Painting Village of Shenzhen. See Winnie Wong, "Imagining the

A 1953 inventory identifies close to ten such portraits along the eastern coast of the United States. We have already referred to those housed at the Peabody Essex Museum. The Museum of Fine Arts (MFA) in Boston boasts a copy from the family of Spooner (Figure 4.5), an associate at Russell & Company, the primary business concern through which Houqua traded with his worldwide partners. One of the descendants of Daniel Nicholson Spooner who gave the portrait to the MFA wrote that the portrait "was painted for my grandfather and given him by Houqua who was an intimate personal friend."[35] The Low family of New York, whose nineteenth-century ancestor traded for Houqua through Russell & Company, also holds a copy of the portrait. Yet another family associated with Russell & Company, the Delanos, owns a copy.[36] Another copy, featuring an aging Houqua, is in a private collection in Washington DC.

Among Houqua's trading partners, the Forbes maintained the most intimate and lasting relationship with Houqua and his heirs. The Forbes continue to hold on to at least one copy of Houqua's portrait in Milton, Massachusetts.[37] The aging Houqua depicted in this copy, similar to the one in the Museum of Fine Arts in Boston, features an old and serene Houqua. The older Houqua in these paintings confirms the production of simplified portraits against a plain dark background during later years as Houqua broadened his network of circulation, both of his portraits as well as of his goods and capital. Within the trading network that Houqua had developed, the Forbes held a special place. Displayed alongside the portrait of Houqua in the sitting room of the Robert Bennet Forbes house in Milton, Massachusetts, is a gemstone that is believed to have been set on top of Houqua's Mandarin cap depicted in the portrait and is said to have been presented by Houqua's son to the Forbes in memory of the old merchant.

In addition, additional portraits of Houqua must have been kept on hand or reproduced posthumously for distribution. In a letter dated May 31, 1845, two years after Houqua's death, Jamsetjee Jeejeebhoy wrote from Bombay to thank Houqua's son for "two portraits of [his] late respected Father."[38] These extant portraits, along with the surviving

Great Painting Factory in the Studio of Lam Qua" (paper presented at "'China Trade' (1760–1860) Merchants and Artists: New Historical and Cultural Perspectives," Macau Ricci Institute, Macau, March 2–3, 2011).
[35] Correspondence with Mrs. Motley and Mr. Hipkiss, Folder of Chinese School, Port of Canton, 50.3790, Museum of Fine Arts, Boston.
[36] This copy, which was passed down through the generations in the Delano family, is featured prominently on the cover of Grant, *The Chinese Cornerstone of Modern Banking*.
[37] Elma Loines, "Houqua, Sometime Chief of the Co-Hong at Canton (1769–1843)," *Essex Institute Historical Collections* 84, no. 2 (April 1953): 99–108.
[38] Jamsetjee Jeejeebhoy Papers, University of Mumbai Library, #354.

Figure 4.5. Portrait of Houqua by an Unknown Chinese Artist. Oil on canvas, 29½ × 22 in. Photograph © 2016 Museum of Fine Arts, Boston.

records related to their production and distribution, highlight their use both to solidify Houqua's business connections as well as to extend his trading networks.

Houqua and his family could not have accomplished these business initiatives through the distribution of his portraits without the presence of the community of artists in Canton. Indeed, Houqua did not control the process by which his likeness came to be simplified and reproduced. Instead, development of the way in which he was portrayed reflected the artistic and stylistic choices of the painters. Houqua did not commission all of the portraits, some of which accentuated different aspects of the subject. Nonetheless, textual evidence in the correspondence between Houqua (and his family) with his business associates, as well as the distribution of his many portraits, especially in America, underscore how Houqua effectively leveraged the creations by the artists in Canton to project a visual representation of himself that produced sufficient consistency for the making of a global icon.

Judging from the lasting relations between John Murray Forbes and Houqua's family, the portrait indeed served its purpose. Not only did John Murray Forbes dutifully handle the business Houqua entrusted to him,[39] but the descendants of the Forbes also came to be reminded of the great Chinese trader with whom their family partnered. William C. Forbes wrote in 1940, "Houqua so impressed the Americans with whom he came in contact that his name has come down for generations as the last word in probity, sagacity and generosity." Writing more than a century after the families initiated their partnership, William C. Forbes attributed the family's memory of Houqua to his portrait, which continued to be displayed prominently in the homes of his partners. "His painted portrait hung on the walls of many American houses," noted William C. Forbes, "highly prized as the symbol of all that is praiseworthy in public and private relations."[40] This testimony from the mid-twentieth century suggests that Houqua left a lasting imprint in the minds of his partners' families.

Several factors were responsible for Houqua's ability to canvass with this vast collection of his portraits the important ports on the east coast of America where Sino-American merchants made their homes. That these merchants from the various ports all traveled to Canton and remained there for protracted periods of time to conduct international trade alongside Houqua provided the basis for the relationships the portraits served

---

[39] Baker Forbes, L, Subseries III, Box 16, f.9–10.
[40] Forbes, "Houqua, the Merchant Prince of China, 1769–1843," 11.

to cement. The sheer number of similar portraits underscores Houqua's conscious effort to leave a lasting impression among his partners as he continued to build his international networks. To execute his strategy of portrait distribution to his many American partners, Houqua relied on their rapid replication that was made available in the Canton studios of native Chinese artists who produced portraits in Western style.

Had it not been for the presence of these native artists and the constant flow of Western traders in and out of Canton, Houqua would have required a different strategy, which most likely would have assumed a different form, to cultivate trust with his partners. Regardless of the form it might have assumed, it was a critical business strategy for trading partners to engender among themselves the trust necessary to ensure orderly business transactions.[41] To achieve such trust, global traders had to improvise.

Rosenthal and Wong propose a framework to understand the mechanism of commercial exchanges whereby trade that encompassed short distances and short time frames could rely on informal arrangements, whereas long-distance exchanges that extended over long periods of time required formal arrangements or had to be carried out on a cash basis.[42]

---

[41] Houqua's strategy amounts to a "branding" effort in the nineteenth century. The gifting of his personal portraits fits the criteria of what a modern-day branding guru considers to be a successful brand: not generic but personal; not merely a narrative but a personal story; not only symbolic but iconic; not making a statement but telling a story; not defined in attributes but wrapped in mystery. Kevin Roberts, *Lovemarks: The Future beyond Brands* (NY: PowerHouse Books, 2005), 70. Of course, Houqua knew nothing of the modern theories of marketing and branding. Nor did he have at his disposal any branding or image consultant. Nonetheless, the portraits displayed in the homes and offices of his business associates reminded them of their business adventures in Canton where they had met the iconic Houqua and to whom many owed their commercial fortune.

Note that my interpretation of Houqua's gifting of his portraits differs from Frederic D. Grant Jr.'s assessment of the general distribution of portraits by Hong merchants. I agree with Grant that "[t]he hong merchant of the port of Canton, China was one of the first great international brands. That brand was marketed both as an image and as a reputation for value and creditworthiness" (*The Chinese Cornerstone of Modern Banking*, 263). Grant argues, however, that the merchants' portraits were "somewhat misleading – or perhaps the appropriate word is aspirational" largely because "[t]he trend in portraiture runs contrary to economic reality." Indeed, most other Hong merchants also distributed their portraits, even as their businesses were foundering. However, as Grant acknowledges, Houqua's business, unlike that of his Hong merchant peers, was on the rise. In Houqua's case, his portraits reinforced his image of commercial reliability and sustained his family's relationship with his trading partners. The prominent display of Grant's family copy of Houqua's portrait on his book cover is one example of such longstanding ties.

[42] Jean-Laurent Rosenthal and R. Bin Wong, *Before and Beyond Divergence: The Politics of Economic Change in China and Europe* (Cambridge, MA: Harvard University Press, 2011), ch. 3.

To a large extent, this framework helps explain the early-nineteenth-century Canton trade, especially Houqua's dealings with the EIC. However, how could Houqua work with his American partners on such an informal basis when the risks of time and space with the Americans expanded far beyond his business dealings with the EIC with which he dealt on formal terms? The answer lies in the measurement of distance. In Houqua's calculations, the risks he had to bear in regard to the spatial separation were not measured in terms of miles or kilometers, but in terms of the psychological distance between him and his allies, a distance shortened by the deep-rooted trust that he had perpetuated with his allies through such devices as the gifting of portraits after their extended interactions in Canton.

To sustain connections over long distances and to assuage the anxieties caused by the time delays between communications, Houqua chose to project his iconic image through the distribution of portraits to his partners. This strategy served the important function of cementing his ties with his partners over the long term. The strength of these ties was tested time and again during periods of short-term disruptions that threatened to jeopardize the stable flow of business, thereby posing serious risks to the trust that had taken years to nurture.

Trying Times

The longstanding presence of John Perkins Cushing and the Forbes brothers in Canton was interrupted in 1840 when Bennet departed Canton only one year after taking up his position. This was a difficult period for Houqua because not only did he sense a heightened risk exposure abroad due to the absence of the reassuring presence of a member of the Forbes family in Canton but also because of the escalating risks at home due to the Sino-British conflict. Enforcement of the ban on opium trafficking that Commissioner Lin Zexu initiated in earnest in 1839 developed into a full-blown confrontation with the arrival of British warships on China's coast in 1840. The conflict between the Qing government and the British disrupted the flow of global trade. The partners in Houqua's network formerly had been able to rely on expectations of recurring profits from their trade to alleviate the risk of any member absconding with goods or capital. But with the dislocation of the trading network, this bond underwritten by financial motivations was weakened and Houqua could only depend upon the bond of trust that had been nurtured through close and extended interactions with his allies, the personal relationship signified by the portraits that his partners had carried home with them. It was not until the Opium War that these bonds of trust were tested.

Shortly after Bennet's departure, Houqua wrote three letters. The letters, dated June 28, 1840, the day the English "commence[d] the blockade of the port of Canton," expressed his fear that the blockade would be "very rigid." As he expressed uncertainty about the steps the British might take and fear that it would take "a long time before the dispute is settled & trade allowed to go on regularly," Houqua dictated his instructions on the execution of his overseas business to Bennet, John, and John Cushing, his handpicked partners in the Cushing/Forbes family that had transacted business in the West on his behalf for three decades.

In his letter to Bennet, who had reached Macao to await his voyage back to America, Houqua expressed regret over his departure, but at the same time, he conveyed his hope that Bennet would soon return to Canton. Houqua indicated that he was confident that Bennet's partners in Russell & Company would prove capable of handling his business in Bennet's absence "[a]s it is likely that there will not be much business done here for several months to come." Of greater significance, however, were his funds in America and England that the Forbes family had hitherto managed for him. Houqua assigned the task of the proper care of his properties overseas to Bennet, along with his brother John: "You understand that I have a large amount of funds in America & England & I request that you will consider with my old & good friend Cushing & your brother John M. Forbes how to take the best care you can of my property placing it where it will be safe & productive of interest."[43]

To provide an additional measure of proper protection and investment of his assets, on the same day Houqua also wrote to Bennet's brother, John. In addition to voicing his disappointment that Bennet had found it necessary to immediately leave China, Houqua highlighted his concern about the funds that he had invested in America and Europe through the Forbes brothers: "I have now a large amount of funds in America and Europe of which you must take the best care you can [to] place them in safety and where they will be productive of interest," Houqua requested of John, in a manner similar to his instructions to Bennet. Houqua vested in John and Bennet power to invest his capital for both safety and productive returns. These general instructions allowed John and Bennet significant latitude in their execution of Houqua's trust. Not viewing this lack of specificity as an obstacle to the protection of his assets, Houqua considered this latitude a critical factor for success, as it ensured that his trusted partners could readily adapt to the ever-changing commercial and financial landscape in the global marketplace.

[43] MHS Houqua Letters, June 28, 1840.

As for his wish regarding the final destination of his assets, Houqua instructed that John send the funds back to China, but only "after this English business is settled." The money should be sent "to my friends Russell & Co. in Hard Dollars or Bills on Bengal – whichever you think may be best for me," wrote Houqua.[44] He expected that the funds would be sent back to Canton through whatever means John deemed best for him, in the same manner that for decades the Cushing/Forbes family had handled Houqua's transactions. John had served as Houqua's co-pilot as they charted the course for Houqua's investments. This shared experience allowed Houqua to rest assured that John was capable of investing his funds overseas and routing the proceeds to Canton in the most profitable manner when the time was ripe.

Houqua must have considered his funds in America and Europe sufficiently large and important that, in addition to his letters to the two Forbes brothers, he also wrote a third letter, this one to Cushing, asking him "to advise with Mr. J. M. Forbes" on the investment of the funds until their repatriation to China, and "in case of the death of Mr. [John] Forbes and his brother [Bennet], I must also ask you to take care of my property for me." In other words, Cushing was to lend his investment expertise to the Forbes brothers in the management of Houqua's funds and to serve as their substitute should it become necessary. Chaotic times called for multiple levels of safeguards. Houqua called on all three of his surviving partners in the Cushing/Forbes family to protect his assets, jointly and individually if necessary. His faith in the collective enterprise of Cushing, John, and Bennet stemmed not from his dealings with merely one individual, but from the longstanding alliance he had enjoyed with all three blood-related partners. This collective enterprise ensured the continuity of Houqua's trust should any one of the partners meet a sudden death.

Houqua was equally concerned about his own safety. He was well aware of and prepared for trouble ahead as the Opium War loomed on the horizon. "If any accident should occur to me by which I may be prevented from giving instructions regarding the management and disposition of my property in Europe & America," Houqua informed John, Bennet, and Cushing, "my agents Russell & Co. will have my full authority to act as they may think best for and in behalf of myself or my heirs, and you will in such case see that their instructions are properly attended to." With the triumvirate on the American side, Houqua could feel confident about the continuity of the investment network he had fashioned, but only when he was present to dictate his wishes. This was far from certain in light of the combative postures of the military forces in Canton. So Houqua set

[44] Ibid.

up a power of attorney to specify the proper line of command should he become indisposed. The funds, he stated clearly, were to be invested for, and to be returned to, him and his heirs. However, the power of issuing instructions on his behalf in the event of his incapacity went not to one of his sons, but to his "agents" at Russell & Company. These agents could more readily remain in contact with Houqua due to their proximity to Houqua's base in Canton. Equally importantly, compared to his family, these partners in Russell & Company were well versed in international trade and finance and were thus better equipped to handle Houqua's investments overseas.[45]

In an emergency, more than ever before Houqua had to articulate the specifics of the trust that he placed in his partners. He had to specify the chain of command and the order of precedence in terms of his partners for management of his assets. This copious volume of correspondence certainly reflected Houqua's sense of insecurity during these extraordinary times, but it also underscored his continued faith in his trusted partners as a group to continue to conduct his business in a most devoted manner.

The Testing of Trust

To complete the sale of any consigned cargo over such a long distance always took many months. However, during this moment of crisis, time seemed to drag even longer and Houqua grew ever more anxious. To fortify the connections with his partners, he brought to bear their personal relations with his family. "My son joins me in sending compliments to your family," wrote Houqua to Cushing in his June 1840 letter.[46] This greeting from his son resurfaced again in December when Houqua wrote to Bennet. In the same month, Houqua closed his letters to Cushing and John by saying, "My Grandson sends his compliments."[47] Cushing and the Forbes brothers had made the acquaintance of Houqua's family during their stays in Canton and Houqua was eager not to allow these connections between the families to fade during the period of separation. Although he designated his agents at Russell & Company as his repesentatives in financial dealings in the event of his incapacitation, he needed his American triumvirate to keep in mind the fiduciary beneficiaries as they managed the assets entrusted to them. In addition, the death of his seventy-two-year-old wife in 1840 reminded old Houqua in war-stricken Canton that he "must expect to go off the stage . . . before a great while."[48] This heightened sense of mortality (and morbidity) must

---

[45] Ibid.   [46] Ibid.   [47] MHS Houqua Letters, December 27, 1840.
[48] Ibid.

have made it more pressing for Houqua to reinforce his family's ties to his business partners in America so that the relations would transcend the life spans of individual associates and their investment projects would endure Houqua's demise.

Deprived of the reassurance of face-to-face interactions, Houqua and his partners took pains to swap token gifts to maintain the tenuous physical exchange across the oceans. En route to America Bennet made with his own hands an ivory snuff box, which Houqua happily "accept[ed] as a token of your kind remembrance." Anxious to perpetuate the exchange, Houqua requested in his thank you note to Bennet, dated October 20, 1840, that he "send . . . two Barrels of fine Flour by the first opportunity."[49] Barely two months later, Houqua once again requested of Bennet "two casks of fine flour, packed in double casks."[50] The Forbes were quick to oblige as their Russell & Company partners informed Houqua in 1841 of the pending arrival of "two Barrels of Flour."[51] In exchange for the token gifts he had requested of his American partners, in April 1841 Houqua sent tea to his American partners. Through Russell & Company, the Chinese merchant sent to "the care of Cary & Co. New York, 5 packages cont'g 9 boxes Tea for J. P. Cushing, 3 packages cont'g 6 boxes Tea for R. B. Forbes, 3 packages cont'g 6 boxes Tea for J. M. Forbes."[52] Before long, Houqua would enclose with his November 22, 1841 letter to John another "supply of Tea" as he acknowledged the arrival of more flour.[53] Similarly, along with his letter to Cushing written about the same time, Houqua sent "a supply of fresh Tea for your family use" as he believed "[t]he Flour and Beer which you had kindly ordered for me will prove very acceptable."[54] Their exchange of such quotidian items may seem frivolous, especially in the case of tea, as Houqua's American partners were already awash with the tea the Chinese merchant had consigned to them in large quantities. However, such token exchanges served an indispensable function: they provided a mechanism by which the partners communicating across the seas could acknowledge each other's correspondence, provide continuity in the transmission of information, and perpetuate their mutual trust.

The importance of these token exchanges was apparent in Houqua's change of heart regarding the terms of his overseas investments. Before Houqua received a response from his American partners and the enclosed

---

[49] MHS Houqua Letters, October 20, 1840.
[50] MHS Houqua Letters, December 27, 1840.
[51] MHS Houqua Letters, October 4, 1841.
[52] MHS Houqua Letters, April 12, 1841.
[53] MHS Houqua Letters, November 22, 1841.
[54] MHS Houqua Letters, November 21, 1841.

gifts, he had expressed a desire to have his American partners complete the sale of goods he had consigned and to remit the proceeds as quickly as possible. "There have been two arrivals the *E. Peeble* and the *Oneida* but I received none of your letters," complained Houqua to John in a letter dated December 27, 1840, "and I have not written you for a long time – there having been no direct opportunities." In the meantime, warfare intensified in Canton: "The difficulties with the English are still unsettled, and it is impossible to say when they will be." Houqua was unsure of the liquid assets to be required of him and he was eager to call back his funds. "If a *fair* profit can be had on my old shipments," he instructed John, "please close the whole of them without much delay, and take care not to hold too strong." His desire for a quick sale applied not only to tea, but to merchandise of lesser importance as well, underscoring his wish for a quick and complete conclusion to the consignment. "My old shipments of silks & Nankeens," wrote Houqua, "I should like brought to an early close." In addition, Houqua desired that upon a prompt conclusion to the sale of his goods, all proceeds be remitted to him in Canton. To this end, he directed Russell & Co. to give John instructions on "selling and remitting out *all* my funds in your hands" [italics added].[55] In a moment of anxiety when communications seemed to be cut off, Houqua wanted to call back to Canton all his assets in the United States.

Before receipt of the token goods, to underscore his desire to call back his funds to Canton, Houqua issued similar instructions to Bennet, emphasizing his wish for a quick sale, even at the expense of reduced profits. "[D]on't let your brother hold too strong," Houqua told Bennet. The same principle applied not only to the sale of goods but also to the search for a lucrative remittance, and Houqua went so far as to bypass John in locating a favorable exchange as he specified what he considered would be "the value of Rupees and Dollars" when the remittances arrive in Canton. Exchange rates were fine in Canton: "From England I have received large remittances in Company's Bills and Goods, the former nearly all realized at fair rates and the latter promise to pay well by & bye."[56] As the war raged on and he had still not heard from his partners, the speedy recovery of his funds loomed large in Houqua's mind.

The resumption of correspondence from America altered the situation. After having been notified by a partner at Russell & Company of the pending arrival of the first batch of token gifts in late 1841, and perhaps emboldened by the prospect of a resolution between the Qing court and the British, Houqua was back in business, "I am pretty well," he wrote Cushing in October 1841, "& think that if the difficulties with the English

[55] MHS Houqua Letters, December 27, 1840.   [56] Ibid.

could be amicably settled so that both sides could carry on their trade quietly & steadily again, I should have strength & spirit for a number of years more of life."[57] In November, he even informed John, as he thanked him for the flour, that he was contemplating "making some shipments to the United States & England this season if Teas can be had at moderate prices."[58] Perhaps demands for his cash had abated after he lost "by the attack upon Canton in May last one million six hundred thousand Dollars," as he told Cushing.[59] More importantly, however, the Cushing/Forbes had proven to be trustworthy, even in the trying times of an extraordinary crisis. Of course, resumption of China's trade with the West boosted the economic motivation of his American partners to uphold their reputations. However, in the darkest hours when future trading prospects dimmed his American allies showed no inclination of abandoning Houqua. During their wartime exchanges, token gifts provided a symbolic expression of this enduring partnership.

Just as important as his demonstrated loyalty to Houqua, John proved capable of continuing to execute Houqua's trade such that it provided the economic value that underwrote the alliance. For Houqua's shipment to New York and London in 1840, which amounted to "about a million Dollars worth of Tea," as he accounted for Cushing,[60] "John managed very well indeed," Houqua told Bennet. "[U]nder your united care, . . . I anticipate a fine result to the shipments made the present year." This reference to their "united care" highlights Houqua's contingency plans and his trust in their joint efforts. Nothing showcased Houqua's renewed enthusiasm in international trade and his toughened faith in Cushing and the Forbes brothers more than his decision to resume shipments. In the coming season, Houqua planned to ship "three or four hundred tons of new Teas," perhaps more if prices came down, he informed Bennet in November 1841.[61] In fact, the volume of shipped tea turned out to be much more. Houqua told Cushing in December 1842 that in one ship alone he had shipped to New York five hundred tons,[62] and to London another 10,000 chests, "all being bought for me in the Tea country by my own agents." For management of these shipments, he requested Cushing "to give your advice to JM & RB Forbes."[63] The disruption of the Opium War had dislocated Houqua's trading network and tested the delicate trust among the partners. But the vast distance between Houqua and his

[57] MHS Houqua Letters, October 1841.
[58] MHS Houqua Letters, November 22, 1841.
[59] MHS Houqua Letters, November 21, 1841.   [60] Ibid.
[61] MHS Houqua Letters, November 23, 1841.
[62] I estimate that shipment to be worth about half a million taels.
[63] MHS Houqua Letters, December 23, 1842.

partners and the time lag in communications gave the old Hong merchant in Canton pause in his international business dealings. Nevertheless, with his partners already having proven their credit in the business, Houqua did not lose a beat when the seas reopened, and his confidence in his trusted partners became all the stronger after the nerve-racking period of suspended communications. In the aftermath of the temporary cessation of trade, Houqua was all too glad to resume work with his trusted allies.

The three-member team serving Houqua from America had endured the test of extreme conditions. Their lines of communications had been compromised during the military conflicts, and the long voyages had compounded the anxieties that built up during the months of no correspondence. Due to their efforts to reinforce their family ties and their exchange of token gifts, in spite of the military difficulties their business network continued to operate. At the end of this trying period, exchanges between Houqua and his American allies were no longer limited to the swapping of token gifts. As if to symbolize their substantial bonds, from Boston Cushing sent a cow, which Houqua received by mid-1842. "[T]he Cow which you were so kind as to send to me for which I return you many sincere thanks," Houqua wrote Cushing on May 11, 1842. Cushing expressed in no uncertain terms his concern for Houqua's frail condition, especially during the crisis that took a toll on his friend's health. "When landed the Cow was very thin," continued Houqua, "she had a calf then about two months old which was also thin and very weak – but with good care and plenty of good food they have both become quite fat and the cow furnishes us with a most liberal quantity of rich milk."[64] Just like his relationship with Cushing, if nurtured properly, Houqua believed that this expression of his friend's caring attitude would bear fruit in due course.[65]

Undergirding Houqua's trust in his American partners were the financial returns that his partners had generated on his behalf. The respectable performance by John, along with Bennet, in executing Houqua's trade strengthened the trust that Houqua had cultivated with his team of partners in America. As a sign of his faith in his partners, during the period of continued uncertainty in Canton Houqua reiterated his instructions

---

[64] MHS Houqua Letters, May 11, 1842.

[65] Showing similar concern for Houqua, his other trading partners also sent him substantial gifts from overseas. Bennet sent the elderly gentleman a rocking chair and A.A. Low sent him a stove, which Houqua acknowledged to be "a very convenient article & much preferable to our Chinese chimneys... just what I wanted for my inner office room which you will recollect" (MHS Houqua Letters, April 4, 1843 and April 5, 1843). Notably, the senders of these substantial gifts, reflecting thoughtful concern for the comfort of their Chinese partner, were also the recipients of portraits of Houqua.

regarding management of his affairs in America. In June 1842, Houqua sent Cushing a short but formal note:

I have directed Russell & Co. to request you in the event of any accident to John M. Forbes & Robert B. Forbes, to take charge of the business which I have placed & am placing in their care from time to time through Russell & Co., and in so doing you will oblige.

Houqua signed the note with, "Your old friend."[66]

This "old friend" of the American traders continued to play an active role in the trade in Canton. He wrote to Bennet on April 5, 1843 to commend him on his handling of his business in America: "I . . . feel satisfied that you are doing the best for my interest that circumstances permit you to do." Although Houqua expressed a desire to receive a more extensive report on the sale of his teas, especially a final account for the 1841 shipment, he remained completely confident in the Forbes's execution of his trade: "The sale of my Teas generally I must leave to your discretion." He limited this discretion to remittances to Canton where he was in a privileged position to collect market information: "For returns," he instructed Bennet, "I hope you will always be able to send me something better than Mexican Dollars[;] the Discount now is 7% and it is very painful to submit to such a loss." Having "no faith in trade at the northern ports being carried on extensively for several years," Houqua was convinced that foreigners would return to his base in the southern port once they realized that "it would have been best to have been content with Canton."[67] He believed that the tea merchants would be inclined to bring the teas to Canton in the coming season and he would continue to play a role in Canton, despite the abolition of the Hong system.

Cultivation of trust with his partners was Houqua's most enduring business initiative. He made tremendous efforts to study the market dynamics of Sino-Western commerce and to establish himself in the existing trade institutions while also transforming the system to his advantage. His strategy to break out of Canton and to extend his network to America was a bold move that required a constant building of bonds with his partners. Economic considerations contributed significantly to the strength of these bonds during periods of normalcy when it was easy to reap continued profits from the relations. However, the durability of these bonds were tested during the trying times when business was disrupted. To accomplish the feat of building trust that would secure solid trading connections, Houqua capitalized on the flow of global traders

[66] MHS Houqua Letters, June 21, 1842.   [67] MHS Houqua Letters, April 5, 1843.

through Canton, developed lasting relationships with a select number of traders, and projected his image as the authority on trade in Canton by presenting gifts of his portraits to partners and business prospects, thus bringing these connections to bear during the difficult times. Houqua's commissioning of his portraits was more than an exercise in branding his iconic image. Along with the exchange of gifts, some quotidian and some substantive, the gifting of his portraits allowed for an information flow that enabled Houqua and his partners to detect any devious maneuvers in their tight network. The bonds they nurtured in Canton resemble what Trivellato calls "communitarian cosmopolitanism," a worldview that allowed the ethnically distinct Ergas and Silvera to sustain their commercial relations as they maintained both a local and a global dimension in their horizons.[68] Houqua & Co. sustained its connections with a larger repertoire than the shared language of business correspondence that enabled the flow of commercial letters for the Ergas and Silvera; it leveraged non-textual materials that transcended linguistic boundaries to deepen the personal bonds among the business partners.

The elaborate but subtle bonds of trust between Houqua and his partners, in particular with Cushing and the Forbes brothers, endured the test of the most trying times. In the aftermath of the Opium War, Houqua was even more confident in his partners and in his ability to reconstitute a trading network in which he would resume a pivotal role. As he told a British correspondent in April 1843, "I am happy to say that my health is good . . . I am able to attend to business as usual. I am now 75 years old."[69] The difficulties in Canton had indeed subsided by 1843, but nevertheless Houqua would soon need to pass the baton to the next generation of traders, not all of whom would prove to be as enterprising as Houqua had been in the arena of global trade.

[68] Francesca Trivellato, *The Familiarity of Strangers: The Sephardic Diaspora, Livorno, and Cross-Cultural Trade in the Early Modern Period* (New Haven, CT: Yale University Press, 2009).
[69] MHS Houqua Letters, April 2, 1843. Houqua was 75 *sui*, his age calculated based on Chinese custom.

5   To Reorganize or To Be Recognized? Reconstituting Business in the Reconfigured World of Global Business

During the Opium War, military conflicts and political turmoil cost Houqua dearly. In the calculation Houqua furnished for his old British partner W.H.C. Plowden, the EIC official who had carried to Britain Houqua's portrait painted by Chinnery, he claimed that he had lost a factory worth "8 lacs" (eight hundred thousand dollars) and he had paid another "8 lacs" of the Canton ransom. All told, Houqua's losses were in excess of 2 million dollars. In comparison, in that year state expenditures for the Chinese empire totaled just over 58 million dollars.[1] Individually, Houqua endured losses from the Sino-British conflict that amounted to 3.5 percent of the annual expenditures of the entire Qing Empire. Indeed, Houqua was quite relieved that the war was over by 1843.[2]

In the darkest hours of the conflict, John Murray Forbes had suggested to Houqua "to take possession of one of my ships the *Akbar* or *Paul Jones* for the conveyance of yourself and family" to join his partners in America "where every man is only called to pay his fair share of the expenses of the Government," in contrast to the continued exactions that Houqua faced from the Mandarin officials in Canton. Understanding that New England weather would be too cold for Houqua, John proposed that Houqua move to St. Augustine, Florida, which offered "very much such a climate as that of Canton." In Florida, or on "one of the West Indian Islands," Houqua could "for a small sum . . . buy as much land as is covered by Canton and have just such an establishment as [he] pleased." His American allies, with Bennet as captain and Cushing and John as passengers, would stop by on one of their pleasure trips. "Indeed, if you come there you will have us for visitors every winter I think." Even when political changes disrupted the network of trade and dimmed hopes for continued profits, his partners remained committed to Houqua and looked out for his well-being. Admitting that Houqua might consider his suggestion "very

---

[1] He Lie, *Qing Xian-Tong shiqi de caizheng* (State Finances of the Qing Empire during the Reign of Xianfeng and Tongzhi) (Taipei: Guoli bianyiguan Zhonghua congshu bianshen weiyuanhui, 1981), 50.
[2] MHS Houqua Letters, April 2, 1843 and April 4, 1843.

foolish," John nonetheless maintained that "when such great changes have taken place in China, circumstances *may* arise, which would make such a plan advisable."[3] Political turmoil was transforming the world of commerce, thus requiring that Houqua and other players study their situations and position themselves in the reconfigured landscape.

Houqua appreciated the invitation from his American allies to join them in their part of the world. "I should think seriously of embarking for America, to settle down – somewhere near you," he wrote to Cushing, but only "[i]f I were a young man now."[4] It is difficult to know whether Houqua ever seriously considered such a radical proposal, but it is clear that he was not about to embark on such a life-altering journey at the age of 74. He had spent his life fashioning a global network centered around the nexus in Canton, and his centrality in that network pivoted around his command over the institutions in the city. Great changes were in store for China and the world of trade, but Houqua remained convinced of his critical position in Canton.

As uncertainties loomed on the horizon and the new configuration for China's trade with the West had yet to take shape, Houqua assured his partners of the continued importance of Canton. On the structural changes to be introduced and the opening of the Treaty Ports along the coast of China, Houqua informed his trading partner, "The Hong Merchants are to be done away with," and that he was "glad of it." However, he doubted that this institutional change would prove to be as transformative as the Western negotiators had envisioned: "[t]he good of this measure to foreigners," Houqua surmised, "will not be manifest I apprehend to foreigners for some years to come."[5] Houqua was certain that Canton would remain the center of China's trade with the West and he was confident about his continued role in this system.

Houqua did not live to witness the transformation of the world of commerce in subsequent decades. He died within months of the conclusion of the Opium War and did not get to see his American friends again, let alone join them in the West. However, he had made ample preparations ahead of his eventual demise. He had been plotting his succession plans not only according to Chinese custom but also taking into consideration the global dimensions of his business in Canton.

Initially, his American partners agreed with Houqua's insistence on the continued centrality of Canton in China's trade with the West in the aftermath of the Opium War. However, they soon proved to be more nimble than Houqua's son, who remained steadfast in his opinion with

[3] Baker Forbes, G, Box 3, f.24b.   [4] MHS Houqua Letters, December 23, 1842.
[5] MHS Houqua Letters, April 4, 1843.

respect to the centrality of Canton and continued to shore up the city even as its commercial significance flagged.

The different responses by these players in the aftermath of the Opium War illustrate the importance of agility in the rapidly transforming landscape of global commerce of the mid-nineteenth century. Foreigners did not share the attachment of Houqua's family to a specific Chinese site and they did not care where they had to conduct business, as long as it was profitable. Houqua had demonstrated his agility during the early part of the century when the profile of Western traders arriving in Canton shifted, but his successors responded to this new round of challenges differently. As the emporium in Canton was being dismantled, some moved to position themselves spatially in the new configuration of trade. Others capitalized on the elements of Houqua's business enterprise, the value of which endured in the new system of exchange. But Houqua's heirs were determined to stay put in Canton, and thus they were marginalized as the intricate commercial complex that Houqua had woven together began to unravel with his passing.

Houqua's Succession Plan

The strategy of Houqua's family in response to the turmoil of the Opium War depended as much on Houqua's business decisions in the immediate aftermath of the war as the succession plans he had put in place, especially because Houqua died within one year after the end of the war. Houqua's investment of his assets certainly transcended political boundaries, but he never dispatched his heirs away from their home base and they remained in Canton at the time of his death in 1843. Houqua, however, was mindful of the global setting of Canton as he designated the rightful inheritors of his estate. For years before his eventual demise, he brought to bear Chinese cultural practices and contractual arrangements, as well as Western institutions, in structuring and restructuring the organization of his estate.

Recall that Houqua was the third of four sons in his family and that he had started the Yihe Company with Puiqua, his second eldest brother who predeceased him in 1801. His cousin, Geowqua (his Chinese name was Zhao), had also traded with Westerners in Canton in his own name until his bankruptcy in the late 1790s. Therefore, no member of the Wu family could lay claim to the business assets of Houqua except for his brothers and their descendants.

Puiqua died without any sons. As was common in other Chinese families, one of his nephews was adopted into Puiqua's branch of the family to present him with ancestral offerings as if Puiqua were his father. Even though Houqua's two other brothers bore many sons (four in the case of his eldest brother, Bingyong, and five in the case of his youngest brother, Bingzhen), the adoptee was chosen from none other than Houqua's branch. Houqua's second son, Yuanlan, born in 1793, was adopted into Puiqua's branch.[6] Not only was this birth-son of Houqua responsible for the ancestral offerings to Puiqua, but in his capacity as the continuation of Puiqua's line he also stood to inherit Puiqua's share of the family's assets. Unfortunately for Puiqua's branch, Yuanlan died without any sons in 1820. A grandson of Houqua, born in 1819, was again adopted into Puiqua's branch, this time as Yuanlan's son,[7] thus securing for Houqua control over the business assets of the Yihe Company. Therefore, with these successive rounds of adoption, Houqua ensured that, according to the shareholding mechanism within the family as inscribed metaphorically in terms of ancestral lines, he remained the controlling shareholder in the family enterprise (Figure 5.1).[8]

Houqua had assumed control of the company's business with the EIC in 1801 by taking Puiqua's name (see Chapter 2). From the perspective of the EIC, the use of the same name had eased the transition and had guaranteed that Houqua would assume Puiqua's share in the EIC business. After operating for decades under Puiqua's name, in 1827 Houqua requested an official change in the title of his account with the EIC, from his brother's name to his own, by that time spelled in the EIC's records as Howqua. Houqua did not hide his reason from the EIC, which recorded that Houqua "expressed some apprehension of the surviving brothers in his family in the event of his death, making claim to share in the Hong

---

[6] Wu Lingli, ed., *Wushi Putianfang Fulonggong Guangzhou shisanhang zhimai zuyinpu* (The Genealogy of the Wu Clan of Fulong, from the Putian Branch Extended to those Involved in the Canton Trade) (2010), 47; Wu Quancui, ed., *Lingnan Wushi hezu zongpu*, 2a:45b–46a; Wu Ziwei, ed., *Wushi ru Yue zupu*, vol. "3rd branch."

[7] Wu Lingli, ed., *Wushi Putianfang Fulonggong Guangzhou shisanhang zhimai zuyinpu*, 47; Wu Quancui, ed., *Lingnan Wushi hezu zongpu*, 2a:49a; Wu Ziwei, ed., *Wushi ru Yue zupu*, vol. "3rd branch."

[8] In their study of marriage and adoption patterns in northern Taiwan, Wolf and Huang explore how a family would incorporate an outsider into its tight-knit unit (the adoptee, the bride, or the adopted brides in the case of "minor marriages," in which infant girls were adopted and raised along with their eventual marriage partners, the male heirs of their adoptive parents). See Arthur P. Wolf and Chieh-shan Huang, *Marriage and Adoption in China, 1845–1945* (Stanford, CA: Stanford University Press, 1980). Such strategies served to alleviate conflicts within the family, while at the same time pursuing the cultural ideal of continuing the line of descent. Just as important, if not more important, as these social and cultural considerations was the economic function of such adoptions as legal acts allocating shareholders' rights within the family. For Houqua, the controlling shareholder in his family's Yihe business, the successive rounds of adoptions that he engineered for Puiqua's branch provided him with a mechanism to manipulate the family's genealogical configuration to financially privilege his branch in the profit allocations and ownership calculations of the family enterprise.

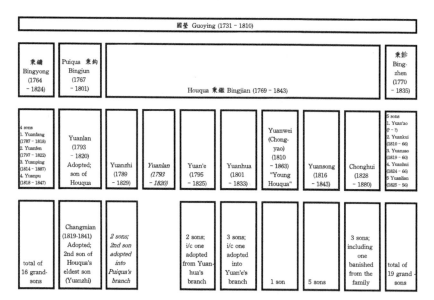

Figure 5.1. Schematic Representation of the Genealogical Records of the Wu Family, from Houqua's Father to Two Generations after Houqua. *Source:* Wu Lingli, ed., *Wushi Putianfang Fulonggong Guangzhou shisanhang zhimai zuyinpu* (Genealogy of the Wu Clan of Fulong, from the Putian Branch Extended to Those Involved in the Canton Trade) (2010), 41–61.

if the name of Puiqua was retained." Understanding his apprehension, EIC officials in Canton consented to Houqua's request without hesitation. The EIC's London headquarters approved this change, affirming that it was in the name of Houqua's late brother that "the affairs of the Hong have been entered in [the EIC's] books for thirty-five years past."[9]

The timing of this request for a name substitution in the records of the EIC was no mere happenstance. Houqua's extensive interactions with the EIC over the years must have allowed him to become so comfortable with the company's officials in Canton that he could have requested a name change at an earlier date. The timing instead reflects his strategy to leverage the global resources at his disposal to execute a plan for succession. Just at this time, Houqua had "at a very considerable expense, obtained permission from the Hoppo to retire from the Hong, and that he had placed his fourth son in charge of the same," according to EIC records.

[9] EIC G/12/231, 17–18; R/10/56, 147a.

When he devised this succession plan some time after 1826, he hand-picked his fourth son, Yuanhua (born in 1801), plausibly at the expense of his eldest son, Yuanzhi, who died in 1829.[10] He ensured that the nominal title of the Hong merchant was to be conferred on this son even though Houqua was not about to disengage from the business or to be relieved from his duties as Senior Hong Merchant.[11] Houqua utilized the cultural devices of Chinese family practices to protect his business assets from unwanted claimants. Unfortunately, the strategy of adopting members of his branch into Puiqua's branch did not put to rest contesting claims to the business that he had started with Puiqua and had built into a formidable venture on his own in the decades following Puiqua's death. Therefore, Houqua had to resort to rectifying the business records with the EIC. His request to the EIC demonstrates Houqua's awareness of the possibility of claimants' use of the ambiguous nomenclature across linguistic and political boundaries in legal and financial disputes. As he endeavored to install his fourth son in the firm's trade with foreign partners in his stead, he sought to set the record straight that the continued use of Puiqua's name in the EIC's records was more an issue of legacy than a reflection of actual ownership. The global setting of Canton offered many business opportunities to the aspiring merchant; however, the inconsistent record-keeping practices of the various participants could also become potential liabilities if they were to be mobilized for the wrong intentions, and Houqua was determined not to let this come to pass.

To formalize the arrangement that he had put together through adoptions and business arrangements with his foreign partners, Houqua also prepared a contract for the division of the family assets. Although undated, internal evidence indicates that this contract was executed in about 1826, around the same time that Houqua requested the name-change with the EIC. Entitled "Negotiating an Agreement on the Division of Family Assets on Behalf of Wu Dunyuan [Houqua] of the Yihe Company which Handles Trade with the West," this document began by tracing the family branch back one generation to Houqua's father:

Our late father, styled Xiuting [Wu Guoying; d. 1810] had four sons. The eldest styled Dongping [Wu Bingyong; d. 1824] and the second eldest styled Hengpo [Wu Bingjun; Puiqua; d. 1801] have both passed away. The third son is styled Pinghu [Wu Bingjian; Houqua; 1769–1843] and the fourth is Nanzhou [Wu Bingzhen; 1770–1835].

[10] Yuanhua, along with one of his older brothers (most likely Yuan'e, who died in 1825), had accompanied Houqua to a dinner in 1815 that Houqua hosted for his European and American guests (PEM Tilden Box 1, Folder 1, 102, October 10, 1815).
[11] EIC R/10/56, 146a.

Named as parties to this agreement were "the sons and grandsons of Dongping of the senior branch [Houqua's eldest brother, had died 1824] and the grandson of Hengpo [i.e., Puiqua; his grandson was thus Wu Changmian (1819–1841), the second birth-son of Houqua's eldest son who was adopted into Puiqua's branch]," along with Houqua and his younger brother Nanzhou. The inclusion of only the four immediate branches in the Houqua family suggests that by the time of this document Houqua had successfully insulated the assets of the family to the more exclusive group, consisting of himself, Puiqua's branch represented by Houqua's grandson by birth, as well as his younger brother, and descendants of his eldest brother.

The document then proceeded to describe the genesis of the family's business:

Our late ancestor [Houqua's father] was by nature diligent and frugal. He worked hard all his life. Although he had saved up some assets, he was always stern in his training of his sons. Even before Hengpo and Pinghu [Puiqua and Houqua] had reached the age of adulthood, he already instructed them to branch off in trade. In the fifty-seventh year during the reign of Qianlong [1792], he solicited foreign business on the order of the Hoppo. Together, Hengpo and Pinghu considered enlisting [as foreign traders]. Having secured the permission of our ancestor, Hengpo [Puiqua] began the operations of the Yihe Company under the trading name of Zhongcheng.

Thus began the operations of the Yihe Company. Houqua and Puiqua had started the business in 1792, nominally under the order of their father who provided some of the startup capital. But why were only the second and third sons involved in the business? "At that time, Dongping [Houqua's eldest brother] was pursuing academic studies and Nanzhou [Houqua's younger brother] was still young," explained the document. Therefore, the senior branch as well as the fourth branch did not play a part in the establishment of the family business. Their claim to the assets was limited to the contribution of their "late ancestor," i.e., Houqua's father, to the launch of the firm.[12]

If their common ancestor's share constituted the basis for their claim, how much did Houqua's father contribute to the enterprise? "Our late ancestor was over sixty years of age," stated the document. "Although he responded to the invitation to become a merchant, he only contributed tens of thousands of taels for licensing and opening expenses." Otherwise,

[12] Pan Siyuan, "Dai Yihe yanghang Wu Dunyuan zuo fenjiachan yiyue" (Negotiating an Agreement on the Division of the Family Assets on Behalf of Wu Dunyuan [Houqua] of the Yihe Company Which Handles Trade with the West), in *Siyuanzu yigao* (Surviving Manuscripts of the Ancestor Siyuan), ed. Pan Siyuan (N.p.: n.p., 1880), 77–79. I thank David Faure and Zhang Wenqin for bringing this document to my attention.

their father "did not contribute the family's assets." That was no small amount of money, but the startup capital for a foreign-trade enterprise required much more and "the capital required for all trade with Chinese and foreign merchants alike was raised and managed by Hengpo [Puiqua] and Pinghu [Houqua]. Only after they exerted their orchestrated effort did the business show any promise."[13] In other words, they might have done their father's bidding in the opening of the Yihe Company, but the enterprise achieved its initial success due to the joint efforts of Puiqua and Houqua, with no contribution from either the senior or the fourth branches.

This was followed by the demise of Puiqua: "Hengpo died in the sixth year during the reign of Jiaqing [1801]" and Houqua began to operate the business "under the new trading name of Dunyuan." Unlike the ambiguous transition in the EIC records that served to ensure that Houqua's family would continue to receive its allocated shares of the British business, this Chinese document depicted a swift handover of the business to complete control by Houqua at the time of the death of Puiqua. "Since then [Puiqua's death], all business, both private and public, was undertaken by Pinghu [Houqua] alone." Did the two other surviving brothers become involved? The document provided a specific answer: "Dongping [the eldest brother] was an official in the capital. And as Nanzhou [the younger brother] also came of age, he too went to the shop to assist in accounting matters." The eldest brother's career in officialdom was a typical diversification strategy that families took to secure a certain level of government patronage and to earn prestige for the extended family. Nor was the fact that the youngest brother participated in the operations of the firm when he came of age no surprise, but the document took care to indicate that his role was limited to his "assist[ance] in accounting matters." Such was the arrangement of the family business in which Houqua played a critical role and "only after over thirty years of diligent and thrifty operations did the business take shape and prosper." In other words, the business traced its beginnings to the closing decade of the eighteenth century when Houqua's father was still living, but it had grown, despite the death of Puiqua, only through decades of labor largely on the part of Houqua alone. "This is the account of the business of the Yihe Company established by Hengpo, prospering after Pinghu assumed leadership," concluded this section of the document as it attributed the success of the firm to the two branches of the family.[14]

The division of the family assets was not to spell the end of their relationship. After all, the document was drafted to include all parties

13 Ibid.   14 Ibid.

who shared their "late ancestor," i.e., Houqua's father. Their ritualistic offerings to this ancestor and all the deceased members of the Wu clan, along with other celebratory occasions, would continue to bind together these Wu descendants. For such purposes, the family lavished extravagant spending before this proposal on the division of the assets, and it would continue to do so. "No mean sums have been spent over the last three to four decades on the construction of the ancestral temple, on weddings, official appointments, and on the general living expenses of the different branches of the family," the document asserted. However, as "the various branches proliferated in headcount and swelled in spending," continued the document, the family had to "calculate our profit and loss and settle our public expenses before satisfying our private requirements" so that they could pay their dues to the state. "As we get accustomed to the [financial] convenience," admonished the preparer of the document, "we forget the labor and hard work it entails." It would be difficult to continue this practice "even though supportable for the time being . . . if we do not plan to settle [our financial arrangements] ahead of time so that each [branch] can plan to operate and economize," stressed the writer of the document as he stated the ostensible reason for this division of the assets.[15]

What triggered this proposal, however, was Houqua's succession plan. Houqua was "getting on with age and he often thinks of retiring." Unfortunately, the office of the Hong merchant "entails tremendous responsibilities that he cannot easily delegate to others." As dispensation of his official duties was exhausting the old merchant, he had to find a successor. The choice of a successor, as portrayed by this document, was not a personal appointment by Houqua, but a unanimous vote in favor of his fourth son. Houqua "gathered together his brothers, uncles, nephews, great-nephews and others to discuss the business of dividing the family's assets and the issue of succession." As a result of "deliberations by the various branches of the family," the group "unanimously agreed on the resolution." As if uncontested, Houqua's fourth son, Yuanhua (born in 1801) was to succeed him as "no one would assume the office of the business but nominated him."[16] By the end of the 1820s, Yuanhua had become the designated successor, at the expense of some of the surviving cousins from the senior and the fourth branches.

Having settled the issue of succession, what remained was the important business of dividing the family's assets. For the rules of this division, "the group recalled that before the business began operations, our late ancestor had always set aside the savings he had accumulated and

15 Ibid.   16 Ibid.

expressed his will that these savings be applied against the expenses of the
ancestral offerings after his death, not to be divided among the descendants and not be invested as capital in the business." This formed the
basis for the joint account to be held by the four branches, even after division of the family assets. "In observance of the will of our late ancestor of
first applying the savings towards ancestral offerings before distributing
to the offspring, the group considered investing the capital in properties
to generate income, prepare a detailed account, and rotate its management among the various branches of the family." The group set aside
this designated amount to underwrite all future family rituals that would
continue to tie together the clan.[17]

Thereafter followed the crux of the discussion: division of the remainder. "After subtracting from the annual rental and interest income
expenses on ancestral offerings and family celebrations," the document
continued, "the remainder will continue to be divided into four shares"
for the four branches. This would include what Houqua had "earned
for the business," consisting of "cash, shops, houses, and rice lands."
It was to consist of four equal shares, determined "in front of everyone," as "lots will be drawn and each branch will take possession of the
assets along with the deeds for its own management." But the document
included an important exception: "It is decided that the remaining assets
and the treasury of the main office as well as the foreign-trade business
of the Yihe Company will be given to Pinghu's [Houqua's] branch for
the operating capital of the business and to pay official duties." That is
to say, what was to be divided was only certain real-estate holdings of the
family, along with some cash. Whatever assets were deemed to be part of
the operations of the business of the Yihe Company, along with all the
liquid assets in the firm, would remain within Houqua's branch.[18]

As Houqua's offspring held two of the four shares to be allocated,
by this agreement in essence Houqua only gave up half of the family's
assets. More importantly, because of the established succession of his son,
Houqua continued to hold on to the part of the family's portfolio that
was actively generating annual income, of which the two other branches
were not to partake. Indicative of the other branches' desire to get their
hands on ready cash, "all were in agreement and there was no objection,"
despite what appears to be a lopsided division.[19]

This was the agreement among the family members and it was to
be all the more effective with acknowledgment by the Chinese state.
Therefore, to seal the deal, Houqua was to "request the withdrawal of
his trading name, Dunyuan, in the tenth month during the sixth year

[17] Ibid.   [18] Ibid.   [19] Ibid.

of Daoguang's reign [November 1826]." As his replacement, he was to "instruct Yuanhua to change his name to Shouchang so as to operate the business, and to declare and report the reason for the division of family assets to the Hoppo for approval and to the local officials for their records."[20] Indeed, Shouchang's name replaced Houqua's Chinese trading name in official documents shortly thereafter.[21] Just as Houqua was careful to implicate the EIC in his succession and asset divisions, he was eager to involve the Qing administration in the execution of his estate plans.

Along with the adoption and the change in registration with the EIC, this agreement shielded exposure of Houqua's branch to any future claims on the assets and income of his business.

Upon the completion of this division, the third branch of the family [Houqua's] alone will assume the responsibilities of all trading businesses, both domestic and foreign, of the Yihe Company along with all official dues and customer accounts. Henceforth, the first, second and fourth branches [those of Houqua's three brothers' households] will have nothing to do with the profit or loss. There should be no excuse for involving them in the payment of duties. The first, second, and fourth branches will be responsible for the management of the assets they receive. Should the fate of the different branches diverge financially, the third branch [Houqua's] should bear no responsibility. There should be no more argument over the assets of the business.[22]

The branches would continue to interact, but only as required ritually and to the extent underwritten by the communal assets that had been set aside.

Compared to the cases of eighteenth- and nineteenth-century household divisions examined by David Wakefield,[23] Houqua's family followed the guiding principles of equal division among the sons and identical treatment of adopted and biological sons. However, Houqua employed

---

[20] Ibid. According to the records of the EIC, this transfer cost Houqua half a million dollars (EIC G/12/236). As early as 1821, the Wu family had already made contributions to the court in Yuanhua's name, for which he was conferred an honorary official title (FHA 02–01–03–09380–012 DG1/8/30). Court documents registered additional contributions to the Qing state that earned Yuanhua further titles during the period between execution of this succession plan and his death in 1833 (FHA 04–01–35–0663–082 DG10/11/2; FHA 03–2888–072 DG10/12/7; FHA 04–01–12–0428–058 DG12; FHA 02–01–03–10014–04 DG13/3/15). The earlier of these documents acknowledged Yuanhua's relations to Yuanzhi (d. 1829), Houqua's eldest son, in whose name the family had made prior contributions to the court.

[21] Zhongguo di 1 lishi dang'an guan, *Qinggong Yue Gang Ao shangmao dang'an quanji*, 8:4288, 4321–4322.

[22] Pan Siyuan, "Dai Yihe yanghang Wu Dunyuan zuo fenjiachan yiyue."

[23] David Wakefield, *Fenjia: Household Division and Inheritance in Qing and Republican China* (Honolulu: University of Hawai'i Press, 1998).

this treatment of the adopted sons to skew the distribution to his bio-logical offspring within the framework of equal male division. The Wu family also allowed for setting aside properties for rituals, as was commonly the case in Wakefield's sample, but the larger carve-out was the business assets of the Yihe Company. This large carve-out was not to be a joint stock corporation organized as a kin-based arrangement (as was the case in the Anhui merchant family that Wakefield studies),[24] but a business concern to be severed from the rest of the Wu family and allocated to Houqua's branch alone. In other words, the agreement of Houqua's family preserved the business in its entirety, just as in cases in which business assets were withheld from division among branches. But Houqua's branch was to be the sole owner of the Yihe Company, to which other members of the Wu clan could no longer lay claim after this division.

In terms of the format and execution of this household-division document, Houqua's family followed the usual pattern and included the customary legal phrases "to provide a touch of legality and 'completeness' to the document," just as in most of the cases in Wakefield's study.[25] However, in a departure from Wakefield's sample, which did not involve the state in the household divisions,[26] Houqua's family engaged both the Hoppo and the local officials in the execution of its agreement, probably not only to notify the proper authorities in their capacity as authorized dealers with Western traders, but more to provide an additional layer of assurance in recognition of the terms of the agreement, just as in Houqua's application for a change in the name of his account in the EIC books.

Houqua might have had some reservations about severing his ties with the branches in such a formal manner. He had endeavored to preserve his hard-earned assets by adopting his own son and grandson into the Puiqua branch, the only other operator of the business whose descendants could be claimants to the assets. However, the common ancestral origins of Houqua and his two other brothers, as well as the occasional involvement of his younger brother in the business, made it necessary that he stem future drainage from the company's account. First, he rectified the lingering issue with the EIC with respect to the name on the account. Having fixed this legacy issue with his biggest customer, he then proceeded with the execution of a formal document specifying the exact division of the joint assets, so much so that "all properties and cash received by each branch of the family" were listed.[27] However, these

---

[24] Ibid., 178–180.   [25] Ibid., 59.   [26] Ibid., 62.
[27] Pan Siyuan, "Dai Yihe yanghang Wu Dunyuan zuo fenjiachan yiyue."

efforts were not all in vain because the successive adoptions that he engineered helped secure for his offspring an additional share in the process of division. Most importantly, he managed to keep intact and retain complete control of his business portfolio and the attendant assets.

This series of steps that Houqua took to protect his assets from unwanted claimants reveals his awareness of the many resources at his disposal in Canton, which he could call upon to serve his purposes. The resources that he leveraged transcended both boundaries of the state and politics, and included specific cultural devices as well as strict contractual arrangements endorsed by various authorities. Despite Houqua's resourcefulness in the execution of his succession and estate plans, there still remained one outstanding issue. As he engineered the configuration of the business after his exit, Houqua did not foresee the possibility that the role of Canton in the world of commerce would be usurped by other ports due to the reconfiguration of global trade. His succession plan did not include any allowance for such a contingency and, despite the portion of his assets that was set aside for investments outside of Canton, as we shall see in the following chapter, his estate remained heavily invested in his base in this southern Chinese city. Houqua did not allow for any provision to steer his family business in a different direction after the conclusion of the Opium War. Had he lived longer, he might have participated in the reconfiguration of the trade routes. However, he never had a chance to envision the transformation of the global commercial landscape.

The Lasting Appeal of Canton to Houqua's American Partners

Neither Houqua nor his American partners ever expected that the world of commerce would be transformed so readily. As noted in the previous chapter, the Forbes left Houqua with no representative from the family after Bennet departed in 1840. During the next two years, Houqua worked with Russell & Company, the firm with which the Forbes continued to maintain a vested interest. When the political turmoil subsided, the Forbes family, not questioning the commercial centrality of Canton in the immediate aftermath of the Opium War, was eager to regain control of its trading house and it quickly dispatched to Canton a cousin, Paul Siemen "Sim" Forbes – a veteran in the world of commerce but without any experience in Canton. Having recently returned to New England after an unsuccessful stint in Latin America, Sim was eager to follow in the footsteps of his cousins by perpetuating the family's business ties with Houqua, whose capital and trading network would guarantee him a respectful fortune. This return of a member of the Forbes family to Canton shortly after the conclusion of the Opium War, especially in light of the pains the family took to stage this comeback, attests to the enduring appeal of Canton and the family's belief in the continued prosperity of this port despite the introduction of the Treaty Ports.

The Forbes's faith in Canton, and in Houqua's critical position there, was even more evident in their determination to surmount significant hurdles as they reconstituted their linkages with Canton and reclaimed their supremacy as Houqua's prime American partner on the ground. Sim's arrival in Canton in 1843 diverged from past practice in that his family in Boston did not have a personal representative stationed in Canton by Houqua's side. In previous cases of personnel transition, the outgoing partner would stay in Canton and introduce the incoming family member to Houqua in person before returning to Boston. Prior to his departure from Canton, John Perkins Cushing had groomed Thomas Tunno Forbes to be his successor as Houqua's partner. Thomas's tragic death in 1829 prompted Cushing to rush back to Canton to install John, Thomas's brother, in his place. John in turn positioned his other brother, Bennet, already a fixture in Canton's international trade, as Houqua's connection to the English-speaking world. Bennet, however, had left Canton in 1840 as the military conflict with the British escalated, leaving Houqua's business to other members of Russell & Company who were not related to the Forbes family. When members of the Forbes family attempted to reassert themselves in Houqua's Canton trading network as the network was reconstituted in the aftermath of the Opium War, Sim's lack of financial resources and his business experience made him a good candidate to represent the Forbes cousins. Houqua's patronage in Canton promised an excellent business opportunity for the financially wanting Sim. John and Bennet considered that they had made their fortunes during their own sojourns in Canton, and thus they did not accompany Sim there. Instead, they dispatched Sim to Canton with letters of reference addressed to Houqua.

Sim went to Canton more on the recommendation of the Forbes brothers than to respond to any business needs of Russell & Company. Before he set out in a search of wealth in Canton, Sim had secured a letter from John and a letter from Bennet. In his longer letter to Houqua, John crafted his request to appeal to the sensitivity of Houqua on the basis of his understanding of the power relationship in Canton. John addressed his letter, dated December 31, 1842, to "Houqua, Chief Hong Merchant, Canton," reflecting his adherence to the former trade convention, despite the new configuration under the recently executed Treaty of Nanjing that abolished the Hong monopoly on foreign trade and expanded China's international trade beyond Canton to a total of five ports. "My dear friend," John explained to Houqua, "this will be handed by my cousin P.S. Forbes, the son of my Father's elder Brother and for whom I have the same regard as for a Brother." John took care to specify his exact relationship to Sim, indicating Sim's father's seniority to his own father, a distinction he had learned was important in Canton through his years by Houqua's side. Nor did he neglect to declare his brotherly love for Sim that went beyond their relations as cousins.

Elaborating on Sim's qualifications, John wrote that Sim had been a commission merchant "conducting a very large business ever since he was 18 years old." Sim began his commercial operations, observed John, "at the same age that I had reached, when you [Houqua] took me under your fatherly care." Throughout Houqua's long career, he had worked with many generations of young American entrepreneurs. He had taken under his wing the Forbes brothers, first Thomas, then John, and then Bennet, to whom he not only provided capital assistance but also advice on international trade. But Sim arrived in Canton at twice John's age when he first came to be entrusted to Houqua; yet John did not fail to point to the early commercial aspirations that the cousins shared and his own luck at having received the tutelage of Houqua.

John testified that Sim had been hard at work since a tender age, chiefly in Latin America. According to John, Sim had "the confidence of some of the first Houses in work, among others of Howland & Aspinwall who ha[d] usually sent *two* or three ships to China yearly." Having served as Houqua's partner in Canton, John was keenly aware of the competitive landscape at that international port and he could bring to bear evidence of Sim's qualifications in a manner relevant to Houqua's world of commerce. John then explained the losses that Sim had endured due to his exposure to high-risk exchanges. Despite these losses, Sim continued to uphold his integrity. With his ample experience as a global merchant, all Sim needed was "an adviser like you to make him remember his former bad luck and take no more risks in future," John wrote to Houqua. John did not hide from his Chinese business partner Sim's business failures. What John thought would help Sim in his future business endeavors was advice from Houqua in his area of expertise – the management of risk in the volatile world of commerce.

As for the Forbes's position in Russell & Company, John informed Houqua that the house had reduced Bennet's share of ownership. As the Forbes brother attempted to install his cousin in the house, John implored Houqua, "I hope you will use your influence with them now that they have almost turned old Forbes out to take our cousin in," believing that the business Houqua funneled through Russell & Company would allow him to wield more power over the house than the two ex-partner brothers in Boston.[28] This appeal from John to Houqua constituted part of the Forbes family efforts to resurrect its presence in Canton after the end of the military confrontation. The brothers did not stay by Houqua's side physically during the difficult times, but they hoped their continued state-wide service to the old Chinese merchant would entice Houqua to install their candidate in a critical position in the reconfigured trading network.

But what if Sim's fellow American traders proved to be a less agreeable crowd? That was the reason for a private letter that John instructed Sim to use if the other letter did not "prove strong enough" and he found himself not "get[ting] on with R&Co. fast enough."[29] However, without the help of a Russell & Company associate to interpret the "private" letter, how was Sim to communicate to Houqua the message that John had prepared as private correspondence between two families? Did Houqua speak or understand enough English for Sim to communicate with him?

John had the answer. He knew full well the system of communication between Houqua and his English-speaking partners. Sim faced a challenge in terms of presenting to Houqua the content of the letters of recommendations because he had never functioned in the linguistically hybrid environment of Canton. John's answer to that challenge was a "translation" of his original sealed letter written in proper English, to be opened in Houqua's presence. He translated the letter into a "key," rendered into pidgin English in the manner that Sim was to read it to Houqua. "[K]eep it . . . till you are acquainted with [Houqua], & try to read it yourself telling him I asked you to read it to him as it is private," John instructed Sim.[30]

In this second letter, also dated December 31, 1842, John began, "Houqua, My dear Friend, My cousin P.S.F. give you this by he own hand." John knew that his partner in Canton understood the rhythm of business on the Western calendar. This cousin, explained John, "have my Father *old* Brother son" [emphasis in the original]. Again, John placed the emphasis on the seniority of Sim's father, reflecting his recognition of this important distinction from his years of work with Houqua. He continued, "he all same one Brother to me – worry [very] near!" This cousin "began do commerce foreign when he have 18 years old, just same old that I was when you began take care of me." Thus far, John's rendition of his letter into pidgin English placed the emphasis on the same factors as the version written in standard English.

---

[28] Baker Forbes, G, Box 3, f.24b.   [29] Baker Forbes, G, Box 4, f.46.   [30] Ibid.

The same is true in the following section as John transliterated certain names and abbreviated others to expand upon Sim's industrious character and his misfortunes: "All this time he have work very hard, & do very large commission pigeon in Souse Merikey – Two or three large N. York houses send him pigion and likee him very much now. One house *paps* you know H&A who *any* year send 2 or 3 ships to China-Cheena." In Houqua's transnational world, not only had the partners become accustomed to the peculiar syntax of pidgin English, but they had also adopted a special pronunciation of proper names and abbreviations of others. Had Sim read the letter in standard English to Houqua, "South America" would not have been comprehensible to Houqua because that continent was called "Souse Merikey." Proper names posed more of a challenge to communicating in non-written pidgin English. This letter that Sim was to read to Houqua indicates that commonly used names had assumed certain standard transliterated pronunciations, while not-so-common names came to be represented primarily by their initials. John's command of these technical issues afforded Sim access to Houqua. This letter in pidgin English provides us with a glimpse into the daily interactions in Canton, the global center of trade during that period. Through this letter, John furnished Sim with training in certain cultural issues and a crash course on the lingo and jargon that he would need in order to operate with one of the most powerful men in international commerce at the time.

John proceeded to explain the financial predicament of "Mr. Forbes" – the use of first names must not have been common among Houqua's Western partners in Canton. "[M]y cousin no look sharp," but more importantly, "what man he trust this side." Sim had placed his trust in the wrong people. "[H]e Partner Father broke" and "he agents London & N. Orleans both broke and three merchants this side no pay for coffee he have sendee!" For what John wrote in the original as "I have perfect confidence in his integrity and he has certainly had great experience as a merchant," in this version, a simple "I lookee he my No. 1 *good man* – and very good merchant" would suffice. There was no floral language in Houqua's pidgin English and business operated largely on the basis of word of mouth. John's request of Houqua was simply, "only mi want you give he good advise & show he no take too much risk another time."

The tricky part required that this letter be marked "*Private*." John requested that Houqua intervene in the power politics of Russell & Company on behalf of the Forbes. "My Brother, long one [Bennet, that is; again, revealing that the use of the first name was not common] hope Russell & Co. take he [Sim] for partner. This house, Russell & Co have cut my Brother down to *one sixteen share* [6.25 percent ownership]!!"

When it came to doing business, little translation was required. The pidgin English shared by Houqua and John effectively handled issues such as numbers, share ownership, and business exposure. To retain ownership of only one-sixteenth and yet to continue to expose oneself to the risk of the partnership was obviously not a fair deal. To rectify this situation of gross injustice, John "chin chin [Houqua] very much [Houqua] show Russell & Company, more better they take [Sim]" so that Russell & Company would have a working partner in Canton and Bennet, "long one," would promise to look out for the interest of the company "this side [i.e., in America]."

John reminded Houqua that their relationship was not confined to the business concerns of Russell & Company. "Shou they [Russell & Company] take he or no take he I show you truly you can trust he all same as me – & spose you help he you help me." Theirs was a business relationship that encompassed a strong sense of personal obligations toward each other. John construed the partnership to include both families and it would only be appropriate for him to conclude his letter, "I *chin chin* you very happy new year & with compliments to your grandson," simply signed "I am your friend."[31]

Bennet, the "long one," also wrote a letter of recommendation to Houqua on behalf of Sim. His letter was shorter than his brother's and spoke of his endorsement of Sim taking his place in Russell & Company. Translated into pidgin English for Sim's presentation to Houqua, it was "my have write to R&Co. chin chin them to take him & cut me, let me go, Russ & Co have now put me down to 1/16 all same four piece new young men, spose my no worth any more, more better they let me go, take my cousin, he understand work and by and bye after a little time he can understand that Canton business very well." Bennet echoed John's request, asking Houqua, "whether he goes into the house or not I ask for him your valuable advice and assistance," or in pidgin English, "spose he go into Russ & Co. house or not, I hope you give him your opinion." To substantiate his greetings to Houqua and his family, Bennet also "put on board the *Paul Jones* some good Beef and Pork and some fine Flour," to be precise, "two R&C Flour counter No. 1 thing," which Bennet "chin chin [Houqua] accept." The exchange of token gifts remained important in underscoring their personal concern for each other.

In Bennet's rendition of his letter into pidgin English, he provided instructions for Sim at the bottom of the letter, "The original I send in your care sealed & you can open it in his [Houqua's] presence after a few days & read it to him as per Key." On the cover, he wrote, "letter to

[31] Baker Forbes, G, Box 3, f.24b.

Houqua to be delivered after a few days – Paul S. Forbes, Esq."[32] A few days later, after his arrival and once he had situated himself in Canton, Sim was to hand deliver the *"Private"* letters to Houqua, presenting to him his credentials with John's and Bennet's endorsements, articulated in a style of pidgin English that he was required to acquire in order to insert himself into Houqua's web of trade so as to facilitate ongoing transactions without the onerous filter of another trading partner.

After Bennet's departure from Canton, the Forbes's associates at Russell & Company marginalized the Forbes's influence at the firm and hence their criticality to the firm's relationship with Houqua. Sim's venture to Canton represented not only a chance for Sim's personal redemption but also an opportunity for the Forbes family to resuscitate its business ties with an important partner whom the family had represented for decades in his business with the West. The cultural sensitivity and the linguistic know-how that John and Bennet demonstrated in their letters indicate that cultural and linguistic differences were not merely hurdles to overcome but also opportunities upon which transnational traders could capitalize as they developed means to circumvent such impediments and to transform them into entry barriers for others. That John and Bennet took pains to overcome all obstacles and to present Sim to Houqua in the most favorable light revealed their hope and confidence in Houqua's ability to reconstitute the Canton network of international trade in the aftermath of the Opium War and in the lucrative business one could expect from a continued partnership with Houqua.

Sim departed Boston on January 4, 1843, just days after he secured the letters from the Forbes brothers. After fifty-three days, his ship sailed past the Cape of Good Hope, and by the end of March, the ship was several hundred miles from the coast of Australia, with Java 1,500 miles to the north. The voyage ended on May 6: "Only this morning, we found ourselves surrounded with fishing junks . . . we came to anchor, being just 111 days from Boston." The journal entry in his diary records that four days later, Sim began the twelve-mile journey up river to Canton. "At 2 o'clock then on the 10 May 1843, I landed in the City of Canton. *At last I am here.*" Early in the morning two days after his arrival in Canton, Sim "went around to see the celebrated Hoqua [*sic*]." Houqua made a return visit two days later. On this special encounter, Sim elaborated in his May 14 journal entry.

Old Hoqua [*sic*] returned my visit – this of course was a great condescension. I was out & just as I came in I met his chair going out. He stopped, put out his tiny hand which I shook & said he had been [kind] to make me a visit. As he could

[32] Baker Forbes, G, Box 3, f.24b; G, Box 4, f.46.

not go up to the 2nd story, Mrs. Palmer & Mrs. Low came down & he paid them (as he did me when I first saw him) a Chinese compliment by asking them "how many years you have" he is 74 years old himself, is very intelligent & shrewd merchant & has been honored by the Emperor with the red button & Peacock feather.[33]

Sim had already acquired a clear sense of hierarchy. That the great merchant would return his visit was a great honor. Houqua arrived in style in his sedan chair, and he was so frail that he could not walk up the stairs to the second level. Two Western ladies greeted him. The style of greetings involved both Western protocol and Chinese elements. Houqua was as comfortable shaking hands with a new arrival from America as he was insistent upon inquiring about one's age when meeting someone for the first time. Sim was aware of the culturally appropriate practice of inquiring about one's age and Houqua deserved respect for having lived to the ripe old age of 74. How could Sim surmise that Houqua was a "very intelligent & shrewd merchant" from such a brief encounter? That observation probably stemmed from the impression he had developed in his conversations with the Forbes brothers and also from his own aspirations to ride on Houqua's coattails in the world of international trade. The Qing Empire might have just been defeated at the hands of the British, but Sim was not about to make light of the imperial honor that the Qing Emperor had bestowed upon Houqua, "the red button & Peacock feather." Nor had Houqua's pride in his honorific accoutrements diminished.

The thrill of meeting Houqua left quite an impression on Sim. Almost a month later when he wrote to his wife, he recounted the encounter: "I had got so far when old Houqua came in & I left off to speak to him, & may as well give you a little a/c of him. He has a hand & waist just about the size of yours which you know is not particularly large...has been a Hong merchant for 52 years & of immense wealth." Sim expressed contradictory feelings about Houqua. In spite of his slight frame, even smaller than that of his petite wife, Houqua had held court in the international commerce of Canton for over half a century, during which time he had amassed a tremendous fortune. His old, fragile figure still loomed large in global trade. "You can judge a little of it," continued Sim as he discussed Houqua's wealth, "when he paid 100,000 dollars for the Peacock feather for one of his sons, the same son died the other day!!" Sim focused on Houqua's ability to spend lavishly on his acquisition of an imperial honor, and that honor was conferred not on Houqua, but on his son who did not even get to enjoy the prestige in life. "I don't know

---

[33] Baker Forbes, K, Box 6, f.65.

if I can say more of him than that," Sim concluded. "He is an intelligent, high minded, liberal Chinaman & would honor any country."[34] Sim expressed no skepticism about Houqua's spending habits. Instead, Sim admired his spending power and his desire for recognition by the Qing state, calling him "intelligent," and "high minded." Perhaps Sim's views of Houqua reflected as much Sim's own desire for wealth and recognition as his acceptance of Houqua's strategy to convert financial resources into social capital under the rubric of the Qing state despite its recent setback. His personal situation and the impression of Houqua that his Forbes cousins had imparted to him go far in explaining his description of Houqua, as well as his hopes in Houqua, a "liberal Chinaman" who "would honor any country." To Sim, China was not a broken country, and Houqua remained at the nexus of a transnational network centered in Canton.

After his encounter with Houqua, Sim surveyed the business world of Canton and was evidently amazed at the sheer volume of trade passing through the city. The ship *Paul Jones*, which carried his first letters to John and Bennet, had outbound cargo worth $250,000. Its return cargo would be another $200,000! He remained hopeful that he could "follow in the footsteps of [his] illustrious predecessors" in this nexus of global trade. To his delight, he was informed by a partner that he was welcomed into Russell & Company. "I think that it was after he saw Houqua that he said [that] to me," Sim told Bennet, acknowledging the instrumentality of Houqua as the kingmaker in the power politics of the American firm. So critical was Houqua's opinion that in their exchange of letters the following month, Sim and Bennet discussed how they should "test the extent of influence over R&Co of Houqua." Houqua was never a partner in Russell & Company. Nevertheless, his informal power reached deep into this company of American partners, allowing him to dictate who was to be admitted to the partnership and who was to be rejected and when. Even in the aftermath of the Opium War, Houqua's trading partners did not question his sway over the world of commerce and the power of his decisions in directing the flow of money in global trade.

"I shall no doubt make enough to return in a few years to live comfortably," Sim promised his wife in a letter dated July 3, 1843, "but I should be satisfied if these things did not depend on as uncertain a contingency." What could be the contingency upon which Sim's fortune depended? "[I]f the life of old Houqua is preserved 4 years longer," prayed Sim. Sim was a realistic, calculating businessman. He was convinced that his prospects would vary "in proportion as [Houqua's life was] lengthened

[34] Baker Forbes, K, Box 4, f.44.

or shortened from that." Houqua was already 74. But just four more years of Houqua's patronage would do; that would more than cover the remaining term of the partnership and generate enough income for Sim to provide his family with a comfortable living back home.[35] To Sim, Houqua's patronage in the world of commerce was his ticket to success.

Houqua is Dead, Long Live Houqua?

Upon returning from Macao on September 6, Sim's world collapsed around him. He arrived in Canton at noon to learn that Houqua had died two days earlier at four o'clock. Members of Russell & Company crossed the river to pay their final respects to Houqua. In accordance with Chinese custom, they saw the corpse before it was placed in the coffin. "I was thus just in time to look for the last time on what remained of this good old man," lamented Sim. As the Russell & Company contingent approached Houqua's house, their frayed nerves suffered from the "hideous noise" from half a dozen musicians. They were ushered along until they came to the entrance of the house where they met with "around at least a hundred of [Houqua's] attendants & several mandarins." Once they took their seats in a large hall, a curtain was drawn from the door of an adjoining apartment. As if to accentuate their horror during this moment of distress, the discordant music resumed and "on the platform with a plain cloth thrown over him was stretched in the cold embrace of death the emaciated form of Houqua." To the left of Houqua's dead body were his children and grandchildren, prostrated with their foreheads to the ground, expressing their grief with groans and cries. Louder than all the others were the cries of Houqua's sons. "By the side of old Houqua lay his Mandarin cap & peacock feathers, the emblems of his worldly distinction." The insignia that were the pride and joy of Houqua in life, featured prominently in his portraits, accompanied his lifeless body in death. "But in his countenance could be seen the last retiring rays of that intelligence with which it had so often been animated while living."[36]

The trepidation of the trading community was encapsulated in the reaction of Edward King, a Russell & Company partner who preceded Sim in approaching Houqua's remains.[37] King "shrunk back with instinctive horror at the appalling sight & well he might, for before him was all that remained of one who had been his benefactor." Mourners continued to file pass Houqua's dead body. Sim and his colleagues were ushered into an antechamber where tea was served to calm their nerves. It did not

[35] Ibid.   [36] Baker Forbes, K, Box 6, f.65.
[37] Recall that King had been the recipient of one of Houqua's portraits.

help – the discordant sounds continued, reminding them of the gravity of the situation.[38]

"The last four days have been gloomy ones," wrote Sim in his journal on September 9, 1843. For Sim, the world had just undergone a tragic transformation. Houqua had died. "It will not be difficult to imagine the feelings with which I viewed his lifeless body," continued Sim, "recollecting that altho' a stranger he had raised his powerful voice in my favour and that alone had heretofore been sufficient. His great characteristic was humanity – and in his unbounded confidence in Americans he has never been equaled, entrusting those with whom he had no ties of country, language, or religion between 2 & 3 millions of Dollars at one time. He might have doubled or quadrupled his fortune by dealing in opium but when asked why he did not do it he said, 'how can have face to look at the sun.'"[39]

His high accolades for Houqua notwithstanding, Sim had had very little firsthand experience with Houqua. He had just arrived in Canton in May and had interacted with old Houqua only on several brief occasions. Yet what are we to make of Sim's exaltation of Houqua in his personal journal, the intended audience of which did not extend beyond his wife? He must have found Houqua's morality laudable but, more importantly, he pined for Houqua's trust which, he had learned from his cousins, transcended cultural boundaries and privileged his American partners. Sim had gone to Canton to appeal to Houqua's generosity and he had hoped to weave himself into Houqua's network of trade in order to secure a comfortable living for his family. For Sim, who had traveled close to four months from Boston to Canton to position himself at the center of Houqua's trading empire, Houqua's passing not only marked the end of a great era but also dashed his hopes of making a quick fortune by leveraging his family's connections with this powerful figure in international trade. From Sim's perspective, this was not merely a transition from the Canton era to the Treaty Port days; it was the sudden disappearance of the world of commerce that hinged upon Houqua and the unexpected spiral into the abyss of global trade.

Before Houqua's earthly remains were buried, his business enterprise was dissected into its prized components. His family members, who stood to inherit his estate, were only the financial beneficiaries of his immense wealth. The critical elements of his business operations, however, were up for grabs. Although these elements constituted an integral part of Houqua's ventures, in the reconfiguring of the world of commerce they served the business interests of various parties. The prime elements in

---

[38] Baker Forbes, K, Box 6, f.65.   [39] Ibid.

Houqua's business were his capital, which provided the indispensable funds for capital-intensive global trade, the widespread name recognition that he had enjoyed, and the privileged position he had occupied in the network of trade. Those inheriting these prized business factors in Houqua's portfolio turned out not to be all the same party.

It was customary for the sons of Hong merchants to inherit their father's trading name. Following this convention, the son who took over Houqua's business in 1843 also assumed the designation of "Houqua." The holder of this new title, however, was not Yuanhua, his fourth son and chosen successor, as designated in the proceedings with the EIC and in the documentation on the division of the family assets. By 1843, his original handpicked successor, Yuanhua, had already died.[40] In fact, Houqua's four eldest sons had all been dead for at least a decade. Even the second youngest of his seven sons, Yuansong, had predeceased Houqua by three months. By the time of his death, Houqua had not only lost five sons but also many of his eldest grandsons. He was survived by only two sons, his fifth, 33-year-old Chongyao (also called Yuanwei), and his youngest, Chonghui, who had barely reached the age of 15 when Houqua died.[41] Of the surviving grandsons born by 1843, all but one were below the age of 15 (see Figure 5.1).[42]

---

[40]   After Yuanhua died in 1833, the records of the Qing court documents reverted back to Houqua's Chinese trading name (Zhongguo di 1 lishi dang'an guan, *Qinggong Yue Gang Ao shangmao dang'an quanji*, 8:4427). The community of foreign traders in Canton had also noted Yuanhua's passing in 1833. *The Canton Register* (6, nos. 13 and 14 [1833]: 73) carried the story on the front page of its September 16, 1833 issue: "The eldest surviving son of the senior security merchant, commonly known as 'young *How-qua*,' died, after a lingering illness, on the 11th Inst. He was the fourth son; the elder three had previously deceased." This record of the date of death is one day late – the Wu genealogy registered it as September 10, 1833 (Wu Ziwei, ed., *Wushi ru Yue zupu*, vol. "3rd branch," 6:16a). There was at least one other Western account of his passing. However, the American trader who recorded the mourning of Houqua's family had mistaken the original chosen successor of Houqua as "[h]is oldest son" who died after having been sick all summer (PEM Tilden Box 1, Folder 2, 67–68, September 12, 1833). Houqua had to resume leadership of his Hong with the passing of his chosen successor. In his petition published posthumously on September 26, 1843, Houqua had asked to retire. "I, the senior hong merchant Wu Tunyuen, am now 75 years of age, and was heretofore established as a merchant for foreign trade in the I'wo hong; but because of my age, I begged permission to retire. My son Shauchang [Shouchang, Yuanhua's trading name] and my grandson Shauyung, successively dying, and my son Tsungyao [Chongyao] and his brothers being at school and unacquainted with foreign business, could not succeed them, wherefore I have been obliged as before to manage the business of the hong" (*The Canton Register* 16, no. 39 [September 26, 1943]: 171).

[41]   Recall that Houqua's second son was adopted by his brother and transferred to that branch of the family. This son, too, had also predeceased Houqua. For a genealogical account, see Wu Ziwei, ed., *Wushi ru Yue zupu*, vol. "3rd branch," and Wu Quancui, ed., *Lingnan Wushi hezu zongpu*, 2a:45b–50a, 9:46b–47b.

[42]   Wu Ziwei, ed., *Wushi ru Yue zupu*, vol. "3rd branch."

Chongyao thus took over Houqua's business enterprise.[43] Chongyao's name had circulated among Qing officials the previous year when Houqua requested that Chongyao be sent on his behalf to help with the negotiations with Britain. In their report to the Emperor, Qing officials had expressed reservations about Chongyao's ability due to his young age and his lack of experience.[44] One year later, upon the death of Houqua, the business community harbored similar feelings. The pre-eminence of Houqua in the international trading community in Canton rendered it difficult for the foreign partners to automatically transfer the position of leadership to his son, with whom they had not transacted extensive business. Personal relationships could not be inherited without question and efforts by either side to enlarge such personalistic ties to encompass the family would work only if the various parties considered their interests to be properly aligned in the resulting network.

To make the distinction between Houqua, the respected merchant who died in 1843, and his son who inherited his business, Sim called the new Houqua "Young Houqua." He was not alone in calling the successor by this name. In fact, this was the designation commonly used among Westerners in Canton during the years of transition, and Houqua's son also came to adopt this designation in his business correspondence as a self-referential term. He signed business and legal documents with "Young Houqua." However, unlike his enterprising father who had pioneered the bold use of his English trading name in executing documents in his signature brushwork, Young Houqua would sign his name as such, but as 央浩官 Yang-hao-guan.[45] In this case, "Yang" did not carry the literal meaning of the character, but was the transliteration of "Young," as in "Young Houqua." Houqua's stature loomed large in the international world of commerce in Canton and his son was not bold enough to assume his father's title. Nor were his business acquaintances forthcoming in conferring that title on his son. As he transliterated the title he had assumed into Chinese characters, Houqua's son abandoned his father's bold venture of signing his name in a foreign script and he retreated to his comfort zone of the Chinese language. This change in signatory practice underscores Young Houqua's departure from his father's outward orientation to the global trading community. Instead of guarding his family's pivotal position in the transnational network of trade, Young Houqua would channel his father's commercial fortunes to buttress a crumbling

---

[43] A biography of Wu Chongyao is included in Wu Quancui, ed., *Lingnan Wushi hezu zongpu*, 4b:2a–b and Wu Ziwei, ed., *Wushi ru Yue zupu*, vol. 1.
[44] NPM 405006060 DG22/6/13.   [45] JM F14/8.

nexus of power as he endeavored to assert the criticality of Canton in a Sino-centric world.

As the Treaty Port system continued to undermine the centrality of Canton in the world of international trade, Young Houqua did not diversify his commercial interests beyond the city into the burgeoning trading posts in the other Treaty Ports. Instead, Young Houqua chose to increase his reliance on Russell & Company in his business dealings with the West and to focus his efforts on asserting the prominence of Canton, but only in the world of Sino-centric culture. As he busied himself with the task of planting Canton firmly on the cultural map of China, Young Houqua ceded his father's position in global trade to the encroaching commercial interests from the West, and allowed the webs of global connections that his father had developed to decay. Young Houqua worked to rescue the city's decline by strengthening a local cultural presence in Canton. At the same time, however, his reaction to the demise of Canton hastened his family's business decline by confining it to a regional ambit and de-globalizing its commercial scope.

The world of trade that centered around Houqua was no more. The subsequent fortunes of the various parties depended on their own adaptations to the new environment. As the aspiring global traders jockeyed for privileged positions, others rested on their previous laurels.

Global Financier or Just a Gold Mine?

Just as it had appealed to John and Bennet, Canton also appealed to Sim and his fellow-traders from America, due to its image as the Gold Mountain that could generate handsome profits. For John and Bennet, Houqua was a valued friend and a key partner in unlocking the potential of Canton. By the late 1840s, however, Houqua's family had become nothing more than a source of financial capital to Bennet and Sim.[46] Young Houqua was able to provide only the financial capital for the Forbes's venture, but not the social connections and business sway that old Houqua had steered in the Forbes's direction. In less than a decade after the demise of old Houqua, Canton had evolved from a Houqua-centered business network, in which the Forbes labored, into a Forbes family franchise backed by the financial resources of Houqua's

---

[46] British and American houses would soon bypass Canton and purchase tea directly from Fujian. See Robert Gardella, "The Boom Years of the Fukien Tea Trade, 1842–1888," in *America's China Trade in Historical Perspective: The Chinese and American Performance*, ed. Ernest R. May and John K. Fairbank (Cambridge, MA: Committee on American–East Asian Relations, Department of History, Harvard University, 1986), 37–38.

descendants. Young Houqua would finance the new commercial king in Russell & Company, but, unlike his father, he would no longer assume the role of kingmaker.

That the Forbes considered themselves to be the controllers of the Canton fortune had become increasingly clear in Bennet's writings of the late 1840s. "[T]he moment you abdicate the throne of the Russell," he told Sim in 1848, "all will be chaos." To Bennet, the Russell enterprise belonged to the Forbes and their presence in Canton held it all together. The linchpin in the business world of Canton, which formerly had been Houqua's prerogative, had now been usurped by the Forbes. The Forbes family was the true guardian of the Canton fortune, so much so that should Sim leave Canton without installing a proper trustee, "[t]he Forbes dynasty will die nasty and be forever extinguished in all its phases," Bennet warned Sim.[47]

Bennet again became financially wanting and in the late 1840s he plotted his return to Canton. His alleged "principal motive was to keep the [Forbes] dynasty, the power in [the family's] hands,"[48] probably merely served as an excuse for his return to Canton. Regardless, this line of reasoning that Bennet employed to lobby for a return trip to Canton struck a chord with his brother John, who had succeeded old Houqua as the new kingmaker in the reconfigured hierarchy of the China trade in Canton. "It strikes me that since he [Bennet] had made the sacrifice of going," John wrote to Sim in a letter dated June 19, 1849, "you & he had better set yr heads together & arrange things so that R&Co shall hereafter be under your joint control & perhaps handed down to yr children – giving me a piece when you both can spare it." A sojourn in Canton was a "sacrifice," one that Bennet undertook only to perpetuate the Forbes's control of Russell & Company. "[T]he House belongs naturally to us & we may as well look ahead & arrange to keep it," noted John. Arrangement of the house of Russell had become the sole prerogative of the Forbes, who no more required intervention from Houqua. However, Houqua's family remained an asset in the eyes of John. "Houqua you must keep hold of," he mentioned to Sim in the same letter. The Forbes had developed confidence in their own operations in Canton, and Houqua was to be a helpful resource, not a critical partner, much like the position of the consulate in Canton. "[I]f it will help do this," noted John to Sim, "it may be an object for us to keep the consulate which I can manage for either you or Bennet." The Houqua connection was to be an asset the

[47] Baker Forbes, K, Box 5, f.46.   [48] Ibid.; MHS Forbes Reel 16, No. 9.

Forbes could utilize, not a power structure within which they needed to operate.[49]

To secure the investment required of him by the partners in Russell & Company, Bennet borrowed from Young Houqua. Reporting to John in December 1849, weeks before his investment in the partnership was due for the year 1850, Bennet wrote, "PS [Sim] & I went to see [young] Houqua about the necessary arrangements to put me in funds for my share of capital according to agreement, say $25,000 for each 1/16 [6.25 percent ownership in the house] represented. He at once agreed to let us transfer $100,000 of his funds to our a/c at 6 per cent interest!! Where can I find any other man willing, without any question, to do this? So, I am all 'fixed.'"[50] It was a good deal for Bennet, and a straightforward one as well. Houqua's family had entrusted their surplus cash to Russell & Company for investment. With Young Houqua's approval, all he needed to do was to record the transfer of the assets on Russell & Company's books under the name of Houqua's family to his own account as his investment in the partnership for 1850.

What is most telling about this transaction between Bennet and Young Houqua is that the latter lacked investment opportunities. The family already owned plenty of land in the area and held silver that did not generate income. Old Houqua had deployed the capital by investing it in the shipment of goods overseas, but Young Houqua was content with earning steady income on his family's assets from a trusted source. Although not for lack of trying (as the following section will show), Young Houqua did not possess the business acumen of his father and was reduced to a *rentier*, never succeeding in charting a new course for the family business that Houqua had bequeathed to him.

Compared to Sim, Bennet cherished his personal relationship with Houqua much more. Russell & Company was to accrue interest on Bennet's capital investment at 6 percent and he could have structured a pass-through transaction at no cost to himself by borrowing an equal amount from Young Houqua at the same interest rate. However, the loan he took out for Sim and himself was a twelve-month note bearing interest at 9 percent. Young Houqua had named 6 percent, but Bennet thought "as I am to get 6 from R&Co. & as we [Bennet and Sim] are really squeezing Houqua, I thought it good policy to insist on his making it 9%." Bennet told John, "I dated the note to Houqua back to 1 Jan'y & so made good my contract with R&Co, the money having been in hand, as it now appears & earning 6% from R&Co. to my credit so that my capital cuts me only 3 pr ct. Houqua would have let me have it @ 6% but I insisted

---

49 MHS Forbes Reel 2, No. 13.   50 MHS Forbes Reel 14, No. 7.

on paying 9%."[51] In other words, Young Houqua had financed Bennet's effort by reestablishing himself in Russell & Company in Canton. Bennet did not bring his own financial resources to reinvest in this new business opportunity in Canton. Nor did his financially capable brother John fund Bennet's venture. Young Houqua, his sole financial backer, probably approached this less as a personal favor than as an investment opportunity and considered 6 percent to be an adequate return. After all, Young Houqua was merely transferring the money he had deposited with Russell & Company to an account in Bennet's name from which he was to accrue interest.

Young Houqua's Attempt to Break into the New System

Young Houqua might have been a passive investor in his financial dealings with the Forbes, but he also made an attempt, albeit with limited success, to leverage his American partners to break into the world of commerce by tapping into new channels afforded by the Treaty Port era. Through his American allies, he expanded from his base in Canton to enter the newly created British colony of Hong Kong where the rules of the game were still evolving. With his American partners, Young Houqua proactively positioned himself in Hong Kong under the new legal and political framework to take advantage of the opportunities afforded by the British system. In the British colonial territories of Hong Kong, R.S. Sturgis appeared as Young Houqua's power of attorney to chart a new course in Chinese interactions with the West when he became an early Chinese plaintiff in a lawsuit against leading British figures there. In 1855, in the Supreme Court of Hong Kong, Young Houqua, under his Chinese Romanized name of Woo Tsung yaou (Wu Chongyao in present-day pinyin), "otherwise 'Howqua,'" filed a suit against David Jardine and other partners of the trading firm Jardine Matheson. For good measure, Young Houqua launched this suit not only against the Jardine partners but also against John Charles Bowring, son of the sitting governor of Hong Kong, John Bowring.[52]

At the crux of the dispute were rents due Young Houqua in the amount of $26,851.25, a meager sum in the grand scheme of Young Houqua's finances and Jardine Matheson's business enterprise. Nonetheless, the suit serves to illustrate the shifting power structure among Chinese and British traders in the world of business, and how Young Houqua, with American counsels, sought to assert control following the new rules of the game. The rents in question related to the property of Houqua's

[51] MHS Forbes Reel 14, No. 7.   [52] JM F23/14.

family in Canton; yet Young Houqua took the suit across the newly drawn political borders to the British colonial jurisdiction. Devised by his American partner, this ingenious use of the system of extraterritoriality by Young Houqua challenged the British by invoking the rules of their own system.[53]

The suit cited that Houqua, the deceased father of the plaintiff, owned "in perpetuity according to the Law of China of a certain piece of ground situate[d] in Canton and of the buildings thereon erected and built called the Imperial Hong with the Appurtenances thereto belonging." On July 1, 1823, Houqua had agreed in writing with Charles Magniac, "then of Canton aforesaid also since deceased for themselves their heirs and assigns" to rent to Magniac the Imperial Hong and premises. It was "declared to be understood," Young Houqua claimed in the suit, that the charges for the repairing of the premises were to be borne by Houqua "unless when the Factories were occupied by tenants." The tenant was to pay rent in one sum at the end of the year. Accordingly, Charles Magniac and his partners, whose business would eventually become the firm of Jardine Matheson, occupied the factory, "paying rent therefore unto the said Howqua deceased down to the period of the late war between Her present Majesty and the Emperor of China." Soon after the war, Houqua died, "leaving the Plaintiff his son and by Chinese Law his sole heir and successor to and sole representative of his . . . real and personal estate him surviving."[54]

Thus far into the framing of this lawsuit, the basic premise of the legal proceedings acknowledge a comfortable juxtaposition of British colonial law and the traditional arrangements of business contracts and inheritance recognized in Canton. Young Houqua's suit cited the "Laws of China" and claimed his father's "perpetual ownership" of the property without any apparent conflict between British legal codes and the manner in which business was conducted in Canton. The sheer occupancy of the premises by Magniac's associates (and later Jardine Matheson) and their initial payments of rent to Houqua's family represented an acknowledgment of Houqua as the rightful owner of the property, and no deeds had to be produced to substantiate Young Houqua's claims of ownership. Equally indisputable was the fact that Young Houqua was the rightful "heir and successor" of the property upon his father's death according to "Chinese law," for which Young Houqua did not provide any citations of legal codes or precedents. The acceptance of such a premise was simply taken for granted.

[53] Ibid.   [54] Ibid.

Magniac's associates returned to the premise after the war and paid rent to November 1, 1843. Allegedly, Alexander Matheson renewed the lease with Young Houqua in 1844 on the same terms as the original lease and signed a document to that effect in 1845. From that time onward through to the date of the suit in 1855, Jardine Matheson occupied the premises and from time to time paid Young Houqua or his agents "various sums of money on account of the yearly rent." On November 1, 1855, Young Houqua delivered to Jardine Matheson a bill representing twelve years of rent, less the payments already made, and demanded payment of the balance, which stood at $26,851.25. On December 8, Jardine Matheson informed Young Houqua's attorney that it did not agree with the calculation, but "had instructed their Canton friends to pay the amount of rent they should find to be due unto the Consular Court pending the final decision of a suit that had been carried on there" against Jardine Matheson by Young Houqua. Young Houqua stated that no suit was pending at the time. Jardine Matheson further complicated the calculation by refusing payment of rent for the period when the premises were "vacant on account of repair." Thereupon, Young Houqua's agent took his case to the Supreme Court in Hong Kong and demanded redress.[55]

The case dragged on to August 1856 when Jardine Matheson "by protestation not confessing or acknowledging all or any of the matters... invoking clauses in acts of Parliament for protection, claiming... each & every of [the defendants] British subjects; that this suit has been instituted against them by a subject of the Emperor of China; that the cause or subject matter of this suit arose at Canton within the dominions of the said Emperor of China." However, the court overruled its appeal on grounds that it was not to be compelled to answer Young Houqua's bill of complaint. On August 15, 1856, the Supreme Court in Hong Kong "ordered that the said Defendants... have one week from this time to put in their answer to the said Bill."[56]

The Jardine Matheson associates had initially responded not by disputing any technicalities on the basis of different legal regimes, but by resorting to their extraterritorial protection. But this strategy backfired. Not only did the Supreme Court in Hong Kong refuse protection to these business elites in the newly established British colony, but it also allowed the colonial arrangement in Hong Kong to serve as an avenue through which Young Houqua, a Chinese merchant operating out of Canton, could seek recourse from a British company whose operations

[55] Ibid. [56] Ibid.

transcended the Canton–Hong Kong border. For Young Houqua, a resident of Canton under the control of the Qing government, this suit represented an audacious move against the powerful business elite operating both in Canton and in Hong Kong on either side of the newly instituted borders. Rather than viewing the extraterritorial rights afforded by the 1842 Sino-British Treaty purely as a legal sanctuary for British traders, Young Houqua's American agent approached the new system as a favorable alternative to the Chinese court in his quest to seek what he considered his due payments under the agreement struck between the two international parties.

When compelled to respond, the Jardine Matheson partners claimed that they had not been involved in the agreements with Houqua or his son. They also claimed that Charles Magniac, and subsequently Alexander Matheson on behalf of Hollingworth Magniac, had signed the agreements not as representatives of the firm but under their own names. Furthermore, the defendants complained that Young Houqua had neglected to repair the premises. To further limit their liability, the defendants cited the statute of limitations for suits and actions, insisting that Young Houqua was not entitled to any accrual beyond six years up to the institution of the suit.[57]

The details of this lawsuit reveal the changing dynamics of business transactions in Canton at the time of the Opium War. Before the war, Houqua had leased his property to the predecessor of Jardine Matheson, a firm with which he had few trade connections. He executed lease documents with the British merchant from whom he received regular rent payments until interrupted by the war. Upon the conclusion of the war and Houqua's subsequent death, Houqua's son, Young Houqua, renewed the lease on the same terms with a Jardine Matheson partner, and the firm returned to the premises to resume its operations in Canton. However, rent payments from the British firm were erratic as the occupants disputed the terms of the lease agreement and their financial responsibilities thereof. Young Houqua's agent then took the case to the newly opened courts in Hong Kong and presented his case in a manner consistent with the expectations of the British court.

When they failed in their initial attempt to have the case dismissed by invoking their rights to be protected as British subjects in China, the partners at Jardine Matheson argued that the agreements, which had been executed by individuals, were not binding for the firm of Jardine Matheson, but only for the involved individuals, thereby calling into question the legal representation of partnerships and successor responsibilities in

[57] JM F23/14, F23/17.

the evolving environment in which interpretations of international transactions remained fluid. For further protection, they sought to reduce
their liability on the technical grounds of the statute of limitations, bringing to bear in the arena of international legal disputes elements that ran
counter to the previous standards of mutual trust and credit.

There is no surviving written document from the 1823 agreement.
However, the 1845 renewal contract has been preserved in its original
bilingual format. Both the Chinese and English versions refer to the
original 1823 lease. The Chinese version of the contract states that Mr.
(Charles) Magniac of England had rented from Houqua's firm the Ewo
Hong (怡和行; Yihe Hang, in pinyin) the Isun Yune Kwoon (日晉元
館; Rijin Yuanguan, in pinyin), which was seven rooms deep and three
rooms wide, along with the entire structure, windows, and doors that
Houqua's firm had constructed with its own capital. The annual rent of
$4,600 was due on each anniversary of the lease. The tenant was not to
hold any contraband goods or illegal merchandise on the premises nor
were bandits allowed to gather therein. Acknowledging that the rent had
been paid in full through 1845, Young Houqua signed an extension of the
lease with the English gentleman Mr. (Alexander) Matheson, acting as
the representative of Mr. (Hollingworth) Magniac and retaining the same
terms of the lease. This is the document that Young Houqua had signed
in Chinese with "Young" romanized as the Chinese character "*yang*."
To his signature, he also added the chop of his firm, the Ewo Hong.
The document was dated the nineteenth day of the seventh month in the
twenty-fourth year of the reign of Daoguang, equivalent to September 1,
1844.

This document, which Young Houqua's legal counsel rendered faithfully into English in his complaint to the Supreme Court in Hong Kong
in 1855, differed in its emphasis on certain details from the English version, which was not signed until March 18, 1845. The English version
also referred to the original agreement of July 1, 1823 between "Howqua
Hong Merchant and Charles Magniac for themselves, their heirs and
Assigns." The document specified that the lease was to cover "the whole
of the Ground and range of Buildings thereon" but, unlike the Chinese
version, it did not go into the details of the space dimensions. There was
no disagreement between the two versions regarding the rent, payment
schedule, or the provision of termination at will. The English version,
like the Chinese version, acknowledged that the buildings were the property of Houqua, but it included the additional clause that "the charges of
repairing the same were to be borne by him, unless when the Factories
were occupied by Tenants." Herein lies the problem with the complaint
that the partners at Jardine Matheson launched against Young Houqua

in 1856: Young Houqua could not be held responsible for the costs of repairs, except for repair work done when Jardine Matheson was not occupying the buildings.

As for the issue whether Hollingworth Magniac had renewed the lease for himself or for his firm, the exact wording in the contract reads: "[T]he foregoing agreement [of 1823]...has been renewed between Young Howqua, as heir and representative of his late Father, and Alexander Matheson, as representative of Hollingworth Magniac, heir of the late Charles Magniac, on precisely similar terms – all past accounts having been settled to 1st November 1843 on which date – annually the aforesaid Ground rent is to be paid to Young Howqua by the Agent of Hollingworth Magniac, his heirs or Assigns." As a renewal of the original lease, this contract specifically named the heirs of the original parties. However, that Hollingworth Magniac was not the only occupant of the premises and that Jardine Matheson had operated out of this location would indicate that the firm could well be Hollingworth Magniac's "assign," from which Young Houqua could expect payment of the rent.

This document straddled two periods of different international understandings. In the earlier period, individuals who were parties to an agreement would uphold their ends of the bargain individually and collectively for their partners, whereas in the later period, businesses were seen as distinct from the individuals executing the contracts. Whereas Young Houqua would attach his firm's chop to his signature and continue to sign documents using his family's trading name, albeit in Chinese transliteration of the same name that his father had signed in his signature brushstroke, his trading partners from Britain would come to dispute the claim of the collective responsibility of the partnership when a partner executed a document in his capacity as the representative of another.[58]

This lawsuit would remain unresolved for an entire decade. Eventually, in 1866, Young Houqua received $9413.67 from Jardine Matheson & Company. In consideration of this payment, Young Houqua signed a document "discharg[ing] Mr. Hollingworth Magniac from all and every claim on [his] part under a certain old lease of the Imperial Hong in Canton to the said Mr. Magniac." As part of the settlement, Young Houqua also agreed to release Messrs. Jardine Matheson & Co. and Hollingworth Magniac "from any and every claim on their part to the further use or benefit of or from the Imperial Hong at Canton under the Lease referred to."[59] The sum received by Young Houqua represented a small fraction of the amount in the suit that he had brought a decade earlier. The difference, although a token amount relative to the scale of the operations of

[58] JM F14/8.   [59] JM F20/7, F20/8.

either Young Houqua or Jardine Matheson, underscored a monumental shift in the power structure of China trade. Young Houqua's American agents had enabled him to seek redress in the balance of power during the two decades after the conclusion of the Opium War. His leverage with the Americans had even allowed Young Houqua to bring his case to the British court in Hong Kong. However, the tide had turned and he could only salvage what remained of his father's tremendous power in international commerce.

Extraterritoriality has also been viewed as the means through which national citizenship was negotiated, as Western sojourners bargained for personal protection with their pledges of allegiance to their home countries.[60] Although this view recognizes flexibility about the budding notion of citizenship as practiced by transnational travelers in the early modern world, it does not acknowledge the instrumentality of merchant alliances in asserting their rights across incipient political divides. In the case of Young Houqua's lawsuit in Hong Kong, what mattered was not the nationality of his American agents or his status as a subject of the Qing Empire; instead, it was the British citizenship of the plaintiffs that made them accountable in the British colonial court in Hong Kong.

Young Houqua and his American associates were resourceful in turning extraterritoriality to their advantage. The Chinese courts in Canton could not force the British tenants to pay Young Houqua the overdue rent. In fact, the Chinese courts would probably not even entertain such a commercial case launched against a foreign resident. Instead, Young Houqua's team took the case to Hong Kong by turning extraterritoriality, which was supposed to protect those British residing in China, into a channel through which a Chinese landlord could hold his British tenant financially accountable. The law, in its various forms that followed the contours of different jurisdictional specifications, did not impose constraints on adroit traders, but rather it provided them with an array of resources as they traversed the world of international trade. That Young Houqua had limited success in Hong Kong, compared to his father's earlier success in American courts, reflects a shift in geopolitical power as British trade, especially in the post–Opium War era, was less dependent on iterative and reciprocal dealings than was the nascent American trade in the opening decades of the nineteenth century. With this shift in geopolitical power, the relative financial distribution among the disputants tilted against Houqua & Co., despite the mediation of legal mechanisms beyond the confines of Canton.

---

[60] Eileen P. Scully, *Bargaining with the State from Afar: American Citizenship in Treaty Port China, 1844–1942* (New York: Columbia University Press, 2001).

Appropriation of a Brand Name

Young Houqua's setback in this legal battle was but a small loss for his family's business enterprise. At about the same time, the family lost a prized possession, the value of which far exceeded that of Jardine Matheson's delinquent payment of rent. It lost its company name in Chinese, Yihe, the very name under which Houqua had operated since the late eighteenth century. This company name, a brand that signified quality and Houqua's trust and credit in the Chinese business world, was taken up by none other than Young Houqua's opponent in his legal battle in Hong Kong, Jardine Matheson.

In its business documents that included Chinese wording, Jardine Matheson had its name transliterated into various Chinese characters, mostly according to the Cantonese dialect. Ja-din (渣甸, Zhadian, in pinyin) or variations thereof was the name of the firm in these documents in the 1830s.[61] From time to time the company had also used a Chinese name that bears no phonetic resemblance to its English name, Yihe 義和,[62] a near homophone to Houqua's Yihe 怡和, but with a distinctive tonal difference in the first character in both Cantonese and Mandarin. This distinction was evidently apparent to the two parties in the 1830s as there is an extant document that includes both of these similar Chinese names of Jardine Matheson and Houqua.[63] However, the use of this tonally different Yihe designation for Jardine Matheson did not gain currency until the 1860s. In various agreements (Houqua's family business was party to some of them), Jardine Matheson continued to use its transliterated name.[64]

The situation changed in the 1860s when Jardine Matheson developed the practice of using its Yihe name more frequently. At first, it continued to use the Chinese name (義和洋行) the first character of which indicated an obvious difference from the name of Houqua's company.[65] But in an 1868 document it came to be known as "the chop of Yi" (怡記), the first character of which was identical to the first character in the name of Houqua's company.[66] Several years later, in 1873, Jardine Matheson adopted Houqua's entire brand as it used both of the Chinese

---

[61] JM H1/10/1, H1/10/8.

[62] Coincidentally, these two Chinese characters became the name of the Boxers during the movement that erupted at the beginning of the twentieth century.

[63] JM H2/3/8. A Chinese source asserts that Jardine Matheson began to use the characters 怡和 when it relocated its headquarters to Hong Kong. Li Guorong and Lin Weisen, eds., *Qingdai Guangzhou shisanhang jilüe* (Chronicle of the Hong Merchants in Canton During the Qing Dynasty) (Guangzhou: Guangdong renmin chubanshe, 2006), 102. However, this source does not offer any precise timing of this usage.

[64] JM H1/49/6, H1/49/8.   [65] JM H1/57.   [66] JM H1/68.

characters in the name of Houqua's company on the chop for its insurance operations.[67] The appropriation of both characters from Houqua's brand spread to other parts of Jardine's business enterprise in the 1870s and 1880s, as the firm used this Chinese name, along with its English transliteration Ewo, in its operations, and it came to be known by this name among its Chinese business contacts.[68] Before the nineteenth century drew to a close, the usurpation of Houqua's brand was complete. The Chinese name Yihe no longer evoked memories of Houqua's business enterprise, but rather denoted the firm of Jardine Matheson, the expanding franchise in China.

John K. Fairbank also notes Jardine Matheson's gradual adoption of the name of Houqua's company in Chinese. He points out that Jardine Matheson did not extensively partner with Houqua, preferring to work with Powqua and others and renting its Creek factory from Mouqua.[69] Indeed, Jardine Matheson rented a factory from Houqua and transacted with Houqua's family, but this business relationship turned sour, as indicated by the lawsuit in Hong Kong. To make the triumph of Jardine Matheson complete, the British company took possession of an invaluable business asset of Houqua's business – its Chinese brand. More than a reflection of the business practices of specific commercial concerns, this appropriation of Houqua's brand evinces the evolving power structure in the world of business during the second half of the nineteenth century. Young Houqua, through his agent, had endeavored in vain to assert his rights in the new courts of the Treaty Port era. Regardless of the outcome of the court case, however, the effort was ill-placed. As Young Houqua was suing Jardine Matheson for delinquent rent, he lost sight of an item that held much greater value – the family's business name. Just as Houqua's American partners capitalized on the use of Houqua's liquid assets, Jardine Matheson claimed ownership of his brand. Far from being a devolution of Houqua's brand name on a former business associate, as Fairbank conjectured, it was a gradual process through which Jardine Matheson developed its Chinese brand, finally capitalizing on the name of Houqua, with whose family the firm maintained a relationship that was far from amicable, at least in the Hong Kong court of law. Houqua's descendants are not known to have registered any legal protest over this appropriation of their ancestor's Hong name, probably because by the closing decades of the nineteenth century, no substantial family business

---

[67] JM H1/70.   [68] JM H4/2/1–2, H1/78/1, H1/79/1.
[69] John K. Fairbank, "Ewo in History," in *The Thistle and the Jade: A Celebration of 150 Years of Jardine, Matheson & Co.*, ed. Maggie Keswick (London: Octopus Books, 1982), 242; John K. Fairbank, *Trade and Diplomacy on the China Coast: The Opening of Treaty Ports, 1842–1854* (Cambridge, MA: Harvard University Press, 1964), 250.

was any longer operating under that name. The business enterprise of Houqua was not dissolved; instead, it was dissected for the parts critical to international commerce, and the heirs in Houqua's family did not position themselves to be the primary beneficiaries of this reorganization.

The Self–De-globalization of Houqua's Family

Although Young Houqua demonstrated an ability to extend his sphere of activities into the newly established British colony of Hong Kong, he retreated from the global reach that his father had achieved. Young Houqua's interest in building a local culture in Canton did not begin only when Canton ceased to be the sole port of call for China's trade with the West. Like many of the merchant families in nineteenth-century Canton, Houqua's Wu family was a generous patron for local scholarship. In fact, the emergence of a local scholarly tradition in Canton during this period reflected a contest of control over the representation of Cantonese culture between recent arrivals congregating in the political and economic centers of Canton and the more established rural elite whose families had built their wealth from the exploitation of agriculture and fisheries in the Pearl River Delta.[70] Thus, the Wu family's sponsorship of local scholarship was embedded in the continuous cultural transformation of Canton. Although Young Houqua was not unique in his support of local culture, his patronage was both financially draining and strategically distracting for the family business that he had inherited from his father.

By the time of the outbreak of the Opium War, Young Houqua had already partnered for years with Tan Ying, who, under Houqua's sponsorship, collected and prepared comments on works by local Cantonese scholars. The most ambitious project that they undertook was publication of *Lingnan yishu* (嶺南遺書, The Surviving Works in the Region South of the Passes), a series of local anthologies, the first installment of which was printed in 1831. In the preface to this first installment, Tan Ying, writing under the name of Young Houqua, spoke of their efforts to retrieve and compile forgotten works for publication. In the preface, they lamented the loss of early Cantonese literary masterpieces from the first millennium and expressed concern about the survival of later works. They sought to edit and publish these local works not only for the benefit of the people of Canton but also to celebrate the Cantonese contribution to the entire Sino-centric culture: "Would this [work of ours] not be an elegant princely offering to the previous dynasties and earn us

---

[70] See Steven B. Miles, *The Sea of Learning: Mobility and Identity in Nineteenth-Century Guangzhou* (Cambridge, MA: Harvard University Asia Center, 2006).

our rightful place in the cultural heartland?"[71] With this 1831 preface in Young Houqua's name, Tan published six works, totaling seventy-nine volumes. The first installment focused on the recovery of writings from the Ming dynasty (1368–1644) and included biographies of celebrated Canton natives, asserting early recognition of Cantonese works in the compilation of the official dynastic history of the Ming. At this time, the prominence of Sino-centric culture and the invincibility of the Great Qing had not yet been challenged. The goal of this first installment was to recognize their native Canton in the official chronicles of the Chinese state.

Thereafter, the collapse of the Canton system rocked the world of Young Houqua. His concern about the downfall of this southern Chinese city mounted in the 1840s, as evidenced by his escalating patronage of local scholarship. His strategy to arrest the decline of his hometown reveals his recognition of the threat to Canton, more in terms of culture than in commerce. The second installment of *Lingnan yishu* comprised eleven works. These selections claimed an early Cantonese participation in the intellectual and political traditions in China. Situated at the interface with its neighbors beyond its borders, Canton had experienced a series of crises similar to the intrusion of the British in 1840. In this second installment, Young Houqua signed off on Tan Ying's selections, which took a decided turn to assert not only recognition of Canton in the Greater Chinese tradition but also the participation, and even the expertise, of local scholars in directing moral cultivation and shaping statecraft during challenging times, especially along the borders.

The 1847 preface to *Lingnan yishu* underscored the challenges of the era as it expressed the slow publication process in the seventeen years since the first installment had been published in 1831. Among the factors causing the delay was "that military threats surfaced repeatedly and that barbarians from overseas have yet to be pacified."[72] The third installment, comprising ten works, appeared in 1850. The postscripts to these works were prepared in 1848. The selections reflected an effort to make sense of the tumultuous world by returning to the basic conceptualization of governing ever-expanding units – training of the individual, regulation of the family, reform of society, and harmony of the cosmos – all admonishing words by local scholars.

The fourth and fifth installments, which were published at the same time as the third installment, followed a similar pattern. The seven works

---

[71] Wu Chongyao, preface to *Lingnan yishu* (The Surviving Works in the Region South of the Passes) (Nanhai: Yue ya tang, 1831–1863), 1b.

[72] Ibid., second preface, 1b.

in the fourth installment focused on more recent local scholarship, with a bias toward practical applications and away from intellectual discourse. The fifth installment, comprising twenty shorter works, showcased local scholars' talent in interpreting the classical texts. The selections in this installment also asserted the inclusion of the south in the territorial footprints of the early Chinese empires. More importantly, the works in this installment exalted local sons who contributed to the Chinese court.[73] Tan Ying and Young Houqua's agitation was clear. Uninspired leadership at the court often led to wasted talent. Young Houqua, along with his Cantonese collaborator, blamed the trouble along the border on the court's inability to tap top-rated talent in their native Canton.

The last installment of the series appeared shortly before Young Houqua's death. It included two longer works by a local scholar that interpreted the ancient classics and other writings by Canton natives. This installment rounded out an impressive collection of fifty-nine pieces of local writings that Tan Ying had amassed in Young Houqua's name over several decades. This expression of a local identity in Canton underwent numerous transformations. Beginning with the assertion of earlier recognition in the first installment published before the Opium War, the tone shifted to the claim of expertise over border issues in the mid-1840s. Thereafter, the emphasis was placed on the local interpretation of the Chinese way of life and celebration of the Cantonese contribution to previous dynasties, only to return in the last installment to the bitter note of local talent suffering at the hands of incapable political leadership.

Young Houqua, who at times served as the Qing court's representative in its dealings with officials from the West,[74] felt that his government had not fully utilized his skills for maximum potential. In voicing his national concern and personal dissatisfaction through narration by the native sons who had endured the injustices of previous regimes, he was expressing his resentment of the uninspired court leadership that had devastated his native Canton. At the same time, the emphasis at various points on "border issues" revealed his position that the presence of non-Chinese was an issue to be contained and controlled, in keeping with the longstanding court policy, but in direct opposition to old Houqua's embracing attitude, which viewed foreigners as partners through whom he could connect with the commercial opportunities outside of Canton. Canton never existed as an isolated island; instead, the city prospered because it served as a nexus which blended together and mediated diverse

---

[73] For Young Houqua's involvement in diplomatic negotiations on behalf of the Qing state, see Frederic Wakeman Jr., *Strangers at the Gate: Social Disorder in South China, 1839–1861* (Berkeley: University of California Press, 1966), 147, 161.

[74] Wu Chongyao, *Lingnan yishu*, fifth installment, postscript, 2b.

interests and differences. Unfortunately, Young Houqua's effort to shore up the local prestige of the city stressed the historical contribution of Canton to the court in the north and to the larger Sino-centric cultural sphere, diminishing its role as a point in the cross-cultural connections and international commercial ties that had served the Wu family so well for over half a century. In the end, local triumphalism could not save the cosmopolitanism from being eclipsed because the commercial interests that had underwritten this cultural transformation degenerated along with the city's fledgling global ties.

In the aftermath of the Opium War, the commercial world in Canton began to unravel. This resulted as much from the new political order and the economic configuration stipulated in the 1842 Treaty of Nanjing as from the September 4, 1843 death of Houqua, the linchpin in the business network centered in Canton. The merchants whose fortunes were closely tied to the development in Canton did not see that the Treaty of Nanjing was spelling an end to Canton as the international center of commerce. In fact, the Forbes, who had retreated from Canton and fled back to America as the military pressure mounted during the Opium War, in the aftermath of the war considered business prospects in Canton favorable enough to dispatch one of their own to reconstitute their business and personal connections with Houqua. Because of their unflagging faith in Houqua's ability to direct global flows of goods and specie, the Forbes brothers were determined to station a personal representative at Houqua's side and they spared no efforts to install cousin Sim as Houqua's new partner, thereby attempting to reassert their power at the international center of commerce. Houqua's sway proved to be powerful enough to dictate the configuration of the American partnership of Russell & Company, to which Houqua's business remained critical. For a while after the disorder of the Opium War, the court of Houqua in Canton was back in business.

However, the untimely demise of Houqua threw the reconfigured order in Canton into disarray. Although Houqua had designed his succession plan elaborately by incorporating various cultural and institutional devices, as well as local and global elements, during his lifetime, he had not anticipated the drastic changes that would befall Canton immediately after his death. Houqua's web of international trade fell apart. After an initial period of disillusionment, those who remained in Canton explored their options. Sim, the new Forbes arrival in Canton, recovered from his distress over Houqua's death and maintained the Forbes's business ties with Houqua's successor. He returned to the United States in 1853, but offspring of the Forbes cousins continued to be stationed in Canton and in the new Treaty Ports. They maintained their close relationship with Houqua's family, mainly for the purpose of leveraging the formidable capital base of Houqua's estate. Business transactions continued, but the personal relationship between Young Houqua and the American partners residing in Canton followed cold calculations of commercial profits.

Young Houqua took over his father's business enterprise, but he could not assume stewardship of the business community that his father had led. His positioning of the family enterprise reflected the centripetal power of a Sino-centric culture rather than the centrifugal forces of the lure of profits. Unlike his father who worked to expand his reach into the global marketplace, Young Houqua placed more emphasis on his role within the Qing Empire in general and in the city of Canton in particular. The transnational business community in Canton lingered on, but its nature experienced a total transformation from Houqua's world of mutual reliance and alignment of interests to an opportunistic environment of individual enterprises in the post–Opium War era. Houqua's intricate networks were relegated to the memory of a different era. As the remnants of Houqua's business empire suffered from the absence of its powerful linchpin, the global dimension of his network became fragmented and various parties jockeyed to appropriate Houqua's capital, reputation, and business connections.

6   Houqua's "Swiss Account" in America
The Legacy of a Farsighted Entrepreneur

At the outbreak of the Opium War, what began as Houqua's regular shipment of consigned goods to his partners in the United States turned into an allocation of his assets for investment in America that was to be shielded from the tumultuous conditions in Canton. During the military conflict that ensued, lines of communications were compromised and the long voyages around the world compounded anxieties among the global traders. As Chapter 4 reveals, throughout this period of uncertainty Cushing and the Forbes brothers demonstrated their credit to Houqua, who had entrusted them with some one million dollars' worth of cargo. The ties between Houqua and the American triumvirate that came to be reinforced during the Opium War, along with the respectable performance of the American partners, in particular John Murray Forbes, in handling the consignments, convinced Houqua to allow his partners discretion over the execution of his trade in America and Europe.

As the seas opened again after the war, Houqua did not lose a beat in resuming his business, and his confidence in his trusted American partners became all the stronger after the nerve-racking period of suspended communications. Houqua died in 1843, just months after the conclusion of the Opium War. At the time of his passing, he had already resumed shipments to his trusted allies, sending them valuable cargoes not only to generate profits but also to shelter his wealth from the prying eyes of Chinese officials who were eager to tap into his wealth to help pay for the Opium War. For the management of such prodigious sums, Houqua issued no particular directive, but had expressed his anticipation of fine results "under [the] united care" of the two Forbes.[1]

Houqua's adroit maneuvers during the last years of his life left a lasting legacy for his family's investments in the international marketplace. The wartime exchanges between Houqua and his team of American partners formed the basis, both monetarily and procedurally, for what would become his estate's trust account in America. Earmarked simply as the

---

[1] MHS Houqua Letters, November 23, 1841.

"ASI" (American Stock Investments) in correspondence with his American associates,[2] for decades this portion of Houqua's estate remained invested in America under the direction of John Murray Forbes.

Previous studies have made tangential references to the portion of Houqua's estate that was invested in America.[3] However, they have not explored the pioneering nature of Houqua's participation in overseas markets in the context of the development of international finance. Nor have they explored the investment of Houqua's estate in America as evidence of a continuation of Sino-American ties forged before the Opium War. In his study of Russell & Company, Sibing He includes the partnership's dealings with Houqua, but because his purpose is to investigate the role of trade and the relationship between the private economic interests of American individuals and the American diplomatic agenda, he does not analyze its development from the perspective of Houqua's estate.[4] Many scholars have traced the impact of foreign trade into the second half of the nineteenth century, but their works primarily examine developments within China during the Treaty Port era, paying scant attention to the flow of Chinese capital amassed in the pre–Treaty Port days.[5] Therefore, scholarship has thus far overlooked the continued interactions of established Sino-American partners in financial markets; moreover, there is a complete neglect of the participation of Chinese capital in overseas markets in the aftermath of the Opium War.

The deployment of Houqua's assets overseas, and the way in which these assets came to be managed in the second half of the nineteenth century, call into question the conventional view of the rigidity of the Canton system, which supposedly confined the Chinese Hong merchants to one city, and the assumption of the fluidity of the international system

---

[2] It was, as we shall see, a misnomer, as the majority of the holdings was in the form of bonds, not stocks.

[3] See, for example, Kwang-Ching Liu, *Anglo-American Steamship Rivalry in China, 1862–1874* (Cambridge, MA: Harvard University Press, 1962), 12, 179n, 180n; Stephen Chapman Lockwood, *Augustine Heard and Company, 1858–1862: American Merchants in China* (Cambridge, MA: East Asian Research Center, Harvard University, 1971), 141n.

[4] Sibing He, "Russell and Company, 1818–1891: America's Trade and Diplomacy in Nineteenth-Century China" (PhD diss., Department of History, Miami University, 1997).

[5] See, for example, Robert Gardella, *Harvesting Mountains: Fujian and the China Tea Trade, 1757–1937* (Berkeley: University of California Press. 1994); Yen-p'ing Hao, *The Commercial Revolution in Nineteenth-Century China: The Rise of Sino-Western Mercantile Capitalism* (Berkeley: University of California Press, 1986); William T. Rowe, *Hankow: Commerce and Society in a Chinese City, 1796–1889* (Stanford, CA: Stanford University Press, 1984) and *Hankow: Conflict and Community in a Chinese City, 1796–1895* (Stanford, CA: Stanford University Press, 1989).

during the Treaty Port era. An understanding of the establishment of the ASI will help us appreciate the fluidity of the world of international trade and finance prior to the Treaty Port days. The fate of this investment and the management thereof illustrate the shift in the dynamics of the global marketplace as flexible transnational partnerships gave way to institutions styled to conform to Western capitalistic standards. Houqua's foresight in sending funds overseas and his American trustee's faithful management of his assets challenge us to rethink the constraints of Chinese capital markets.

Mid-nineteenth-century China might not have offered its domestic investors many investment options other than land and physical assets, but for Houqua, the dynamic investor whose financial dealings had extended to the global marketplace, national divides posed no hurdles as he constructed the portfolio which was to become his estate. Chinese participation was by no means absent in the development of international finance. By tracing the portion of his estate that Houqua entrusted to John Murray Forbes for investment in America, we see not only the enduring ties of transnational partnerships that were forged prior to the Opium War but also a pioneering investment in overseas markets by a Chinese financier, all at a time when Westerners had yet to gain traction in their investments in China.

Such assets overseas came to serve as financial resources of last resort for Houqua's descendants decades after his death. A large portion of these assets formed a "blind trust" under John Murray Forbes's control, sheltered not only from the Qing court and Houqua's descendants in Canton but also from certain American associates investing on behalf of Houqua's family in Russell & Company. It was only after Houqua's family had dipped into many layers of his estate that the extent of the family's investments in America was discovered. That Houqua personally entrusted John with these assets certainly served to insulate the estate from the prying eyes of various parties. However, this account of Houqua's investments in America does not simply attribute their success entirely to a certain grand scheme engineered by Houqua. The arrangement represents the transnational dimension of Houqua's trade and the fluid dynamics of his global business conducted on the basis of personal trust rather than any special initiative that Houqua undertook with regard to his estate. Compared to the personal ties that had underwritten Houqua's establishment of his American investments, the dissolution of such investments entailed many legal releases and indemnities, reflecting the shift to formal arrangements according to Western standards in the post–Canton trade era.

A "Blind Trust" Hidden from Many

Cushing and Bennet were aware of this pool of capital, which was known as the ASI, but John remained the sole manager of these funds.[6] Houqua had adopted a hands-off approach and allowed his American partners ample latitude in the handling of his trade in America and in Europe. This smart move provided the partners with flexibility, while still remaining under the auspices of Houqua. Young Houqua took this a step further and delegated more of the commercial activities to Russell & Company, even for certain transactions conducted locally in Canton. Young Houqua and the future heirs did not participate in the investment process of the ASI and they would only become actively involved in the deployment of these funds when the family's financial needs required that the funds be called back to Canton.

As additional proof of the trust that Houqua had placed in his American team, the initial amount of this portion of his estate was not specified in the documents, and any accounting record thereof was kept only by John. This absence of a specified financial amount paralleled the procedures for Houqua's shipments to America during his lifetime. Although he would recount after the fact to Cushing in 1840 that his shipment of tea to America and England amounted to "about a million Dollars worth of Tea,"[7] Houqua's tallying of the export volume was vague in absolute dollars but concrete in terms of tonnage or chest count. This arrangement reflected the consignment nature of his trade during this period, which did not specify the sale price of the goods ahead of time. The final value of the goods realized from their sale was subject to market fluctuations and execution. Any pretense of a definite calibration, using such currencies as the Mexican dollar, the British pound sterling, or taels, would deny the fluidity of the capital markets during that era and the absence of a functional currency with which traders only generations later could reduce to a common denomination. What truly mattered was the eventual purchasing power the investments would generate for the ultimate beneficiaries of the funds, in this case Houqua's descendants in Canton. It should come as no surprise then that the accounting of the ASI was to become more transparent only when John remitted the funds to Canton.

This trust fund was not only a "blind trust" in the sense that John, as the investment manager, enjoyed complete discretion over deployment

[6] For an account of Cushing's life after his retirement from the China trade, see Henrietta M. Larson, "A China Trader Turns Investor: A Biographical Chapter in American Business History," *Harvard Business Review* 12, no. 3 (1934): 345–358.
[7] MHS Houqua Letters, November 21, 1841.

of the capital, but it also remained dormant for much of the following two decades as Houqua's family in Canton was not financially wanting. During this period, Houqua's family need not go beyond the portion of his estate that had remained in Canton to satisfy the capital needs of the family business and to respond to the needs of Houqua's descendants. In the meantime, John, who would never again return to China, managed the assets by investing the money in America. Cushing had retired from the business, thus leaving John completely in charge of the capital. Bennet would return to Canton again for several stints at Russell & Company, but by the end of the 1850s he too had departed China, leaving the task of communicating with Houqua's descendants to Russell & Company partners who were related to the Forbes. The issue of the trust funds in America surfaced only in the late 1850s when N.M. Beckwith, a Forbes relative by marriage who was serving at Russell & Company in Canton, had frequent discussions with Houqua's heir.

The Different Layers of Houqua's Deep Pockets

The resumption of military conflicts between the Qing state and the European powers in the late 1850s (the "Second Opium War," or the "Arrow War") proved to be just as taxing on Houqua's family as the conflicts of the late 1830s and the early 1840s. The Qing court's financial burden, which Houqua's family was asked to help shoulder, was compounded by the military expenses against the state's domestic enemies during the Taiping Rebellion (1850–64). "The family of Wu Chongyao [Young Houqua] . . . has risen in power through its trade with the West," wrote the court officials in a memorial. "They have accumulated huge profits and become tremendously wealthy. As such, they should strive to support financially the military efforts of the state."[8]

To make matters worse, Houqua, the family's mastermind in international trade and finance, had passed away almost two decades earlier and the family's role in global business had greatly diminished. Instead of reasserting the previous pivotal role of the family business in actively charting the course of business development, Young Houqua, who succeeded his father as head of the family business, had grown reliant on interest from loans to Russell & Company for income. The enormous amount of capital that Houqua had amassed during his lifetime provided an ample resource, which generated sufficient interest income to fund

---

[8] FHA 03–4128–115 XF8/4/12. See also FHA 03–4363–003 XF3/1/24. Houqua's family was ordered to buy rice and ship it to Tianjin as the court's troubles with the Taiping intensified.

the huge expenses of the family as well as to satisfy the exactions of the Qing state. By 1858, however, the Forbes's representative working alongside Houqua's family would report a noticeable erosion in the family's capital and a decided retreat from the commercial and financial markets. In a letter marked "Houqua squeeze," dated August 27, 1858, N.M. Beckwith reported that he learned "from 1340 this morning that he has concluded to back out of the $400M [$400,000] loan." "1340" was the code word that the partners of Russell & Company had developed to refer to Houqua's family account with the firm. "The gradual diminution of the family fund of 1340 for active use, is I think permanent: I don't believe they will return to his business outside," Beckwith concluded. Nor could it be helped, claimed Beckwith. As he deplored the "forced loans" Houqua's family had to make to the Qing court, Beckwith lamented, "war is a calamity which changes the condition of all, and the wealthiest most."[9]

The financial difficulties of Houqua's family during the next several years confirmed Beckwith's prescience. Continued extortions by Qing officials compelled Young Houqua to withdraw from the account with Russell & Company in installments of over $100,000 at a time.[10] A Russell & Company partner tallied up the withdrawals Young Houqua made from the family's account and reported that these withdrawals totaled between 500,000 to 600,000 dollars over a tumultuous thirty-month period ending in September 1861. This prodigious sum had not yet involved any of the ASI funds under the management of John Murray Forbes in America. The Russell & Company partner estimated that half of the total withdrawals went toward "loans" to the provincial government in Canton, whereas the other half footed the bill of "the general & personal expenses of a great tribe of his brothers' widows, nephews, cousins &c&c dependent upon the great 1340 estate." According to this Russell & Company partner, Young Houqua expected to someday recover the money loaned to the provincial government, but his American partners were not so optimistic.[11]

Even though Russell & Company was not charged with total management of Houqua's assets in China, the partners in Canton and Hong Kong were close enough to the family's situation to form a reasonable assessment of its portfolio. Beckwith believed that the estate consisted mainly of rice lands, property in the city, and money that was employed in commercial transactions. The family's holdings of rice lands remained in good condition, but the income from these assets could not provide

---

[9] Baker Forbes, G, Box 2, f.18.   [10] Ibid.   [11] Baker Forbes, G, Box 2, f.19.

adequate support for Houqua's clan unless they were to reduce their expenses. The portion of Houqua's estate invested in city properties suffered tremendous wartime damages; most of what survived was occupied by the family and there was little remaining to generate rental income. As for the part of the estate formerly used in trade, the majority of these liquid funds was consumed by loans to the provincial government, which the partners at Russell & Company did not believe would even pay any interest. The family lacked the capital required for the reconstruction of its city properties and the continued demands by government officials might compel Young Houqua to sacrifice the family's holdings of city properties, Beckwith reported to John Murray Forbes.

The sale of land in the city could provide only temporary relief and Young Houqua might "think the hour of need arrived for which the ASI fund was laid and wish to call it in," Beckwith observed in early 1861.[12] This observation by Beckwith highlighted his understanding of Houqua's intention of leaving a portion of his estate in American investments, to be returned to Canton only as a last resort. Although Beckwith was not privy to the details of the American funds, informed by his conversations with Young Houqua and his correspondence with John Murray Forbes, he understood the "ASI" funds to be an emergency pool of capital for Houqua's descendants. Judging from the rapid depletion of the family's other assets, the moment might have come for the repatriation of Houqua's investments overseas.

Withdrawals made by Young Houqua soon surpassed the floating surplus that he had invested through Russell & Company. Unfortunately, the family had no other resources at its disposal and could only call on Russell & Company for its repeated rounds of capital needs. During these difficult years, Russell & Company had frequently been unable to readily meet the demands of Young Houqua, but he wanted to access his family's funds with the house as soon as the partners could make them available. Given that a good portion of the withdrawals went to meet the insatiable demands of government officials, the partners at Russell & Company could not help but sense the injustice of the dissipation of the family assets, out of concern both about Houqua's estate and about the liquidity crisis that these withdrawals inflicted on their own operations. "Everything has been done that could with any propriety to exhibit fully to him the position of his affairs & the inevitable result that would follow his large and steady calls on us for funds," lamented one partner.

12 Ibid.

The resistance by Russell & Company partners notwithstanding, there was no getting around the issue that for decades Young Houqua had enjoyed the stupendous estate of his father and "was never much inclined or interested in business operations." Unlike his father who built the family's assets through aggressive dealings in international trade and finance, Young Houqua confined his transactions largely to the lending of the surplus funds in Houqua's estate to Russell & Company. That arrangement had served both Houqua's family and Russell & Company well. For the former, it generated interest income and for the latter, it provided a reliable source of capital. This symbiotic relationship ended as the interests of the two parties diverged toward the end of the 1850s. Houqua's descendants needed more cash than the interest generated from the funds, but Russell & Company had not found a replacement for their much-needed capital. Unfortunately for both parties, Young Houqua had "no where [sic] to turn for relief except to his funds with R&Co." The partners at the house felt that he could not be denied. "We cannot deny him & it would be of no use to do it – he knows his rights, the refusal would become known & our credit would suffer to a greater extent than the values of all his loans," understood a Russell & Company partner.[13]

As the cash that Houqua's estate had lent to Russell & Company began to dry up, the partners brought up the possibility of returning the family's assets in America to respond to the needs in Canton. Beckwith, who had to respond to the numerous calls from Young Houqua in Canton, claimed not to understand "how the American investment is situated nor who has the control of it, nor anything about it." He requested help from the Forbes overseas to release those investments so that the capital calls of Young Houqua would not precipitate a liquidity crisis for Russell & Company's operations in China.[14]

The correspondence between Beckwith in Canton and the Forbes overseas revealed that even the partners charged with the handling of the finances of Houqua's family in China knew little about the size or the nature of the assets Houqua had entrusted to John Murray Forbes in Boston. However, Beckwith appeared to appreciate the need to shield the assets from a rapid drawdown by Houqua's family, both for the preservation of Houqua's estate for as long a period as possible and for the continued use of such resources for the operations of Russell & Company in China. Based on his limited understanding of Houqua's mandate and John's interpretation thereof, Beckwith suggested that the investments

[13] Ibid.   [14] Baker Forbes, G, Box 2, f.18.

in America be returned to China. Upon repatriation, he proposed that the assets be locked up in real-estate investments that would keep the estate secure for the long term yet would generate income for the needs of Houqua's family. Given the turmoil in Canton, Hong Kong might provide a safe haven for the repatriated assets, Beckwith reasoned. "It would be a good thing for the *decaying family* of 1340, if they had half a million invested permanently in Hong Kong instead of Canton, so that they could only call for the interest." Of course, it was not only a solution for Houqua's estate but also a smart move to safeguard the capital base of Russell & Company. "[I]t would be safer for [Houqua's family] & good for the [Russell] house & might preserve the clan for an indefinite period."[15]

Reaching into the Secret Compartment of Houqua's Deep Pockets

By the conclusion of this episode of Qing conflict with the Western powers in 1861, John Murray Forbes, who had served as the safe-keeper and investor of Houqua's estate, finally succumbed to the repeated appeals for the return of Houqua's funds in America. He thought it best to return the funds to Houqua's descendants. "[John] thinks it better that the [ASI] funds should be wholly withdrawn by 1340," Beckwith related to another Forbes associate, "and the a/c closed up – or – put in the shape of a *terminable trust*, by which the interest only could be called for till the termination of the trust, and thus the principal paid over to the heirs at Law." On this matter, John instructed Beckwith to consult with Young Houqua and see if they could set up the trust as he envisioned it. Houqua had entrusted the funds to John for long-term investments because he did not expect any need for the capital in the foreseeable future – his assets in Canton would more than suffice. As such, John had managed the money to maximize its appreciation over the long haul. However, two decades had passed and the capital needs of Houqua's family had grown more pressing, so in his capacity as the trustee of these assets John shifted his emphasis. Instead of the focus on potential long-term appreciation, John became more concerned about preservation of the assets, while recognizing the demands on the funds for the continued maintenance of the expenses of Houqua's family. Hence, he proposed that a formal trust be established from which interest would be paid to the family and the principal would be preserved until the trust's termination.

[15] Ibid.

Beckwith, however, complained that it would be challenging to create such a trust properly and that it was "difficult to make 1340 understand matters of this kind," blaming it on the lack of clarity to him of the details of John's arrangement with Houqua. He voiced his resentment that he knew "nothing or so little about the origin & intention, as to those various loans, & funds," which he supposed "all hung together." He felt that he was so ignorant that he would be "working in the dark."[16]

It is ironic that the funds originated from ad-hoc shipments that Houqua had made to his partners in America, all on an informal basis, but the conclusion of this trust began with a proposal to formalize the arrangement, rendering it "proper" according to legal standards and resorting to legal definitions to dictate its final dissolution. This drastic difference in the treatment of these assets at the beginning and at the end partly reflects the eroding personalistic ties between the Forbes in America and Houqua's descendants in Canton. This erosion of ties notwithstanding, John had faithfully managed the assets and expressed a commitment to account for the portfolio as a distinct account separate from other assets at his disposal. Perhaps this change is more a reflection of growing confidence in the use of legal channels as a framework for structuring financial dealings, at the expense of personal relations and connections.

To John in America and Russell & Company in China, Houqua had left two different pools of capital. John had invested for Houqua's estate funds of a size unknown to those in China, thereby protecting the assets from premature dissipation. The other pool of capital, left in Canton, had continued to finance in part Russell & Company's operations and to generate income which, together with withdrawals of the principal, funded the expenditures of Houqua's descendants for two decades. That the assets in Houqua's ASI account were recorded only in John's books in America shielded them from the prying eyes of Houqua's family, the Qing court, and even Russell & Company partners who were eager to leverage Houqua's estate to fund their own capital needs. At this point, however, partners on the ground in China were anxious to aggregate what remained of Houqua's capital held by the Forbes and Russell & Company. "If the whole fund, say loans of $200M & $100M & the ASI fund, could all be placed in trust – for an indefinite period or a limited period during which interest could be called for," suggested Beckwith in a letter dated January 14, 1861, "it might be better for *all sides*." "All sides" referred to Houqua's family, which stood to benefit from the interest, John, who could rid himself of this continued burden, and the

[16] Baker Forbes, G, Box 2, f.19.

Russell partners, who could then access the capital by borrowing from the funds. Beckwith, however, was not sure if Young Houqua *"would or could make a Trust so that the loans could be used in business, or whether he could or would make a separate trust of the ASI fund – & c & c."* Whether lumping together the funds in America with the capital Houqua's family had lent to Russell's operations in China or not, Beckwith questioned how Young Houqua would react: "He *might* be glad to have the subject brought up, & have things put in a more permanent & formed shape, and *might* be disturbed by the proposition, and think it meant an advantage to the other side." It could be a windfall for the Russell & Co. partners in China as it would provide an exceptional capital base to their operations, but in light of the uncertainty of the response from Young Houqua, Beckwith wondered if he should not just "let well-enough alone, and take chance for the future."

Sizable as Houqua's estate was, the Canton portion was rapidly dissipating due to the combined living requirements of his family, the deterioration of the asset values during wartime, as well as the continued exactions by the Qing state. In order to continue producing ready cash for Houqua's descendants, the family's contacts in China would soon have to reach into the deep pockets in America that Houqua had created for the protection of his estate. According to a Russell & Company partner in Hong Kong, John Murray Forbes began sale of the ASI in March 1862. Liquidation of these American investments started off at a measured pace for two reasons. First, stock prices fluctuated with the onset of the Civil War in America. Second, the capital requirements of Houqua's descendants were sizable, but did not require the immediate liquidation of the entire portfolio in America. The Russell & Company partners in Hong Kong were delighted that the sale of these American investments coincided with "a general rise in value of stocks in consequence of the [U.S.] government victories." The plan was "to begin sales early & not be obliged to force anything but to move out gradually [so as to] have the money within reach when the need arises." The partners in Hong Kong were counting on the return of the ASI funds, but, according to their calculations, the balance of the loans from Houqua's family would meet their capital needs for the near term. Perhaps with anticipation of tapping into another pool of funds, Young Houqua was "as friendly with the house as ever."[17]

Young Houqua died in 1863 at the age of 53, after leading the Wu enterprise for two decades. At about the time of his death, the Wu family again partnered with Russell & Company in an attempt to recover a

---

[17] Ibid.

large sum that the Qing government had extracted from the family in the midst of the renewed Sino-Western conflict and the Taiping Rebellion. Young Houqua had handed over 320,000 taels to provincial officials in 1858. In 1864, Russell & Company demanded payment of the principal with interest from the officials, claiming that Young Houqua had taken that loan from Russell & Company on behalf of the Qing government. At the interest rate stipulated, the amount outstanding had grown to 470,000 taels. Concerned that the original debenture with the seal of the Guangdong Maritime Customs might fall into the wrong hands of the Americans, Qing officials acted quickly to suppress the issue and refused to present any repayment. Although they had executed the original debenture, the local officials claimed that they did not believe Young Houqua expected repayment because "after all, [he] was a subject of China." After Young Houqua had died, Qing officials argued that his earnest heirs should settle this payment in their service to the state, lest the state should levy on the family all the financial contributions the state could have demanded in the intervening years.[18] As we understand that Houqua's heirs had bankrolled much of Russell & Company's business, the real lender to the Qing state must have been Houqua's family. By manipulating the mechanics of the transaction, Russell & Company was simply serving as the collecting agent for Houqua's family, just as Cushing's American associates were the agents for Houqua in the 1810s. In a manner similar to Houqua's lending to the Hong startups through the EIC, the foreign status of Russell & Company was supposed to enhance the collectability of the loan. However, this arrangement engineered by Houqua's heirs and Russell & Company did not produce the desired results. The Chinese merchant family was all the more powerless in the face of a financially troubled Qing court. Its American partners could no longer offer any escape from the predicament.

Anxiety about the Wu family's financial needs soon subsided, either because extractions of Houqua's estate by Qing officials abated or because the gradual sale and remittance of funds from America proved sufficient to respond to its needs. In either case, Houqua's family remained an important stakeholder in Russell & Company throughout the 1860s. In 1865, the house recorded liabilities of 200,000 dollars toward "1340," and this loan would remain outstanding into the late 1870s.[19] In addition, the various Russell & Company offices would

---

[18] NPM 092028 TZ2/10/21; 093331 TZ2/12/14; 094599 TZ3/1/28; 099032 TZ3/9/10; 099033 TZ3/9/10; 100798 TZ3/11/24; FHA 03–4889–096 TZ4/7/9.
[19] MHS Forbes Reel 37B/No.18, Folder 1–3.

continue to conduct trade on the account of the ASI, probably with the funds remitted from the United States. The office in Shanghai shipped drills for the "ASI account" in 1868, for which the partners even purchased insurance in the name of the ASI.[20] Moreover, in addition to the $200,000 loan due "1340," the house often carried on its books liabilities such as "Houqua's funds for T[ea]" in the range of $100,000, not an insignificant amount when the partners' capital totaled around half a million dollars and the total assets of the firm barely exceeded two million dollars.[21]

Houqua's family continued to make withdrawals from its account with its American partners in the 1860s and into the 1870s, albeit in smaller amounts and at more infrequent intervals. For instance, the partners in Shanghai noted in an April 13, 1870 correspondence that "Houqua has made a call on us for $50000 which are [sic] met."[22] No complete records survive to enable us to tally up the total withdrawals Houqua's descendants made during this period, but the archival entries make it clear that in 1874 these capital calls crescendoed into an orchestrated program which yielded $300,000.[23]

The Size of and the Holdings in this Treasure Trove

The 1874 records also revealed for the first time the exact holdings in the ASI. Of sales in 1874, the largest investment in a single business concern was in "CB&Q." Some 26 percent of the proceeds from the 1874 sales came from the disposal of "CB&Q," "CB&Q7s," or "CB&Q7%" (Chicago, Burlington, and Quincy Railroad 7 percent bonds), which yielded anywhere between $97 and $106, plus the accrued interest for each bond at $100 face value, depending on the date of sale. Another 5 percent of the proceeds came from the sale of "Bur & Ills RW RR 8% Convts" (Burlington & Illinois Railway Railroad 8 percent Convertible Bonds), also realized along with the accrued interest.

Most of the smaller holdings were also in railroad companies. The sale of bonds in "Ill Gd Tk" (Illinois Grand Trunk Railway) constituted 5 percent of the total. Yet another 5 percent came from the sale of "Phil Wil & Balts" (Philadelphia, Wilmington, and Baltimore Railroad), which yielded some $53 per unit of investment with no accrued interest, reflecting perhaps that the investments in this concern were in the

---

[20] Baker Forbes, L, Subseries I, v.L–13.
[21] MHS Forbes Reel 37B/No. 18/ Folder 1–3, Accounts and Other Documents between Francis Blackwell Forbes and Russell & Co., 1868–86.
[22] Baker Forbes, G, Box 2, f.19.   [23] Baker Forbes, L, Subseries III, Box 16, f.9.

form of stocks rather than bonds. However, the ASI holdings in "Am. Central" (American Central Railway), the sale of which constituted 11 percent of the total proceeds, definitely included both stocks and bonds. There were also the "Am Central 8s" (8 percent bonds) and the "Am. Central Shrs" (shares, or stocks). In addition, there were investments in "Quincy Warsaw Shrs" (Quincy and Warsaw Railroad shares), "Dixon P&H" (Dixon, Peoria, and Hannibal Railroad), and "Carthage & Bur" (Carthage and Burlington Railroad). Proceeds coming from investments labeled "Ottawas" accounted for 14 percent, and another 4 percent from "Nebraska," both of which were business enterprises involved in the construction of railroads. All told, these investments in railroad companies represented some three-quarters of the portfolio liquidated in 1874.

In addition to railroad investments, the other notable holdings of Houqua's estate in America were U.S. government debt. The sale of three series, named "US 6% 1881," "US 5/20 1867," and "US 10/40 1867," completed on August 12, 1874 at premiums varying from 113 ¾ and 118 ⅜ per bond of $100, fetched an aggregate amount of $50,206.25, representing close to 20 percent of the total proceeds of the 1874 sales.[24] Apparently, through the assets Houqua had entrusted to John Murray Forbes, the descendants of Houqua who stood to benefit from the ASI were unwitting participants in the financing of the Civil War in America, just when the family was also held responsible for China's own civil war, the Taiping Rebellion.

It is important to note, however, that Houqua's descendants appeared to be largely oblivious to the nature of the ASI holdings. Nonetheless, the nature of this "blind trust" that Houqua left in John Murray Forbes's care represented the total confidence that Houqua and his family had in John's ability to invest on their behalf without any periodic reporting of the holdings. Our knowledge of the precise holdings in the ASI comes not from John's briefing of the beneficiaries of the ASI on the investments but from internal records in America regarding the sale of the ASI assets.

It should not come as any surprise that John invested Houqua's American assets in such ventures because they reflected significant economic developments in the United States at the time and thus they comprised a substantial portion of the opportunities available to investors in America during that period. Surely Houqua's estate contributed to the construction of railroads in America rather than in China. However, the sense

[24] Ibid.

of crisis in national economic development in China did not arise until after Houqua's passing. For the transnational investor in the early- to mid-nineteenth century, the search for profits knew no national boundaries and did not follow any patriotic agenda. Although not transparent to Houqua's heirs, the transnational partnership between the two financiers-cum-investors, Houqua and John Murray Forbes, allowed the management of Houqua's estate to transcend political boundaries, and it extended Houqua's investment options beyond holdings in physical assets, land, and real estate in the local area of Canton, the only vehicles for wealth accumulation according to our conventional view of China's capital markets at the time.

Correspondence between the Forbes in Boston and Russell & Company's officers in Hong Kong indicates that the sale in 1874 was to produce $300,000. In a letter dated August 4, 1874, signed in Chinese by Haoguan (浩官) and in parentheses by "Houqua," Houqua's heir instructed the Forbes in Boston to send to "Messrs Russell & Co.... Three hundred thousand dollars United States currency ($300,000 U.S. currency), which draft please honor to the debit of the A.S.I. account." Trusting the Forbes in Boston to decide the manner in which to "disperse of such bonds or stocks belonging to this fund as may seem best in [their] judgment," Houqua's heir issued instructions on the liquidation of one-half of Houqua's ASI holdings.[25] "ASI quite satisfactory, Howqua has authorized us to withdraw from America *one half* [italics added]," the partners in Hong Kong communicated to the Boston office on July 24, 1874.

In response, the Boston office reported on August 17, 1874 that it had "accordingly begun sale of the securities," that they planned to "continue sales as fast as they can be made without injury to the account and trust," and that they expected to be "able to close the necessary account within a month or two."[26] The aforementioned sale of securities in railroad companies and U.S. government bonds did indeed close within the next several months, between July 29, 1874 and October 27, 1874 to be precise. That the financial records approximate the intended withdrawal communicated in the correspondence confirms that the balance of Houqua's investments in America stood at some $600,000 (twice the withdrawn amount of $300,000) before the withdrawals in 1874. Along with the withdrawals made before this orchestrated liquidation program, total ASI investments should have been anywhere between three-quarters of a million and one million dollars.

[25] Ibid.   [26] Baker Forbes, L, Subseries I, v.L–14.

One cannot be certain about what percentage of Houqua's estate was represented by the ASI. The oft-cited estimate of Houqua's net worth that is provided by William Hunter, an associate at Russell & Company, who asserted that on one occasion in 1834 Houqua offered the figure of $26 million, taking into consideration "his various investments in rice-fields, dwellings, shops, and the banking establishments known as shroffs, and including his American and English shipments."[27] There is no evidence to confirm Hunter's assertion about Houqua's calculation and the illiquidity of many of the investments that constituted Houqua's portfolio would have rendered any estimation approximate at best. Nonetheless, if we base our calculations on this oft-cited estimate, the ASI would have represented some 3 to 4 percent of Houqua's assets, not a significant portion of his overall net worth, but a respectable diversification in markets overseas, especially in light of the investment conditions at the time.[28]

Dissolution of the Trust and the Gradual De-Personification of the Relationship

The tone of Houqua's heir as he issued instructions to liquidate one-half of the ASI holdings was more formal than any previous documentation concerning the American investments. However, even the wording of the August 4, 1874 letter, signed "Houqua" and Haoguan in Chinese (浩官), continued to underscore the intimate connections between the two families that had functioned so well as trade and investment partners. Acknowledging the origin of the funds that had been entrusted to John Murray Forbes during Houqua's lifetime, this son of Houqua, who assumed the role as the second representative of Houqua's estate after the death of his brother in 1863, wrote, "I now confirm all that you have done with the funds originally placed in your hands by Messrs Russell & Co. for investment on account of my Father." He then expressed his gratitude to the Forbes for their service, "avail[ing] of this opportunity

[27] Hunter, The "Fan Kwae" at Canton, 48.

[28] Although their portfolios included some of the same American securities, Houqua's estate sharply contrasted with the investment portfolio of his partner Cushing. Whereas Houqua's ASI investments represented an impressive diversification from Chinese holdings in investments overseas, by the late 1830s Cushing turned away from foreign investments as he increased his focus on American investments (Larson, "A China Trader Turns Investor," 351). The increased allocation of American assets, albeit to different degrees, served the portfolios well, largely reflecting the changing landscape of international finance at the time. Noteworthy here is the agility that investors showcased as they traversed the world of investment opportunities.

to express my approval of your management of said funds for my Father during his life, for my brother during his life, & for myself during the time you have been responsible to me."[29]

By 1874, management of the ASI had already endured for over three decades, witnessing the passing of both Houqua and Young Houqua, his fifth son and the first heir to his estate. This first heir had become acquainted with John Murray Forbes during the latter's stay in Canton. His brother, Houqua's seventh and only surviving son by 1874, who became the second representative of Houqua's estate, was only 14 years old at the time that the ASI was established at the conclusion of the Opium War. Therefore, he had never worked alongside John (see Figure 5.1).[30] Without any formal accounting of the balance of the trust on a periodic basis, Houqua's family had entrusted its management to the Forbes in Boston for over three decades, communicating only inter-mittently through their representatives in Canton and Hong Kong. On this occasion when the family requested repatriation of one-half of the investments, Houqua's last surviving son thanked the Forbes in America, whom he had barely known personally but in whom he had placed tremendous trust because of the confidence his father and brother had shown toward them.

Even after the withdrawal from America of one-half of the ASI funds, the balance of Houqua's estate invested by the American partners remained significant. Benefiting from the continued accrual of interest and fluctuating with market valuations, Houqua's account with Russell & Company in 1877, recorded under the name of "JMF Trustee 'H,'" stood at 428,978 taels, or some $600,000 at the exchange rate of $1 to 0.72 tael, representing over one-third of the company's outside liabilities.[31] This amount probably included some of the assets repatriated in 1874 but not yet distributed to Houqua's family. Repatriation of the assets to Hong Kong and Canton was but a first step in the program. Once the capital reached the local offices of Russell & Company, the partners there were charged with local investment of the money for income generation and capital preservation on behalf of Houqua's family before the funds were liquidated to meet capital requirements. No doubt, the investment of such funds in China not only served the purposes of Houqua's family but also alleviated the perennial capital needs of Russell & Company.

[29] Baker Forbes, L, Subseries III, Box 16, f.9.
[30] He was actually Houqua's seventh son by birth, but his second son was adopted by Houqua's brother. For a genealogical account, see Wu Ziwei, ed., *Wushi ru Yue zupu*, vol. "3rd branch," 6:49b, and Wu Quancui, ed., *Lingnan Wushi hezu zongpu*, 2a:46b.
[31] MHS Forbes Reel 37B/No. 18, Folders 1–3.

Therefore, despite the express intention of Houqua's heir to retrieve one-half of the investments in America, the fate of Houqua's family and Russell & Company continued to be intertwined due to their financial dealings.

Without much fanfare, the Forbes in America resumed the sale of Houqua's ASI in 1879. They received a telegram in Boston, sent on March 1, 1879, notifying them, "Houqua wishes you to sell at your discretion investments for his account. Net proceeds can be held awaiting documents." Another telegram, dated March 14, 1879, stated that "all documents connected with ASI have been signed."[32] A letter sent from the Hong Kong office of Russell & Company via San Francisco, dated March 17, 1879, confirmed the message in the telegram as it reiterated "Houqua's desire to have the balance of the ASI account remitted to China." As for the reason for this final withdrawal, the letter offered the following: "The demands of his family for increased allowances makes [sic] him anxious to take advantage of any favorable opportunity to add to his income." The beneficiaries of Houqua's estate in China had gone through the previous remittance at a rapid pace; the $300,000 repatriated in 1874 had only lasted for five years.

As based on Figure 6.1, it is evident that this sale in 1879, just like the sale in 1874, responded not to opportunities for cashing in on price appreciations in the investments, but instead responded to the needs of the beneficiaries of the ASI. American Railroad stocks had dropped in value, having lost over 20 percent in value since 1874. However, during the same period bonds had seen a rise in value. Nonetheless, the order from Canton was not to select securities for sale based on their valuation, but to dump everything in the portfolio to generate cash for repatriation and ready access.

However, Houqua's descendants were not the only beneficiaries of the repatriated ASI. As the remainder of the ASI was returned to China, Houqua's heir agreed to offer a loan in Shanghai to be secured "by the hypothecation of Real Estate," most likely for the use of the partners of Russell & Company there. It is therefore reasonable that in relaying the gratitude of Houqua's heir to the Forbes in America "for the care taken of his property & for the handsome increase realized," Russell & Company partners in Hong Kong and China added their own thanks and expressed their hope that "when the present loan expires Houqua may be induced to again place the care of his interests in your [the American Forbes's] hands."[33] On the one hand, financial ties between Houqua's estate and his former partners in America were severed, whereas, on

[32] Baker Forbes, L, Subseries III, Box 16, f.10.   [33] Ibid.

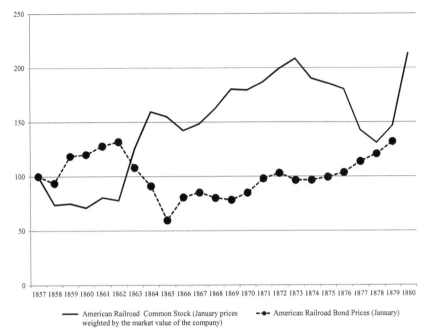

1857 1858 1859 1860 1861 1862 1863 1864 1865 1866 1867 1868 1869 1870 1871 1872 1873 1874 1875 1876 1877 1878 1879 1880

—— American Railroad Common Stock (January prices   --◆-- American Railroad Bond Prices (January)
weighted by the market value of the company)

Figure 6.1. Indices of American Stock and Bond Prices during the Investment Lifespan of the ASI, 1857–1880. *Source:* Frederick R. Macaulay, *Some Theoretical Problems Suggested by the Movements of Interest Rates, Bond Yields and Stock Prices in the United States Since 1856* (New York: National Bureau of Economic Research, 1938; rpt., London: Risk Books, 1999), A208, A221.

the other hand, the mingling of assets between Houqua's heirs and the operations of Russell & Company in China was intensified.

Extant records for this second tranche of the sale are even less complete than the orchestrated 1874 liquidation. The ASI portfolio must have continued to include many railroad securities because in 1878 the Forbes were still crediting the ASI for interest payments from holdings such as Nebraska Railway Bonds and Chicago Burlington & Quincy Railroad. Also remaining in the portfolio was U.S. public debt: the ASI received interest in the amount of $675 for "27000$ US 10/40 Bonds" on March 7, 1879. On the same day, the Forbes also recorded receipt "for sales of securities of ASI under orders from Russell & Co. Hong Kong who are to produce authority in due course," $6,096.25 from the sale of "US 6% Bonds of '67," and $10,210.25 from the sale of "Republican & RR 6% Bds 102." In less than one week, the ASI account received proceeds, net of commissions, of $34,446.79 for the sale of "Ottawa Oswego & FRV RR Bonds," shares of "Burr & Mo Riv RR in Neb," "Leav. Lawrence & Gal. RR Bonds," "Nebraska R'y Bds," and "Ch. Bur & Q RR 7%." Recorded over the next several days were further sales of ASI holdings: $9,016.25 for 75 shares of "Bur & Mo Rev RR," 1,445 shares of "Ch. Burr & Q RR," and a total of $32,025.62 for 105 shares of "Phil Wil & Balt RR," 25 shares of "Bur & Mo Rev RR," and $9,000 face value of "Eastern RR Bonds." Thereafter, the ASI would continue to record proceeds from additional sales, many in installments of over $100,000, but these entries did not include details on the sold securities. Summing the proceeds of these sales, an entry on April 30, 1879 credited the ASI account "[f]or prds of former & as rec'd Ap'l 30 '79 to fd to latter, sales under orders from Russell & Co att'y for Houqua owner of the securities" in the amount of $490,772.24.[34]

What had begun informally as Houqua's consignment entrusted to John Murray Forbes, along with his brother Bennet and cousin John Perkins Cushing, concluded with formal documentation certifying dissolution of the account. Included in the Forbes's records of the ASI is a document dated July 12, 1879, signed by Wu Chonghui Haoguan in Chinese (伍崇暉 浩官)[35] with a red dot seal.

This legal document opened with the drafter's vague understanding of the genesis of the American investments of Houqua's estate: "[b]efore the fifteenth day of August in the year one thousand eight hundred and forty-two, certain sums of money were deposited with and remitted to and put into the hands and possession of John Murray Forbes, now of Milton, in the State of Massachusetts, for care and investments by How Qua, a merchant of China, which sums of money with all additions and increments thereto." The drafter took pains to specify in this document, which was deemed to be legally effective, the names and places of residence of the parties involved, John Murray Forbes and Houqua (the latter rendered here as two separate words, and with a "w"). However, for the date of the establishment of this trust, the document could offer nothing more definitive than that Houqua had entrusted the capital to John by a certain date in 1842. Nor was the writer capable of specifying the exact amount entrusted. But he knew that the capital came in various installments as "additions and increments." This lack of specificity reflects the origins of the capital in the fund generated by Houqua's consigned goods to America on different ships at various times, and the fact

[34] Baker Forbes, L, Subseries I, v.L–22.
[35] Baker Forbes, L, Subseries III, Box 16, f.10.

that at the time, Houqua could not be sure of the proceeds that the sale of such goods would produce.

The text continued, "except so far as they have been paid or transmitted to the legal successor of the said How Qua, or his lawful attorney, [the sums] have come to the possession of the partnership consisting of the said John Murray Forbes, and his sons William Hathaway Forbes and John Malcolm Forbes doing business under the style and name of J.M. Forbes & Co." Thus began the crux of the document when Houqua's surviving son, the signatory of this document, acknowledged receipt of the remitted funds from time to time by "legal successors" of Houqua. The remainder of the capital apparently went only to John Murray Forbes and his two sons, who together had formed a partnership to function as trustee of the assets. The archives of Russell & Company and the Forbes records clearly indicate that not all Russell & Company partners were privy to the nature or the size of the trust. The exclusivity of the information actually went further: even John's brother Bennet and his cousin John Perkins Cushing did not exercise their roles as consultants to John in the management of the funds.

A description of the event that had precipitated the closure of the funds follows: "[i]t is now intended and desired that all the moneys due from the said firm of J.M. Forbes & Co. to the estate of the said How Qua or to his heir or successor, or to the person entitled by the laws of China to receive the same, shall be paid, and all accounts arising from the dealings of the said John Murray Forbes and of the said J.M. Forbes & Co. with the said How Qua and with his successors, heirs, or legal representatives, shall be settled, adjusted, and the said John Murray Forbes and J.M. Forbes & Co. discharged from all liability therefor." Houqua's heir had initiated this liquidation process and the recipients of the funds had to be the legal beneficiaries of the trust. John and the company he had formed with his two sons were thereafter to be released from all responsibilities. The document was to serve as a representation of Houqua's surviving son as the legal heir to Houqua's estate. It did not matter that at the time of the trust's creation the beneficiaries were ill-defined because its establishment was predicated on mutual understanding between Houqua and John Murray Forbes as to who Houqua's true heirs should be. After all, John had worked alongside Houqua and knew his family. However, by 1879, many of the personal relationships had dissolved with the deaths of many of the numerous parties on the Forbes side who had succeeded as the contact person for Houqua's family. Therefore, by signing this document, Houqua's surviving son indemnified John and his two sons against conflicting claims of any rightful inheritance of Houqua's estate.

In establishing the trust, the parties who were known personally to one another needed only an implicit understanding of the purpose and the nature of the funds. In closing this financial arrangement, however, the Forbes brought to bear what they considered to be effective legal protection to avoid further claims against them on the basis of their having served as trustees to Houqua's assets.

This only surviving son of Houqua continued,

Now therefore, I Ng Shing Fai [Wu Chonghui, in pinyin] How Qua, of Canton, in China aforesaid, do for myself, my heirs, executors, administrators, successors, and personal representatives of every name and description, covenant with the said John Murray Forbes, William Hathaway Forbes, and John Malcolm Forbes, their heirs, executors and administrators, jointly and severally, that I am the lawful successor, heir and personal representative of the said How Qua first named, and of his first successor and heir Ng Shing Yow How Qua, that I am the person lawfully entitled by the laws of China to demand, collect and receive all debts and demands due to the estate of the said How Qua first named and to his first successor and heir aforesaid or either of them; and that I will indemnify and save harmless the said John Murray Forbes and the said partnership of J.M. Forbes & Co. from and against all claims by or on account of any and all moneys paid by them or either of them to me or my lawful attorneys on account of debts due to said How Qua first named or his first successor and heir aforesaid, asserted by any person whatsoever.

This is a carefully drafted legal document specifying the various involved parties. Houqua, who had established the ASI, did not need to provide his Chinese name at the outset. Nor was his Chinese name necessary in this legal document. It was acceptable for the Forbes to refer in internal documents to the successive heirs of Houqua's estate simply as "Houqua." However, it would not suffice in this legal document. The signatory "Ng Shing Fai How Qua" had to represent himself as the heir to "the said How Qua first named," following his brother "Ng Shing Yow [Wu Chongyao, in pinyin] How Qua." Just as important as the specification of the parties involved on Houqua's side, it was imperative to indemnify *only* John Murray Forbes, his two sons, and their company against future claims. The financial dealings of Houqua's family with John's family in America had ceased, but that only channeled more of the remitted funds through Russell & Company, with which Houqua's family remained financially entangled. Of course, this indemnity did not extend to other Forbes family members or to Russell & Company associates. Extending the indemnity would not only have misrepresented the financial calculations in Canton but also would have implicitly precluded future use of the capital from Houqua's estate in the operations of Russell & Company.

Nothing could be left to chance for the execution of such an important document. The signing of the document was witnessed by the U.S. Consulate in Canton who certified that "Ng Shing Fai Houqua," whom he had "personally know[n]" executed the document "as his free act and deed."[36] As evidence of his witnessing of this act, the Consul signed and pressed his official seal on the document. The deliberate use of official paraphernalia on this document is evident. John and his sons had demanded this legal document, along with the additional reassurance of confirmation by the U.S. Consulate, to guard against any legal proceedings that might be launched against them for further demands in conjunction with the ASI. Unlike the personal letters between the Forbes and Houqua, which established the trust, preparation of the documents of dissolution was to be handled by American legal professionals rather than amateurs. For the "[l]egal service on a/c A.S.I.," in particular, on "consultations, advice, and examination of papers, in relation to settlement with estate of How Qua and drawing contract of indemnity," Messrs. J.M. Forbes & Co. had paid E.R. Hoar $150 by April 30, 1879. This set of documents might not have held much legal power in China, but it would have been effective in a U.S. court of law should need be. The search for profits knew no national boundaries, but protection from legal claims was highly specific to territorial jurisdictions.[37]

That the conclusion of the ASI entailed such a carefully crafted legal document echoes Lydia Liu's observation on the power dynamics imbued

---

[36] Ibid.

[37] By September 23, 1879, the ASI account was closed in the books of Messrs J.M. Forbes & Co. However, in its stead Russell & Company opened an account called "John M. Forbes Jr. Trustee," which took over "everything pertaining to" the ASI account. This namesake of the person who had personally partnered with Houqua was not his own offspring, but his cousin. John Murray Forbes Jr. (1844–1921), along with his brother Francis Blackwell Forbes ("Frank") (1839–1908), who were active in Russell & Company in the 1880s. As John wrote to Frank on January 18, 1881 when he was preparing for a return trip to China, he was to "come to Shanghai en route to Hong Kong in order to go into the future arrangements of R&Co. with you & to see about 1340 Trust funds." This new trust, which took over from the ASI in 1879, continued to channel the unfinished business of the ASI for the next several years. On December 1, 1882, John M. Forbes Jr., in his capacity as "Trustee for Houqua," recorded receipt of $1,312 and additional securities, which included "Certf No. 24831 for 4 sh. Chicago Burlington & Quincy," as well as railroad bonds with a face value of $40,000 and coupons from 4 to 6 percent. Baker Forbes, L, Subseries III, Box 16, f.10; MHS Forbes Reel 27/No. 5/ Folder 7/116 docs/ Business letters from John Murray Forbes Jr. (1844–1921, FBF's brother), in Boston, New York, and China, 1879–1906, January 18, 1881.

in translations of international law.[38] Although the document Houqua's heir signed was designed for efficacy in an American court of law, just as in the case of the translation into Chinese of Henry Wheaton's *Elements of International Law* for the Qing, it represented not only a textual and diplomatic event but also an epistemological shift that helped to justify the subjugation of Chinese participants in relationships that had begun on more equal footing. Houqua had executed with his signature brush stroke documents written in English that carried no greater weight than the contracts he signed in Chinese.[39] Business partners in pre–Treaty Port era Canton had communicated in pidgin English (and pidgin Chinese) with no obvious cultural insinuation so as to bridge the language gap and to facilitate economic exchanges.[40] By the 1870s, such fluid juxtaposition of linguistic media had given way to a vision of the global in which Western concepts dominated, all with the pretense of a mission to civilize the uninitiated into a reified universal regime.

Thus ended the investment of Houqua's estate overseas thirty-six years after his death. However, the lasting legacy of Houqua's investments with the Forbes through Russell & Company endured. Even after repatriation of the assets, the financial entanglement between Houqua's estate and Russell & Company lasted another twelve years and it was not dissolved until the failure of the latter in 1891. On August 4, 1890, W.H. Forbes, who was struggling with the financial collapse of Russell & Company, wrote to his cousin, Frank: "The Houqua Trust is giving us most trouble & as this account account [*sic*] it has become necessary for Tomes [Charles Alexander Tomes (1854–1933)] & myself to go into bankruptcy here."[41] As the Forbes weighed in on the matter, John Murray Forbes, who had worked alongside Houqua, thought that it might be possible "to tide them over, as it was said that about $300,000 would do this." However, he soon realized that "the liabilities were very much greater." The partners then became convinced that it was impossible "to interest friends in a limited company without full details as to the liabilities & position of the house." First among the factors they listed as major hurdles for any rescue effort was "[t]he complications with Houqua."[42] Their

---

[38] Lydia H. Liu, *Clash of Empires: The Invention of China in Modern World Making* (Cambridge, MA: Harvard University Press, 2004), ch. 4.
[39] See Chapter 3.   [40] See Chapters 3 and 5.
[41] MHS Forbes Reel 29/No. 6/Folder 2 Letters to Francis Blackwell Forbes from Russell & Co. Officials, Including G[eorge]. H. Wheeler, William Pethick, F. D.[W.?] Hitch, and F[rederick]. D. Bush, about the Failure of Russell & Co. and Other Subjects, 1861–92, August 4, 1890.
[42] MHS Forbes Reel 29/No. 6/Folder 2 Letters to Francis Blackwell Forbes from Russell & Co. Officials, Including G[eorge]. H. Wheeler, William Pethick, F. D.[W.?] Hitch, and

predominant concern about the partnership's indebtedness to Houqua's family, relative to the $300,000 infusion that they thought could have kept the firm afloat, suggests that Houqua's family could have continued to tie up half a million dollars or more in Russell & Company as late as 1891, comprising repatriated proceeds from the ASI and any remnants of surplus capital that Houqua's family had lent to Russell & Company.

Russell & Company did not survive the crisis of 1891, and along with the collapse of the firm were the lasts remnants of Houqua's investments in America through his American partners who were deployed both overseas and locally. Half a century after the beginning of Houqua's investments in America and almost as long after his death, Houqua's descendants received the last payment for the capital that their illustrious ancestor had entrusted to his allies in international trade and finance. According to Charles A. Tomes, who started a new partnership from the ashes of Russell & Company, the Shanghai property of Russell & Company was sold for 400,000 taels. After commissions and fees, "all the Howqua family gets is about Tls 300,000."[43]

The End of the Partnership

The final fate of Russell & Company revealed the critical role that Houqua's funds had played in the financial operations of the partnership. Compared with the practice of renegotiating the composition of Russell & Co. partners and the associated recurring reconstitution of the partners' capital, Houqua's estate formed the most permanent source of capital for the operations of the firm. Without the loans from Houqua's family, the firm would not have outlasted the many partnerships that had gone bankrupt during the various global financial crises in the nineteenth century. Nor would the firm have operated on the same scale. However, Houqua's family generated handsome interest income from the loans and, more importantly, benefited tremendously from an arrangement that sheltered the family's assets from both official extractions and dissipation by Houqua's descendants.

This symbiotic relation worked better when the assets remained in the United States under the care of Houqua's personal friend and partner, but even he could not prevent Houqua's heir from calling back

F[rederick]. D. Bush, about the Failure of Russell & Co. and Other Subjects, 1861–92, June 16, 1891.
[43] MHS Charles A. Tomes Letterbooks, 1886–1914, Box 2, Book 1: Letters, 1892–95, September 15, 1893.

the money for use by the family. John Murray Forbes did not receive a clear mandate from Houqua, at least not in any document articulated legally or otherwise. However, he invested his partner's funds as he knew best in the world of opportunities in American economic development and these investments preserved the capital and generated profits in a manner consistent with the commercial and financial strategies that Houqua had employed during his lifetime. In keeping with the reason why Houqua initiated these American investments, for decades John protected the funds from unwarranted withdrawals. Despite the less than optimal conclusion to Russell & Company, the ASI enriched Houqua's descendants through the various rounds of repatriation and measured distributions.

Judging from the repatriation of the ASI, Houqua's trust in his American allies paid off. It might have been a stroke of luck that John Murray Forbes, who outlived Houqua by more than half a century, enjoyed a long life and honored the trust that Houqua had placed in him. However, such personalistic ties should not be considered a suboptimal business arrangement in the context of early- to mid-nineteenth century global commerce. In an environment where the enforcement of legal contracts was highly territorially defined, Houqua took the pragmatic approach of viewing legal recourse as a last resort and instead he relied on his ability to assess and balance risk and to carefully select partners. The use of the legal apparatus, not in the establishment of the ASI but in its conclusion, partially reflects the erosion of the personal ties between the Forbes and Houqua's family and partially is indicative of the increasing popularity of institutional arrangements in global transactions as the nineteenth century unfolded. As much as the severance documents ossified the fluid dynamics between Houqua and his American partners, their use also underscores the compartmentalized operations that separated the Forbes in America from their associates at Russell & Company in Hong Kong and China. In the end, as Russell & Company collapsed, such institutional arrangements might have limited the losses for the Forbes in America. The demise of the former joint venture between Houqua's family and the Forbes ended not only because Houqua's descendants failed to live up to the enterprising talents of the great Chinese merchant but also because the later partners of Russell & Company proved to be less capable than their predecessors in overcoming the turmoil in the international marketplace. Institutional arrangements were no substitute for personal talent.

This "Swiss Account" Houqua established with his American trustees served to separate fiduciary ownership of the assets of Houqua's heirs from management of the assets entrusted to U.S. partners who commanded a better flow of information. On an informal basis predicated on personal ties, Houqua structured this separation of ownership from management, a separation that later became popular under the formal arrangement of business incorporation. In this regard, Houqua was truly ahead of global trends and his business maneuver reflected less of an orchestrated attempt to structure professional management distinct from ownership than a calculated strategy based on his tremendous trust in John Murray Forbes. Indeed, if Houqua's successors had proved to be as adept as he was in directing the development of global trade and finance, they might have leveraged Houqua's wealth to promote economic development in China and China might not have taken a different path at the fork in the road of the Great Divergence.[44] This was Houqua's predicament, but it also affected the course of China's development. Houqua enjoyed a long life of 74 years, but because of that, he also outlived all but two of his seven sons, among whom were the heirs he had groomed for his succession.[45] Succession issues notwithstanding, Houqua's actual accomplishments demonstrate how this Chinese merchant operated on an equal footing with his Western partners well into the nineteenth century.

That the Chinese capital market was less vibrant relative to its counterparts in certain European and American cities in the nineteenth century was only a limitation for the narrow-minded Chinese investor, but not for an enterprising global entrepreneur such as Houqua who saw the world as a canvas upon which he could fashion his investment portfolio. For Houqua's generation of investors, loyalty to one's country did not need to confine productive resources to politically defined spaces. Albeit a modest percentage of his total assets, the ASI he entrusted to his American partners served not only to diversify his holdings internationally but also to protect his assets from official exactions and premature withdrawals. His investments in America first served as his ticket to break free from British ascendency, then as a shelter from exactions by Chinese officials. National divides certainly presented constraints to nineteenth-century

---

[44] Houqua's business engagements and investments in conjunction with his global allies *and* in opposition to his international rivals represented a critical juncture in China's economic development vis-à-vis certain Western economies. At an individual level, his story forms the pivotal moment of China's economic decline relative to the West that historians have analyzed on a macroeconomic scale. For the macroeconomic factors behind the Great Divergence, see Elvin, *The Pattern of the Chinese Past*; Huang, *The Peasant Family and Rural Development in the Yangzi Delta, 1350–1988*; Pomeranz, *The Great Divergence*; Wong, *China Transformed*; Bozhong Li, *Agricultural Development in Jiangnan, 1620–1850* (New York: St. Martin's Press, 1998).

[45] Wu Lingli, ed., *Wushi Putianfang Fulonggong Guangzhou shisanhang zhimai zu yinpu*, 51.

traders, but for the resourceful Houqua, circumvention was not only possible but economically rewarding. Rather than viewing spatial separation as a form of risk, Houqua saw it as a source of protection, bridged by the personal connections he had cultivated with his handpicked allies.

The contribution of the ASI to the portfolio of Houqua's estate was immense in light of the global investment environment at the time. This enduring partnership between Houqua and his American partners, in particular with John Murray Forbes, provides testimony to Houqua's investment sagacity. Houqua deployed capital for long-term investments through his trusted partners and extended his portfolio to overseas markets during periods of geopolitical uncertainty. His trust in his allies enabled him to ascertain his risks over the long haul, well beyond the usual mindset of calculating profits by each shipment. His global perspective not only enabled his investments to transcend national boundaries and to profit from opportunities overseas but also allowed the portfolio to leverage political divides to shelter the funds from unwanted attention. Long before it became fashionable to set up offshore "Swiss Accounts," Houqua, in dealing with his trusted American partners, had designed investment vehicles for similar purposes by leveraging his faith in his allies and his ingenuity in the world of early modern global finance.

Conclusion

Fusing Networks: Local, Regional, and Global

The story of Houqua & Co. is at once local, regional, and global. Houqua's business success certainly amplified economic vitality in Canton. However, this analysis of his business success is less an examination of the Canton system than a study of the impact of an exceptional operator within this system who, through his personal business endeavors, set in motion changes that had ramifications for both China's development and the global system at large. Through the study of Houqua and his successors I have reexamined an episode that has been studied in detail as an issue of high politics and international conflict with a view toward the social, cultural, and economic forces that animated changes at the macro level. Houqua's business story sheds new light on China's place in the world before the introduction of a Western-centric world order and informs us of the birth of global trade in the early modern world. His success in global business illustrates the construction of networks of trust for the purpose of facilitating economic exchange before the advent of an enforceable, unified international system of arbitration. The experience of his successors tells the story of the diverging economic fortunes of global traders formerly operating on equal footing. This is a story not only of an exceptional individual but also of the dynamic setting of transnational business when regional networks negotiated connections in the emerging modern world.

By 1800, China's integration into the global economy was evident in the flow of goods through Canton. Long before the introduction of the Canton system in the mid-eighteenth century, China had traded with a wide array of Western partners through various trading-network configurations. However, the sale of Chinese tea crescendoed toward the turn of the nineteenth century and formed the bedrock for an ongoing economic exchange between China and the West. No bulk commodity had ever before commanded such persistent appeal or generated sales in such great volume in successive years.[1] In this regard, the sale of Chinese tea under the Canton system ushered in an era of global integration between China and the Western world at a level of regularity and predictability unprecedented in the history of China's economic dealings with the outside world. This track record of China's consistent annual exchanges with the West by the turn of the nineteenth century refutes the notion that the Chinese economy was forced open by the West in the aftermath of the Opium War.[2] Even before the imposition of a Western-centric system of economic exchange, China was by no means, and certainly not economically, disconnected from the rest of the world. However, this connection with the West, at least at this level of integration, was not achieved centuries earlier in China's ad-hoc exchange with its peripheral partners. China merged with global trading routes in earnest at about the turn of the nineteenth century, just as the flow of goods and capital accelerated in the emerging modern world, decades before the Western powers dictated the opening of China's Treaty Ports.

Global business flows require the coordination of an organizational structure or a configuration of networks. In the era subsequent to the period of analysis undertaken in this study, the emergence of the modern firm privileged a more hierarchical corporate organization that facilitated administrative coordination, engendered professional management, and allowed more permanence for business entities.[3] However, during the earlier era of global exchange when Canton served as a nexus, few participants relied on such corporate organizational forms to regulate business flows. The rare exception was the British East India Company, and even in that case the organizational form contributed just as much to

---

[1] From the vantage point of a painting by Vermeer that opens many windows into the world of the seventeenth century, Timothy Brook examines the emergence of the interconnectedness among people in different parts of the world at "the dawn of the global world." See Timothy Brook, *Vermeer's Hat: The Seventeenth Century and the Dawn of the Global World* (New York: Bloomsbury, 2008). As Brook masterfully portrays, these global encounters were certainly becoming more predictable. However, it would take another century before the exchange of curious items blossomed into sustained trade in certain bulk commodities that the connectedness with China became demonstrably regular and the exchange was appreciably significant in economic terms.

[2] A classic discussion of this notion can be found in Fairbank, *Trade and Diplomacy on the China Coast*. See also John K. Fairbank and S.Y. Teng, "On the Ch'ing Tributary System," *Harvard Journal of Asiatic Studies* 6, no. 2 (June 1941): 135–246, in which they highlight the breakdown of the tributary system as it failed to accommodate the maritime trade of the West, thereby ending the modern period of Chinese exclusiveness. For yet another example, see Peter Ward Fay, *The Opium War, 1840–1842: Barbarians in the Celestial Empire in the Early Part of the Nineteenth Century and the War by which They Forced Her Gates Ajar* (Chapel Hill: University of North Carolina Press, 1975).

[3] Alfred D. Chandler Jr., *The Visible Hand: The Managerial Revolution in American Business* (Cambridge, MA: Belknap Press of Harvard University Press, 1977).

the procedural management of business as to the formalization of the symbiotic political and commercial interests (the latter being an important differentiation between British and Chinese partners in the Canton trade, about which I will elaborate upon later). With the exception of this important outlier, organization forms did not dictate business operations in the global trade of Canton; instead, business flows followed the routes of networks underwritten not by formal rules but by personal connections. Entities that did not assume formal corporate organizational forms participated in global trade as family businesses (or business structures expressed in the idiom of family relations) and fixed-term partnerships (such as Russell & Company), which had to be reconstituted at the end of each term. These business entities, be they corporate organizations, family enterprises, or fixed-term partnerships, had to be connected together to form circuitries of goods and capital and to generate economic profits for the participants.[4]

Despite the critical functions these networks served in the early period of global trade, studies of business networks have focused on configurations predicated on commonalities in provincial or ethnic origins, thereby lavishing attention on regional networks and rarely venturing into analysis of global arrangements. In the case of analyses of the West for the period under question, the focus on the regional favors networks consisting of business entities built on the (largely Anglo-Saxon) belief in the sanctity of property rights, law, and free markets. In the case of Chinese businesses, examinations of networks highlight the role of overseas Chinese in trade and commerce in an area that remained Sino-centric in its cultural orientation or limited to East and Southeast Asian in its geographical reach.[5] In this study, I underscore the global dimension of the Canton trade and emphasize the active efforts by the key participants to rewire the circuitries of business flows to their own advantage as local conditions and worldwide geopolitical developments disrupted the business networks and presented new opportunities for shrewd entrepreneurs. What bound together the participants in Houqua's network was not any ethnically defined commonality but the culture of the pursuit of profit.

[4] The story of Houqua provides an international context to discussions of Chinese corporate structure that have attracted the attention of Chinese business historians. See, for example, Wellington K.K. Chan, "Tradition and Change in the Chinese Business Enterprise: The Family Firm Past and Present," in *Chinese Business History: Interpretive Trends and Priorities for the Future*, eds. Robert Gardella, Jane K. Leonard, and Andrea McElderry (Armonk, NY: M.E. Sharpe, 1998), 127–144.

[5] See, for example, Kwok Bun Chan, ed., *Chinese Business Networks: State, Economy and Culture* (Singapore: Prentice Hall; Copenhagen: Nordic Institute of Asian Studies, 2000) and Gary Hamilton, ed., *Business Networks and Economic Development in East and Southeast Asia* (Hong Kong: Centre of Asian Studies, University of Hong Kong, 1991).

Global networks link preexisting regional formations. As regional networks merge, the participants must reconcile the different rules governing business flows in their respective areas if they want to formalize a set of regulations that can be applied on a transregional basis. Otherwise, they will improvise and negotiate the regional standards to serve their own business interests. A good example of this pragmatic approach to business in Houqua's fluid world of global trade is his view toward the application of law in different jurisdictions. In the absence of any reliable recourse in any court of international law, Houqua and his partners demonstrated their practical business sense to resolve financial disputes. As some of his American business transactions went sour in the 1810s, Houqua, with the help of Cushing's business affiliates in the United States, considered pursuing debt collection through legal channels in America. This business endeavor, which extended Houqua's business presence to the other side of the globe, underscores the collective ability of Houqua and his trusted partners to tap into the resources afforded them by the legal regimes in different countries. More revealing, however, was their decision not to prosecute debtors who would have found it impossible to pay. That decision is indicative of their sense of financial pragmatism and of their view of legal institutions as a means of last resort.

This flexible appeal to regional regulations stands in sharp contrast to the dogmatic application of what was to be touted in later periods as international rules. The imposition of a Western-centric mode of business transactions has drawn our attention to the important role of contracts and the critical function of laws. Such a focus on contracts and laws has generated academic interest among scholars of Chinese business history to find an equivalent that might have provided order and structure to commercial transactions in China before the introduction of the Western model.[6] Informal arrangements, such as the policing of business conduct through reputation in ethnic groups, served similar purposes, although such informal arrangements would only work in established networks of business associates.[7] However, in the evolving business world of Houqua, who charted an ever-expanding geographical network, these institutions, legally defined or ethnically constructed, provided no lasting solution.

To penetrate the vast markets overseas, Houqua depended on his cultivation of trust with handpicked partners. Houqua placed no greater trust

---

[6] See, for example, Zelin, Ocko, and Gardella, eds., *Contract and Property in Early Modern China*; Faure, *China and Capitalism*.

[7] My discussion in Chapter 4 offers an in-depth comparison with Greif's analysis of another group of long-distance traders. See Greif, "Reputation and Coalitions in Medieval Trade," "The Organization of Long-Distance Trade," "Contract Enforceability and Economic Institutions in Early Trade," and *Institutions and the Path to the Modern Economy*.

than that in John Perkins Cushing and his Forbes cousins who succeeded him. As Cushing planned his exit from Canton, this partnership continued with an almost unbroken chain of personal relations with Cushing who was stationed by Houqua's side. This constant stream of representatives from among Cushing's American relatives, many of whom also stayed for years in Canton, perpetuated Houqua's dealings with a tight-knit group of American merchants that constituted an informal business institution. The mutual understanding between Houqua and his American partners allowed for an enduring relationship and minimized the pains (or transaction costs) associated with each round of personnel changes. The mutual trust between Houqua and his select American partners was all the more impressive because, unlike other tight-knit business partnerships that involved people of similar backgrounds, their partnership transcended ethnic, social, and cultural boundaries. Economic motivations certainly propelled the relations that Houqua maintained with his American team, at least during the early stages. With the promise of bigger transactions and higher profits every year, no rational economic actor would jeopardize these business ties and instead would seek to perpetuate the relationship by ensuring the supply of an unbroken chain of business confidants to work alongside Houqua.

Ties that link regional formations to form global networks are delicate and bonds among such business partners are more easily established than they are sustained. How then did Houqua cultivate enduring trust that seemingly defied economic calculations? As he did not rely on legal channels of conflict resolution, it is not surprising that Houqua did not place a preponderance of trust in the fine print of business contracts. After all, how could one take into account all the business contingencies for transactions that traversed such immense distances and covered such long stretches of time? Instead, Houqua allowed his American confidants remarkable latitude in their execution of his trade. Without any reliable institutional framework, established legal infrastructure, or standardized business routines with which to organize his alliances, Houqua had to improvise connections to bridge his Canton-based trading hub with the overseas outposts manned by his trusted partners. The orchestrated dissemination of his portraits allowed Houqua comfort that his business partners were constantly reminded of their business sponsor in the faraway port of Canton. His iconic image transcended linguistic boundaries in securing and cementing business ties with his partners, especially those in America. The extant portraits of Houqua still hanging in the living rooms of descendants of his former American partners provide testimony to the enduring connections that he nurtured with his allies in the United States. The bonds of trust that Houqua cultivated with such handpicked partners came to be embodied in his portraits, speaking volumes about their mutual understanding of their business ventures that no written contract could replicate. In addition, the exchange of token gifts allowed for cordial acknowledgment of their continuing business ties when months of separation (from both his partners and his goods) tried Houqua's steel-tempered nerves during decades of daring business exchanges. At the conclusion of the Opium War, Houqua took care to assure his partners of the commercial viability of his network, ensuring them there was no end game for their business dealings. A mutually beneficial economic calculation provided the material underpinnings to the trust that endured in their trading network. However, it would not be fair to discount the personal connections between Houqua and his select partners.

The operations of Houqua and his partners in specific areas around the globe bespeak the requirement for a local presence in any global or regional configuration. Business networks cannot function in the absence of the stabilizing force of anchors. In Houqua's case, his critical position in the global network of trade pivoted around his presence in Canton. For ease of control and revenue collection, the Qing state had mandated that Canton be the sole legal port of call for Western traders in China. On the one hand, this official mandate allowed Houqua and other enterprising traders to capture tremendous profits by placing themselves at this funnel for China's trade with the West. On the other hand, the system also dictated that Houqua and the other Hong merchants position themselves in Canton to handle their China trade, thereby proscribing their geographical mobility alongside entrepreneurial business seekers among the Chinese diaspora.

Just like the Western merchants arriving at the port of Canton, the Chinese diaspora demonstrated its impressive ability and willingness to travel far and wide to exploit economic opportunities. Until the advent of navigational techniques toward the second half of the eighteenth century, which allowed Western seafarers to circumvent local knowledge in the South China Seas, these Chinese migrants dominated the region by fashioning a network of trade that linked together the various ports stretching from the coast of southeastern China to Southeast Asia. However, the business requirement that tea from China be transported as soon as possible to consumers in the Western world privileged the Western vessels. Furthermore, the need for Houqua and the other Hong merchants to be stationed in Canton reinforced the structural framework that allowed for the dominance of Western vessels in and out of Canton.

Scholars analyzing the role of the state in national (or local) economic development often question whether governments spearhead, or at least guide, the industrialization of their economies.[8] Houqua's story reminds us that even at an early stage state policies conditioned, sometime inadvertently, configurations of commercial exchange that affected economic development. The spatial configuration of Houqua's network was largely a reflection of the differences in institutional support provided by the political regimes that underwrote the commercial ventures. Operating on an equal footing, Houqua and his partners from the West provided their respective linkages that were critical to the completion of the trade. Houqua commanded access to the goods from China's interior desired by Western consumers, whereas his Western partners dominated the sea routes from Canton to the markets in the West. This specific configuration of global connections in the early nineteenth century spurred the desire of Western countries to penetrate the Chinese marketplace by breaking out of the Chinese-controlled stranglehold in Canton. The gentlemanly capitalists in Britain partnered with their political authorities at home and generated the twin engines of military and economic expansion.[9] Houqua's dealings with the Qing state followed a different path. In exchange for license to profit from funneling China's trade with the West, Houqua agreed to sporadic "contributions" that the Qing Mandarins exacted from him. However, this arrangement between Houqua and the Qing state did not result in a productive symbiotic relationship between the merchants in Canton and the political base in Beijing. Rather, it led to transactional exchanges between a subject of the empire and the state bureaucracy that did not generate a roadmap for extended growth. The policy of the Qing state provided no expansionist impetus for its merchants and structured a defensive posture for China's trade with the West by confining the Western traders, as well as the Hong merchants, to Canton. Houqua stands out as an unusual case of business success in the face of such institutional hurdles only because he undertook business initiatives to break free from this confining arrangement.

The connections between the local network to the regional and the global are not static. Entrepreneurs must devise networks to reconfigure business flows to circumnavigate the hurdles they face. Anchoring himself in Canton for the global flow of goods and capital, as sanctioned and required by the Qing state, Houqua had to fashion a transnational network that would enable him to extend his reach and to project his

---

[8] See, for example, Rondo Cameron, *Banking in the Early Stages of Industrialization* (New York: Oxford University Press, 1967).

[9] For a discussion of the development of "gentlemanly capitalism" in the case of Britain, see P. J. Cain and A. G. Hopkins, *British Imperialism: Innovation and Expansion, 1688–1914* (New York: Longman, 1993) and P. J. Cain and A. G. Hopkins, *British Imperialism: Crisis and Deconstruction, 1914–1990* (London: Longman, 1993).

presence at important nodes of trade where he would never set foot. To accomplish this formidable task, Houqua leveraged the constant flow of Western traders through his city of Canton. From his early days, officers of the British East India Company had already provided him with a stable avenue for the deployment of his goods and capital. The longstanding presence of the EIC in Canton provided the requisite comfort for Houqua to structure transactions with the British that entailed tremendous risks. These risks stemmed from the terms of the agreements over the delivery of the goods and receipt of the payments that stretched over vast territories around the world and took months to complete. To alleviate these risks over time and space, Houqua had the reassurance of the established presence of the EIC in his hometown. However, reliance on this one creditworthy partner did not favor Houqua in the power dynamics of the trade in Canton. Just as the British EIC had to nurture alternative vendors among the Chinese Hong merchants, Houqua had to cultivate alternative trading channels to counteract the mounting hegemony of the British.

To channel business flows to their advantage, business enterprises have to rewire the circuitries of trade to bypass the points of resistance in the network. At a minimum, redirecting business opportunities to alternative points of distribution will alleviate the problem of overpowering partners. In Houqua's case, he found an answer in the American traders who became increasingly active in Canton during the opening decades of the nineteenth century. These new arrivals from America allowed Houqua to circumvent the British in his dealings with the West. They shared many of the business practices of Houqua's British partners. No less important was that they shared the same language, thus lowering the linguistic barriers for Houqua as he developed new relationships with these aspiring new China traders. The opportune arrival of the Americans on the scene of international trade in Canton provided Houqua, the enterprising trader, with an alternative onramp as he merged his China trade with the global economy. As the regional networks of Europe and the United States encountered the Chinese regional economy, the local exchange in Canton completed a circuitry of global business flows negotiated by the various participants to serve their own economic interests.

The Elements of the Flows

In addition to the active positioning and repositioning of traders, global exchanges in Canton in the early nineteenth century entailed a specific pattern in the flow of goods and capital. Enabled by technological advances and conditioned by geopolitical forces around the world, commercial and financial exchanges gathered momentum by 1800 and coalesced in Canton, the port through which China funneled its trade with the West. At this emporium, Houqua, the Chinese merchant who engineered the flows and made himself the nexus around whom this exchange pivoted, directed the flow of traffic of international exchange and captured tremendous economic profits through transactions completed both in Canton and in other global locations.

Economic exchanges are predicated on a mutual desire for goods produced by the trading partners. In this regard, the Western traders' enduring search for an export item of appeal to China underscores the difficulties in structuring lasting two-way trade. Houqua and his fellow Chinese exporters could count on Western demand for Chinese tea, even though the discovery of tea as a global commodity resulted less from any grand design by Chinese exporters than by chance. Conversely, their trading partners from the West, from the British East India Company to the American merchants, struggled. The British had to force Houqua and their other Chinese partners to accept woolen products, bundled as part of their tea purchase agreements, even though these woolen products did not find a receptive end market among Chinese consumers. In the face of the concentrated buying power in British hands at the time, Houqua and the other Hong merchants could not but accept these undesirable woolen products as part of the deal, treating any losses from the woolens as business operating costs. Similarly, early U.S. traders in Canton attempted to sell American ginseng and fur, neither of which could sustain sales in sufficient volumes to pay for their tea purchases. Emperor Qianlong showed no modesty in his 1793 edict on the occasion of Macartney's mission; however, his claim that "our Celestial Empire possesses all things in prolific abundance and lacks no product within its own borders" represented more than imperial arrogance to the foreign traders in Canton.[10] To the American merchants, and to a lesser extent the British merchants as well, the Emperor's statement underscored a commercial reality. The failure of the Western products to penetrate Chinese markets resulted largely from cultural factors. What one country produces and finds valuable to its own domestic market, consumers in another country may not consider appropriate for local conditions. Decades after what Western powers deemed their forced opening of the Chinese markets, Western traders continued to search in vain for merchandise to export to China. That lack of success on the part of Western traders contributed to the idea of China being closed economically to the outside world. The

[10] E. Backhouse and J.O.P. Bland, *Annals and Memoirs of the Court of Peking (From the 16th to the 20th Century)* (Boston: Houghton Mifflin, 1914), 326.

experience of Sino-Western trade during this early period reminds us that the imposition of an open market by means of military might is unable to solve the problem of culturally undesirable merchandise. The difficulties of Western traders to sell to the Chinese market, despite the crumbling barriers, also challenge any resource-based explanation for the economic divergence of China from the industrializing West.

This problem of finding a reciprocal product for two-way exchange was as much an issue during Houqua's times as it is today in our world of modern commerce. Mutually beneficial exchanges require the availability of desirable merchandise on each side that holds comparable economic value for balanced trade. The absence or insufficiency on either side of such merchandise demanded in sufficiently high volumes leads to balance-of-trade issues all too common in today's world. Political rhetoric cannot be the solution, and bringing military might to bear only alters the power structure without solving the underlying economic problem.

To sustain two-way trade without viable merchandise in both directions is an untenable proposition. The British finally found an answer in the opium produced in India. The Americans also found a variant in Turkey for inclusion in their China-bound freight. It was the addictive quality of these substances, tea and opium, that guaranteed the annual return of the buyer. Obviously not comparable in the effects of their consumption, tea and opium nevertheless both commanded a loyal base of repeat customers who generated reliable sales and produced a predictable pattern of global exchange. However, the legal regimes did not allow for simple symmetrical trade. That the opium trade was illegal in China prohibited Houqua and the Hong merchants from entering into the opposite side of the tea trade and required that their trading partners structure business configurations that facilitated this problematic exchange. The British East India Company continued to be the buyer of tea from China and it funneled the proceeds to British traders who purchased opium in India for export to China. As for Houqua's American partners, they also structured their operations (e.g., with one Forbes brother dealing in opium and another handling Houqua's legitimate transactions) so as not to implicate their Chinese trading partner in the opium business. Enterprising businessmen improvised structures to respond expediently to the political and legal requirements. Notwithstanding these expedient arrangements, the opium issue nevertheless percolated to the surface every now and then and caused problems for both Houqua and his Hong merchant brethren. Indeed, opium was what precipitated the conflict that ended the Canton system that had undergirded China's trade with the

West through 1842. The lack of legitimate merchandise of comparable value and appeal for reciprocal trade was not only problematic for the involved trading partners, but it was also inherently destabilizing for the network of trade.

The circuitries of business goods and capital in global networks of trade can only be sustained with a balanced transmission of economic articles. That Houqua and his fellow Hong merchants were denied the business opportunity of participating in the opposite side of the tea-opium trade (whether they found the opium trade morally offensive or not) motivated them to explore other avenues of profit. Houqua found the answer in capital markets, both locally in Canton and internationally in his American partners' web of global finance. Locally, he deployed the mass capital base that he had accumulated to fund the operations of the British East India Company, which faced a perennial problem of capital insufficiency. In particular, while the EIC endeavored to nurture new talent among the Hong merchants to alleviate its dependence on Houqua and other well-funded Hong merchants, the British officers in Canton, who had to provide financing for the new Hong merchants, repeatedly found themselves in positions of capital shortage. Houqua would then lend funds to the British company and earn a dependable source of interest income on the loans. Although the new Hong merchants were the financial beneficiaries who had to rely on these loans for their operations, the EIC remained the borrower of record for loans from Houqua, thereby ensuring the timing of the loan repayments. At an interest rate of 1 percent per month, or 12 percent per annum, these loans generated a stable and profitable income stream for Houqua, who bore but marginal risks of default and non-payment due to the credit standing of the EIC. Expanding beyond his commercial activities of selling Chinese goods to Western buyers, Houqua diversified into the financial market of providing funds for his British partner.

The flow of goods came to be elaborately connected to the flow of capital. Not only was this move by which Houqua redefined the scope of the business indicative of his entrepreneurial talent, but it also demonstrated the understanding and skills select Chinese businessmen commanded of capital markets in China. The capital market in Canton by no means resembled any image of retarded financial development; instead, it was a site of vibrant financial exchange that transcended nationalities and involved enterprising startups as well as established multinational companies.

The circuitries of capital flows for the Canton trade were not confined to the local area. In addition to leveraging local opportunities, Houqua tapped into international capital markets, as he viewed the payments he received from his sale of tea overseas not simply as a unit of account but also as a commodity that generated profits.[11] He received various forms of metallic monies as well as bills on foreign entities. Rather than consistently converting these funds into Chinese silver taels, Houqua exhibited remarkable comfort in trading the funds for profit at financial centers around the world. Silver monies were not created equal and monies represented commodities, the trading of which afforded profit opportunities for international dealers. Houqua was informed of the discounts and premiums of various forms of silver currencies and he instructed his partners to capture the profits by buying and selling on his account. Not only was he aware of the different monetary regimes, Houqua showcased an eagerness to apply such knowledge for economic gain through dealings in different metallic currencies and commercial papers. His successes in arbitraging silver currencies reveal his expert understanding of currency regimes that macroeconomic analyses of silver flows between China and the West cannot capture.[12] For Houqua, the expert currency dealer, profit opportunities extended far beyond the bi-metallic currency regime of copper coins and silver taels in China. Houqua also traded in bills of exchange through his partners at the centers of international finance. This Chinese financier was no stranger to what amounts to the predecessor of today's foreign-exchange markets. Through Houqua's networks, China was linked to financial markets worldwide, long before Western banks had established operations in Asia. His sophisticated dealings in international capital markets, just like his financial dealings in Canton that transformed the business landscape, underscore the fact that China was intricately linked to the financial centers in the West and that enterprising Chinese who dealt adroitly in the global marketplace of finance managed to profit from such participation.

Thus constructed, the configurations and interweaving of people, goods, and capital that Houqua and his partners fashioned to facilitate global flows assumed a pattern specific to this period of global interactions.

---

[11] This observation echoes David Faure's analysis of the Chinese accounting system's emphasis on cash flows rather than the provision of a capital summary. See David Faure, *Emperor and Ancestor: State and Lineage in South China* (Stanford, CA: Stanford University Press, 2007), 230–231.

[12] For a detailed macroeconomic analysis of China's mounting issue of silver circulation in a global context, see Lin, *China Upside Down*. Houqua's story supports von Glahn's general observation that the elite in China understood monetary markets. In fact, Houqua's understanding of economics beyond China's boundaries far exceeded Chinese intellectuals' appreciation of the role of silver in statecraft. See von Glahn, *Fountain of Fortune*.

Directing the Flows and the Shaping of History

As a principal participant in his global network of trade, Houqua was instrumental in the configuration and reconfiguration of business flows, and his story informs our understanding of this juncture in historical development. The success of this Chinese entrepreneur on the global stage also refutes any notion of China's passivity in the merging of regional economies as the modern world took shape. In addition, Houqua's sophistication in dealing with financial markets in the burgeoning world of global finance dispels any assertion of inadequate Chinese understanding of, or lack of Chinese participation in, capital markets during this early period. Moreover, as the strategic positioning of Houqua and his partners anchored their web of exchange, the geographical movement of these people and the cultivation of their trading network tell the story of how business partners transcended political, social, and cultural boundaries and improvised systems of exchange that sustained their economic activities against the backdrop of the tumultuous currents of geopolitical developments.

The creation of organizational structures and the fashioning of networks entail not only the initiatives of individual participants but also the contingency of historical developments. Just as corporate and banking organizations proliferated in the century following the collapse of the Canton system with the development of the enabling technologies of railways, telegraphs, and radios, based on Houqua's initiative China's participation in international commerce came to increasingly involve American traders due to the fortuitous geopolitical environment in the West that allowed for an expanding U.S. presence in Canton.

Permanence, or at least continuity, is a major challenge to any business configuration underwritten not by an institutional structure but by the business acumen of particular individuals. However, as a compromise for such continuity, the personalistic configuration gains agility. The success of Houqua & Co. pivoted largely around the entrepreneurial ingenuity of Houqua. This reliance on a single individual, the loss of whom could spell the demise of the business, also marked the strength of the enterprise. The centrality of a single individual not bound by an institutional framework allowed tremendous flexibility for Houqua's business maneuvers. Houqua held court at the global business center of Canton from the turn of the nineteenth century until his death in 1843. During this long period of business success, he witnessed dramatic changes in international trade as a result of both the geopolitical upheavals in Europe, which tilted the balance in Britain's favor, as well as the brewing military conflict at home as the Qing government faced threats from the Western powers. Houqua repeatedly had to reposition his business enterprise to cope with and to profit from these global currents.

No corporate charter or document of incorporation could have accounted for all these contingencies or have guided the business development of Houqua's China trade business. He was, of course, not oblivious to the structural dimensions of the business world. His understanding in this regard is most evident in his estate planning for which he brought to bear strategies customary to Chinese formal asset-division contracts that conformed with local practices as well as an official application for a change in the account name with the British EIC, reflecting his transnational outlook and the global nature of big business in Canton. However, such formal arrangements could only guarantee his desired distribution of profits and equity ownership upon his death. For the daring and nimble business maneuvers that accounted for the global trade accomplishments that Houqua sustained, there was no institutional substitute for the entrepreneurial bent of Houqua himself.

Although formal organizational structures can help perpetuate business flows, the enterprising ingenuity of visionary entrepreneurs who chart the course of business is irreplaceable. Houqua, with the help of his select American confidants, was responsible for the tremendous business success of their collective enterprise. Despite the challenges befalling the business world in Canton, Houqua and his partners steered the flow of goods and capital away from catastrophic mishaps that could have undermined the entire venture, and also charted new courses of business to reap profits from unexplored territories. To survive and to prosper in such a volatile environment required the balanced approach to risk-taking that Houqua had mastered. He fostered ties with the Americans until he found trusted partners. He entrusted vast amounts to these partners for deployment around the world and he did not worry about repatriation of the proceeds for tabulation at home. Instead, he allowed the capital to be reinvested for gains in locations far away from his native Canton. His audacity, and the impressive performance of his calculated business moves, were truly exceptional for a Chinese trader or, for that matter, for any trader at the time.

The death of an entrepreneurial founder is always trying for business, be it a corporate organization or a sole proprietorship. Houqua died in 1843, months after the conclusion of the Opium War and the demise of the Canton system. During his last months, he busied himself with reconstituting his business networks to continue his role as the gatekeeper of China's trade with the West. Canton did not readily fade away and Western traders, most obviously Houqua's American partners, promptly returned to carry on their business with their old Chinese partner. One will never know how Houqua's fortune, as well as China's economy, would have unfolded had he partaken in the subsequent Treaty Port era.

Houqua's long life of some three-quarters of a century contributed to the durability of his business empire, but it also saw the passing of all but two of his sons. Young Houqua, his fifth son and the only one who was old enough to succeed him in the business world at the time of his death, proved to be not as enterprising as his father.

In business, Young Houqua intensified the family's reliance on the American partners. Although these American partners continued to generate income for the family for decades after Houqua's death, the lack of a forceful entrepreneur to succeed Houqua deprived the family of any central role in global business dealings. The family continued to flex its muscles by leveraging the immense wealth that Houqua had amassed during his lifetime and his American partners would advise the family on strategies to tap into the resources available in the reconfigured world of business. However, among his blood relations, Houqua had no successor to inherit his critical function of balancing the interests among the partners linked together in his transnational business web. Young Houqua, in an effort to perpetuate the status of Canton on the world map, privileged not the commercial centrality of the city on a global scale, but the cultural participation of Canton in the Sino-centric world. He put an emphasis on the inherent value of what he considered to be the cultural legacy of China's long history, which would inform the family's choices in times of difficulties. Such lessons from the venerable sages of his Sino-centric world proved to be no match for the pragmatically-minded Western entrepreneurs arriving in China with an express mandate from their governments to expand their paired interests in commerce and politics. Houqua had managed to channel goods and capital for profits around the world alongside the gentlemanly capitalists of the West, but his son revealed more of an inclination of a scholarly Chinese gentleman and less of a proclivity for capitalist endeavors.

Houqua's ground-breaking overseas investments also invite comparison with the investment strategy of the mounting capital accumulating in China today. Just like Houqua, savvy Chinese investors are diversifying into international markets. However, these overseas investments remain but a small portion of their overall portfolios because returns at home are expected to be much greater than what can be earned overseas. Similarly, Houqua's family kept the majority of its wealth close to home, investing it in businesses and properties in the vicinity of Canton. This proved not to be a winning strategy because much of the wealth was wiped out during the Opium Wars and the Taiping Rebellion. In retrospect, it is easy to criticize such plans, but few could have anticipated such upheavals and the imminent danger they brought to Canton, which had been the established nexus of global trade for a century. Houqua's investments in America served the intended purpose of diversification, just as the overseas assets diversify the portfolios of Chinese investors today. However, the fortune of Houqua's family underscores the significance of business and investment strategies not only for profits during times of normalcy but also in the event of seismic changes in the global environment.

The introduction of the Treaty Port system represented a radical shift in the basis on which global networks could be fashioned, but Houqua did not live to take part in this reconfiguration that affected not only his family fortune but also helped to shape the manner in which China's economy interacted with the rest of the world. To be fair to his successors, Houqua's daring ventures into global trade, buttressed by the connections he cultivated with select partners and his expert assessment of risks, provided no easy blueprint for those who had to continue to chart a business course in the face of the new institutional challenges. Analyzing the development of global trade and finance at the level of the critical players highlights the contingency of the lot of the national economy on specific individuals. From the standpoint of commercial exchange, Chinese merchants continued to operate on an equal footing with their Western counterparts until the 1840s. The subsequent divergence in their paths stemmed not from systemic issues of economic cycles, but from the personal potentials of particular individuals who found themselves in a position to craft the terms of engagement in global exchange.[13] Backed by their stronger military might, by the second half of the nineteenth century Western business interests began to triumph over Chinese aspirants, but there is no evidence of the superiority of an institutional business structure to personal configurations in a fluid environment. Western institutional forms came to dominate global business only because of the imposition of a Western-centric infrastructure.[14] The ascendancy of the West did provide a new framework for the transaction of business, but it also stymied efforts that had grown indigenously in China to navigate the constraints on transnational trade.

Analyses of China's economic development during the period after the Canton era often highlight the country's grudging acceptance of

---

[13] For attribution of China's economic demise in the nineteenth century to systemic factors in economic cycles, see Andre Gunder Frank, *ReOrient: Global Economy in the Asian Age* (Berkeley: University of California Press, 1998).

[14] For an example of institutional borrowing in the reverse direction, see Grant, *The Chinese Cornerstone of Modern Banking*. Grant argues that the idea of U.S. Bank Deposit Insurance originated in the Canton system.

technologies and institutions of Western origin. Such efforts to adapt Western things required the assistance of Western tutors or, at best, overseas Chinese, particularly from Nanyang, who had experience handling foreign inventions.[15] Although these analyses rightfully portray the ascending importance of a Western-centric world order, it is perplexing that one seldom questions the absence of any mention of the role played by members of the Canton-based merchant families who for most of the preceding century had served as the interface between China and the West.

The Canton system in the first half of the nineteenth century facilitated a period of global exchange, just as its successor, the Treaty Port system, would do so in the second half of the century. These systems of global interactions, like other structures deemed to be global in nature, encompassed certain nodes of exchange connected by webs threaded together by personal and institutional undertakings. Conditioned by the opportunities and challenges presented by the political climate at the time, the configuration of the web fashioned by Houqua during the first four decades of the nineteenth century wove China's economy into a system of exchange that encompassed many of the important centers of commerce and finance in the West. Houqua was indeed an exceptional participant in this configuration, and without his contribution global trade, and China's involvement therein, it would have taken a vastly different shape. Today, we can continue to learn from the success of Houqua & Co. in the structuring of its partnership, especially as the long-established Western-centric rules of engagement are becoming increasingly inadequate to contain the ever-expanding transnational networks of interactions and as China is staging a reemergence on the global scene.

---

[15] See, for example, Michael R. Godley, *The Mandarin-Capitalists from Nanyang: Overseas Chinese Enterprise in the Modernization of China, 1893–1911* (Cambridge: Cambridge University Press, 1981).

Epilogue

In weaving together his global network, Houqua never had to travel outside of China. The allure of Canton was sufficient to draw his partners to him. To satisfy the curiosity of those in the West, a special arrangement in 1848 made it possible for Houqua to grace the Western consumer with his presence. Those who wanted to meet this master of global trade, whose operations had facilitated the shipment of tea into their homes, had to go no farther than the City of London. Following the route that had taken many a box of his tea to the West, Houqua did make it across the oceans from Canton to London and would remain there for decades. Visitors seeking an audience with Houqua would find him in the good company of Shakespeare and Voltaire, for in 1848 Madame Tussaud expanded the budding exhibit to 136 sculptures and included its first Asian celebrity, Houqua.[1] In Madame Tussaud, Houqua would remain the sole representative of the Orient for almost half a century.

The Madame Tussaud guidebook explains that Lamqua, a Canton-based artist, had expressly fashioned this likeness of Houqua for Madame Tussaud and Sons. Lamqua was precisely the same Chinese artist whose production of multiple Houqua portraits allowed Houqua to disseminate his likeness to his trading partners as a reminder of the quality of the tea that he sold and as a reflection of the reach of his network. Houqua was introduced as "the celebrated tea merchant," underscoring the widespread recognition of his name in England.[2]

In fact, in England a label for "Houqua's Tea" (sometimes spelled "Howqua's Tea") gathered momentum in the middle of the nineteenth century. An advertisement for the label boasted a caption in large

---

[1] There is no mention of Houqua in catalogues as late as 1847. See *Biographical and Descriptive Sketches of the Distinguished Characters Which Compose the Unrivalled Exhibition of Madame Tussaud, & Sons* (London: Printed for Madame Tussaud and Sons, 1847).

[2] *Biographical and Descriptive Sketches of the Distinguished Characters Which Compose the Unrivalled Exhibition of Madame Tussaud and Sons* (London: Madame Tussaud and Sons, 1851).

upper-case font, with white letters against a black boxed background, which read, "HOWQUA'S TEA / IN PACKAGES." It also cited the endorsements in local newspapers:

It was justly remarked by a great writer that "he who supplies the public with any article of general consumption on better terms, or better in quality, than they have before been able to procure it, deserves that patronage from his countrymen which their own interests should secure him." This observation has been brought to our mind by the great treat [of] a cup of *Howqua's tea . . .* a cup of *really good and genius tea* – *Brighton Gazette*, October 29.

. . . that excellent article known as "Howqua's mixed black tea." The reputation this tea enjoys, is, we can venture to say, from our own knowledge, well merited, and we safely recommend it to our readers as a most agreeable and economical beverage – *Brighton Herald*, October 31.[3]

These Houqua labels must have held such a significant commercial value that legal battles erupted in England over use of Houqua's name in the marketing of tea. In May 1837, a Mr. Willcock, a representative of John Rhodes, the self-alleged one-time commander in the East India Company's maritime service, sought an injunction in the Vice Chancellor's Court to restrain William Brocksopp from selling tea under the label "Howqua's mixture" or "Howqua's small-leaf gunpowder." The tea was being sold in packages that Willcock asserted were an imitation of those sold by John Rhodes Pidding. Willcock presented affidavits by Pidding and others that stated that Pidding had participated in the China trade for twenty-nine years, during which time he "had intimately known Howqua, the chief of the hong merchants at Canton, and had become acquainted with a mixture of black tea which Howqua made for his own private use and with the chops or marks which distinguish[ed] the fine qualities of teas forming that mixture." In other words, Pidding asserted that through his personal acquaintance with Houqua during his years in Canton, Houqua had purportedly shared with him the recipe for the special blend that Houqua had reserved for his own consumption. This case came to be widely publicized in England as newspapers in London, Bristol, Manchester, Ipswich, Southampton, Worcester, Exeter, and Colchester reported the court's decision.[4]

[3] *Brighton Patriot and Lewes Free Press* (Brighton, UK), November 24, 1835.
[4] *The Standard* (London), May 9, 1837; *The Bristol Mercury* (Bristol, UK), May 13, 1837; *The Manchester Times and Gazette* (Manchester, UK), May 13, 1837; *The Ipswich Journal* (Ipswich, UK), May 13, 1837; *Hampshire Advertiser & Salisbury Guardian Royal Yacht Club Gazette, Southampton Town and Country Herald, Isle of Wight Journal, Winchester Chronicle, and General Reporter* (Southampton, UK), May 13, 1837; *Berrow's Worcester Journal* (Worcester, UK), May 18, 1837; *Trewman's Exeter Flying Post or Plymouth and Cornish Advertiser* (Exeter, UK), May 18, 1837; *The Essex Standard, and Colchester,*

Pidding's case was dismissed only several weeks after the initial injunction was issued because there was no indication of his ties to the namesake of the powerful brand. However, this legal case in Britain indicates the tremendous recognition of Houqua's name and explains why he would be no stranger to the British tea drinker, who could meet him face-to-face at Madame Tussaud. In fact, recognition of Houqua's contribution to the global marketplace would prove to be more enduring among British consumers than in his native China, as British newspapers continued to carry advertisements of teas named after Houqua well into the 1870s when the influence of Houqua's family in China had waned and its fortune had dwindled.[5]

Proud as Houqua's sculpture might have sat as he received visitors at Madame Tussaud, the British perspective toward Houqua, whose name had stood for quality tea, began to give way to an appreciation of Houqua and his namesake product as an exotic, mysterious object that the West brought into focus by confronting them face-to-face. Adorned with the same clothes and ornaments that Houqua had worn in life, the Houqua in Madame Tussaud was "to give an idea of the peculiar appearance and costume of China." "Peculiar" might be the key word here for this Houqua sculpture found a home in the "Seventh, or Armour Room," which gathered together an "Interesting Group of historical characters, in magnificent suits of Armour and Costumes, in order to convey an idea of the splendor of ancient times; the whole faithfully in character, every attention having been paid to the person represented."[6] Splendid as Houqua might have been considered, he was also hailed from "ancient times," housed in the same room with individuals who had died centuries earlier, even though his family had not yet even observed the tenth anniversary of his passing.

An article in a British periodical reporting on this new addition to the Madame Tussaud exhibition reflects the British reception at the time. The article describes Houqua's sculpture thus: "[a] Chinese gentleman in the original clothes he wore at Pekin [sic], and who must have accordingly parted with his wardrobe to some Chinese old-clothesman in order to enable Madame Tussaud to represent him with the accuracy that is always professed in the saloons of Baker Street. The individual in *quesito* is supposed to have been the generous HOWQUA." The Tussauds had accurately forecast that public interest would gravitate toward Houqua's

---

Chelmsford, Maldon, Harwich, and General County Advertiser (Colchester, UK), May 26, 1837.
[5] See, for example, *The Belfast News-Letter* (Belfast, Ireland), January 17, 1878.
[6] *Biographical and Descriptive Sketches of the Distinguished Characters Which Compose the Unrivalled Exhibition of Madame Tussaud and Sons* (1851).

curious costume, which, to them, marked the authenticity of the replication. This view paralleled the underlying principle behind the production of Houqua's portraits: the culturally distinct costume was to be the hallmark that distinguished Houqua. Equally telling in the article is the geographical reference. The Canton system had broken down only six years earlier, but the reference to China had already shifted away from the old commercial cosmopolitan city of Canton to the political center of "Pekin."

Among the viewing public in Britain, what resonated most from Houqua's likeness was, not surprisingly, the association of his name with brands of tea. "We believe," the article continued, "that HOWQUA's last moments were divided between CAPTIN PIDDING and MADAME TUSSAUD, by his giving to the first recipe for combining the hundred teas, and making the latter the legatee of his Chinese wrap-rascal, and Pekin twedish trowsers, in which he is now to be seen side by side with HER MAJESTY, JENNY LIND, PIUS THE NINTH, TAWELL, BURKE, HARE, and the other waxen *illustrissmi* and *illustrissimae* of our era."[7] Based on this introduction to the wax sculpture, the writer imagined Houqua's last act of dividing his legacy. He was supposed to have bestowed on Pidding his secret recipe from which he had amassed his tremendous fortune. He was also supposed to have entrusted his comical outfit to Tussaud in order to earn the right to stand in the exhibit alongside celebrities more worthy of a wax sculpture.

Returning to the early guidebook, which provides a glimpse into the life of this worldly figure, the visitor would learn that "Houqua was peculiarly distinguished among the Hong merchants for his exceedingly cheerful disposition." Apparently, the British people were aware of the Hong merchants in China. This description of Houqua, however, was a tongue-and-cheek portrayal of the Hong system in Canton: that Houqua could have been construed as "exceedingly cheerful" implied that most Hong merchants suffered from a broken system. That Houqua prospered in such a system, without the benefit of the imperial infrastructure that the British merchants had come to enjoy in their expanding empire, was exceptional, true testimony of Houqua's resourcefulness and ability to succeed against all odds. The guidebook continues to instruct the visitor that Houqua was to be remembered "for his great attachment to the English nation." That is meant to be an ambivalent statement. Houqua was certainly attached to the British nation because Britain represented to him the single largest market for his global merchandise; however, the guidebook conveniently makes no mention of Houqua's ingenuity in

[7] "A Lass of Wax," *Punch* (London), July 8, 1848, 19.

subverting the mounting British hegemony in the global market for tea, which formed the basis for his "cheerful disposition." "He died in 1846," concludes the guidebook erroneously.[8]

The penetration of Houqua into a realm accessible by the British public extended his global reach as those who had never journeyed to the place of origin of their tea could now come within close range of this famed procurer in Canton. The sculpture put a face, along with Houqua's small Oriental frame and his Mandarin garb, to his namesake brand that had for years signified quality tea. Houqua had certainly initiated this process as he dealt reliably with traders from around the world, many of whose homes were tastefully appointed with his portrait. This posthumous extension of his global fame, however, did not unfold on his own terms or those of his family. Just as Captain Pidding made his contentious legal and marketing claims on the basis of his dubious ties to Houqua for his own economic benefit, this wax sculpture of Houqua generated name recognition for the sale of his namesake products, but it did not provide any financial returns to his successors. The value of his global brand would come to be totally appropriated and the network he had developed for his international trade would be rerouted to conform to the imperial contours of the British Empire.

In the first several decades after his inclusion in the exhibit, Houqua gained in status at Madame Tussaud and Sons. By 1866, he had moved up the list to Number 56 in a larger collection of 313 sculptures. On one side of Houqua, the visitor would find the mother of Queen Victoria, "Her Royal Highness the Duchess of Kent," whose death in 1861 was "deeply lamented by the nation." On the other side of Houqua stood George Washington, "dressed as the President of America," whose memory was "held in great veneration by all nations, as he wielded the power that Providence gave him for the good of his country." Keeping his "peculiar appearance and costume of China," Houqua stood between these two great figures who were well-liked by their respective countries, and he was recognized "for his great attachment to the English nation," explains an 1866 guidebook.[9]

Thereafter, Houqua's standing continued to rise as the British must have enjoyed his company. By 1873, Houqua assumed a position as the second statue to greet visitors at Madame Tussaud's exhibit. The first American president managed to keep pace with Houqua as he stood in

---

[8] *Biographical and Descriptive Sketches of the Distinguished Characters Which Compose the Unrivalled Exhibition of Madame Tussaud and Sons* (1851).

[9] *Biographical and Descriptive Sketches of the Distinguished Characters Which Compose the Unrivalled Exhibition and Historical Gallery of Madame Tussaud and Sons* (London: G Cole, 1866).

the number 3 position. The mother of the reigning monarch, however, had fallen behind.[10] For decades, Houqua remained the only Asian face in the exhibition until he was joined, toward the turn of the century, by the Empress Dowager of China, the Emperor of China, and Li Hongzhang, the chief minister of the Qing court. The appearance of these three, however, did not displace Houqua. Against the lineup of the new arrivals, Houqua, "the celebrated Chinese tea merchant" held his own. However, the guidebook no longer emphasized his "peculiar appearance and costume." The novelty of Houqua had worn off as his curious appearance was no longer rendered unique because Western spectators could then examine the costumes of a better-dressed Chinese high official and regally clothed royalty. However, Houqua's commercial legacy endured. He was "[g]reatly distinguished among the *Hong Kong* merchants for his exceedingly cheerful disposition" [emphasis added].[11] The British public would continue to recognize Houqua's contribution to the global tea market, but the memory of the Hong merchants faded, yielding to the new configuration of trade through the Treaty Ports and the British colony of Hong Kong. The guidebook includes historical references, such as to the Hong merchants, who were not incomprehensible to a British audience, in the form of accessible but erroneous reinterpretations, inadvertently reflecting the usurpation of the command of Canton in the web of international trade by British powers as conveyed by the reference to Hong Kong.

Houqua would be joined by another Cantonese in the second decade of the twentieth century as representation of the Qing court yielded to representation of Sun Yat-sen, the leader of the revolution that overthrew China's last imperial dynasty. Unlike Houqua, however, Sun did make it to London in his lifetime, and during his ten-day stay in London in November 1911, he requested and "was permitted to visit Madame Tussaud's Exhibition one Sunday morning to inspect this model of himself which had just been added." There, the two of them remained, with Houqua being the last of the cast donning a Mandarin garb, standing in front of Sun to greet visitors as he had for more than half a century.[12]

Although the interpretation of Houqua's success was to be filtered through the lens of subsequent developments, the memory of Houqua

---

[10] *Biographical and Descriptive Sketches of the Distinguished Characters Which Compose the Unrivalled Exhibition and Historical Gallery of Madame Tussaud and Sons* (London: Printed by M'Corquodale & Co., 1873).

[11] George Augustus Sala, *Madame Tussaud's Exhibition* Guide (London: Madame Tussaud and Sons, 1909).

[12] *Madame Tussaud's Exhibition: Catalogue* (London: Printed for Madame Tussaud & Sons, Ltd., 1918, 1920, 1925).

as the "celebrated tea merchant" outlasted the dynasty in which he lived, and he stood firm alongside the heroes of later national movements, bringing into relief the boundaries of the political divides that Houqua had so successfully transcended and had profitably maneuvered with his global network. His wax sculpture might have rekindled in the minds of many more Western visitors to Madame Tussaud the memory of his transnational trade had it not been lost to the only power to which Houqua would succumb – nature. The passing of this reminder of Houqua's legacy occurred in 1925. On March 18, a great calamity befell the Madame Tussaud Exhibition as a fire engulfed the collection and within an hour, "little was left except smoke-blackened walls and a heap of ruins."[13] In life, Houqua had rebuilt his business in Canton after many a fire had destroyed the city. In death, however, he could not but be subjected to the mercy of nature.

As the Madame Tussaud collection rose from the ashes of the 1925 fire, some of Houqua's old neighbors would again make an appearance. Voltaire took his place in the French section. Washington assumed his leadership among the American presidents. Shakespeare assumed his rightful position in the literary corner.[14] But the representation of Houqua was no more. After enduring more than three-quarters of a century, witnessing the comings and goings of notable figures, Chinese or otherwise, Houqua's memory was erased from among the cast of important international characters. His likeness, a product of Chinese hands, had followed the global routes of the tea trade from Canton to the consumer markets in the West, reminding tea drinkers of the great distances that Houqua's network covered. The initial observations of his "peculiarities" and the celebration of his ties to England would secure his place of honor in this British exhibition and there Houqua endured the rising tides of British supremacy and the changing order of international politics that altered the memory of him as recorded in the guidebooks. However, not once during his seventy-six years of residence in the exhibit in London was Houqua to take leave from his Western audience. Only an act of nature could destroy this representation of the global marketplace centered in Canton and relegate Houqua's memory to a bygone era.

---

[13] *The New Madame Tussaud's Exhibition: Official Guide and Catalogue* (London: Madame Tussaud and Sons, 1930), 13.
[14] *The New Madame Tussaud's Exhibition: Official Guide and Catalogue* (London: Madame Tussaud and Sons, 1928).

Bibliography

ARCHIVAL SOURCES

Baker Forbes. Forbes Family Business Records. Baker Library Historical Collections. Harvard Business School.

Baker Perkins. Perkins & Co. Records. Baker Library Historical Collections. Harvard Business School.

CHS Oliver Wolcott Jr. Oliver Wolcott Jr. Papers. Connecticut Historical Society, Hartford, Connecticut.

EIC East India Company Records. The British Library. London.

FHA Number One Historical Archives of China 中国第一历史档案馆. Beijing.

Jamsetjee Jeejeebhoy Papers. University of Mumbai Library, #354.

JCB Brown. The Records of Brown and Ives, 1796–1914. The John Carter Brown Library.

JM Jardine Matheson Archives. Cambridge University.

MHS Charles A. Tomes Letterbooks. 1886–1914. Massachusetts Historical Society

MHS Forbes. Forbes Family Papers. Massachusetts Historical Society.

MHS Houqua Letters. Houqua's Letterbook. Massachusetts Historical Society.

MHS Samuel Cabot Papers. Massachusetts Historical Society.

NPM Archives of Qing Memorials. Taipei: National Palace Museum Archives.

PEM Log 148. Journal of the U.S. Frigate *Congress*. Peabody Essex Museum.

PEM Shreve. Benjamin Shreve (1780–1839) Papers, 1793–1848. MH20. Peabody Essex Museum.

PEM Tilden. Bryant P. Tilden (1781–1851) Papers, 1815–1837. MH219 Series I. Bryant P. Tilden Journals: Bound Journals. Peabody Essex Museum.

RIHS Carter-Danforth. Carter-Danforth Papers. Manuscripts Division. Rhode Island Historical Society.

RIHS Dorr. Thomas W. Dorr Collection. Manuscripts Division. Rhode Island Historical Society.

RIHS Edward Carrington. Carrington Papers. Manuscripts Division. Rhode Island Historical Society.

REFERENCES

"Abstract of the Answers and Returns Made Pursuant to an Act, Passed in the Forty-First Year of His Majesty King George III – Enumeration Abstract, 1801." www.histpop.org/ohpr, accessed May 6, 2008.

Appearance Docket. 1817 (December Term)–1823 (December Term), 303. Records of the Supreme Court (Eastern District). Division of Archives and Manuscripts. Pennsylvania Historical and Museum Commission.

"Assessing Kenneth Pomeranz's *The Great Divergence:* A Forum." *Historically Speaking: Bulletin of the Historical Society* 12, no. 4 (September 2011): 10–25.

Atwell, William S. "International Bullion Flows and the Chinese Economy circa 1530–1650." *Past & Present*, no. 95 (May 1982): 68–90.

Backhouse, E. and J. O. P. Bland. *Annals and Memoirs of the Court of Peking (From the 16th to the 20th Century).* Boston: Houghton Mifflin, 1914.

Basu, Dilip Kumar. "Asian Merchants and Western Trade: A Comparative Study of Calcutta and Canton 1800–1840." PhD diss., Department of History, University of California, Berkeley, 1975.

Belfast News-Letter (Belfast). January 17, 1878.

Berrow's Worcester Journal (Worcester, UK). May 18, 1837.

Berry-Hill, Henry and Sidney Berry-Hill. *Chinnery and China Coast Paintings.* Leigh-on-Sea, UK: F. Lewis, 1963.

Biographical and Descriptive Sketches of the Distinguished Characters Which Compose the Unrivalled Exhibition of Madame Tussaud, & Sons. London: Printed for Madame Tussaud and Sons, 1847.

Biographical and Descriptive Sketches of the Distinguished Characters Which Compose the Unrivalled Exhibition of Madame Tussaud and Sons. London: Madame Tussaud and Sons, 1851.

Biographical and Descriptive Sketches of the Distinguished Characters Which Compose the Unrivalled Exhibition and Historical Gallery of Madame Tussaud and Sons. London: G. Cole, 1866.

Biographical and Descriptive Sketches of the Distinguished Characters Which Compose the Unrivalled Exhibition and Historical Gallery of Madame Tussaud and Sons. London: Printed by M'Corquodale & Co., 1873.

Bouvier, John. *A Law Dictionary Adapted to the Constitution and Laws of the United States of America,* 5th rev. ed. Philadelphia: Printed for the Estate of John Bouvier, 1855.

Brighton Patriot and Lewes Free Press (Brighton UK). November 24, 1835.

Bristol Mercury (Bristol UK). May 13, 1837.

Brook, Timothy. *Vermeer's Hat: The Seventeenth Century and the Dawn of the Global World.* New York: Bloomsbury, 2008.

Cain, P. J. and A. G. Hopkins. *British Imperialism: Crisis and Deconstruction, 1914–1990.* London: Longman, 1993.

    British Imperialism: Innovation and Expansion, 1688–1914. New York: Longman, 1993.

    British Imperialism, 1688–2000, 2nd ed. 1993. repr., Harlow UK: Longman, 2002.

Cameron, Rondo. *Banking in the Early Stages of Industrialization: A Study in Comparative Economic History.* New York: Oxford University Press, 1967.

Canton Register (Canton) 6, nos. 13 and 14 (1833).

Canton Register (Canton) 8, no. 49 (December 8, 1835).

Canton Register (Canton) 16, no. 39 (September 26, 1843).

Cassis, Youssef. *City Bankers, 1890–1914*. Trans. Margaret Rocques. 1984. repr., Cambridge: Cambridge University Press, 1994.

Catalogue of Pictures, in the Athenæum Gallery, 1829. Boston: s.n., 1829.

Catalogue of the Twenty-Third Exhibition of Paintings in the Gallery of the Boston Athenæum. Boston: Eastburn, 1850.

Chan, Kwok Bun, ed. *Chinese Business Networks: State, Economy and Culture*. Singapore: Prentice Hall; Copenhagen: Nordic Institute of Asian Studies, 2000.

Chan, Wellington K. K. "Tradition and Change in the Chinese Business Enterprise: The Family Firm Past and Present." In *Chinese Business History: Interpretive Trends and Priorities for the Future*, ed. Robert Gardella, Jane K. Leonard, and Andrea McElderry, 127–144. Armonk, NY: M. E. Sharpe, 1998.

Chandler, Alfred D., Jr. *The Visible Hand: The Managerial Revolution in American Business*. Cambridge, MA: Belknap Press of Harvard University Press, 1977.

Chang, Te-Ch'ang. "The Economic Role of the Imperial Household in the Ch'ing Dynasty." *Journal of Asian Studies* 31, no. 2 (February 1972): 243–273.

Ch'en Kuo-tung 陳國棟. "Qingdai qianqi Yue haiguan de liyi fenpei (1684–1842): Yue haiguan jiandu de juese yu gongneng" 清代前期粵海關的利益分配 (1684–1842): 粵海關監督的角色與功能 (The Accrual of Benefits in the Maritime Customs in the Early Qing [1684–1842]: The Role and Function of the Hoppo). *Shihuo yuekan* 食貨月刊 (Shih-Huo Monthly) 12, no. 1 (April 1982): 19–33.

"Yue haiguan (1684–1842) de xingzheng tixi" 粵海關 (1684–1842) 的行政體系 (The Administrative Structure of the Maritime Customs at Canton [1684–1842]). *Shihuo yuekan* 食貨月刊 (Shih-Huo Monthly) 11, no. 4 (July 1981): 35–52.

Ch'en, Kuo-tung Anthony. *The Insolvency of the Chinese Hong Merchants, 1760–1843*. Taipei: Institute of Economics, Academia Sinica, 1990.

Cheung, Sui-Wai. *The Price of Rice: Market Integration in Eighteenth-Century China*. Bellingham: Center for East Asian Studies, Western Washington University, 2008.

Chin, Kong James. "Merchants and Other Sojourners: The Hokkiens Overseas, 1570–1760." PhD diss., University of Hong Kong, 1998.

Cohen, Paul A. *China Unbound: Evolving Perspectives on the Chinese Past*. London: RoutledgeCurzon, 2003.

Conner, Patrick. *George Chinnery 1774–1852: Artist of India and the China Coast*. Woodbridge (Suffolk, UK): Antique Collectors' Club, 1993.

"Lamqua, Western and Chinese Painter." *Arts of Asia* 29, no. 2 (March–April 1999): 46–62.

Continuance Docket, 1818 (July Term)–1825 (December Term), 197. Records of the Supreme Court (Eastern District). Division of Archives and Manuscripts. Pennsylvania Historical and Museum Commission.

Corning, Howard and Sullivan Dorr. "Letters of Sullivan Dorr." *Proceedings of the Massachusetts Historical Society*, third series, 67 (October 1941–May 1944).

Croizier, Ralph C. *Koxinga and Chinese Nationalism: History, Myth, and the Hero*. Cambridge, MA: East Asian Research Center, Harvard University, 1977.

Cushman, Jennifer Wayne. *Fields from the Sea: Chinese Junk Trade with Siam during the Late Eighteenth and Early Nineteenth Centuries.* Ithaca, NY: Southeast Asia Program, Cornell University, 1993.

Deng, Kent G. "A Critical Survey of Recent Research in Chinese Economic History." *Economic History Review,* new series, 53, no. 1 (February 2000): 1–28.

Dermigny, Louis. *La Chine et l'Occident: le commerce à Canton au 18e siècle, 1719–1833.* Paris: S.E.V.P.E.N., 1964.

Dolin, Eric Jay. *When America First Met China: An Exotic History of Tea, Drugs, and Money in the Age of Sail.* New York: Liveright, 2012.

Downs, Jacques M. *The Golden Ghetto: The American Commercial Community at Canton and the Shaping of American China Policy, 1784–1844.* Bethlehem, PA: Lehigh University Press, 1997.

Eberhard, Wolfram. *Social Mobility in Traditional China.* Leiden: E.J. Brill, 1962.

Edelstein, Michael. *Overseas Investment in the Age of High Imperialism: The United Kingdom, 1850–1914.* New York: Columbia University Press, 1982.

Ellis, Henry, Sir. *Journal of the Proceedings of the Late Embassy to China, Comprising a Correct Narrative of the Public Transactions of the Embassy, of the Voyage to and from China, and of the Journey from the Mouth of the Pei-ho to the Return to Canton,* 2nd ed. London: John Murray, 1818.

Elvin, Mark. *The Pattern of the Chinese Past.* London: Eyre Methuen; Stanford, CA: Stanford University Press, 1973.

Essex Standard, and Colchester, Chelmsford, Maldon, Harwich, and General County Advertiser (Colchester, UK). May 26, 1837.

"Extract from the Port Folio of a Canton Supra-Cargo, Painters of Canton." *National Gazette and Literary Register* (Philadelphia) 4, no. 381 (August 5, 1823).

Fairbank, John K. "Ewo in History." In *The Thistle and the Jade: A Celebration of 150 Years of Jardine, Matheson & Co.,* ed. Maggie Keswick, 241–255. London: Octopus Books, 1982.

——— *Trade and Diplomacy on the China Coast: The Opening of the Treaty Ports, 1842–1854.* Cambridge, MA: Harvard University Press, 1953.

Fairbank, John K. and S. Y. Teng. "On the Ch'ing Tributary System." *Harvard Journal of Asiatic Studies* 6, no. 2 (June 1941): 135–246.

Faure, David. *China and Capitalism: A History of Business Enterprise in Modern China.* Hong Kong: Hong Kong University Press, 2006.

——— *Emperor and Ancestor: State and Lineage in South China.* Stanford, CA: Stanford University Press, 2007.

Fay, Peter Ward. *The Opium War, 1840–1842: Barbarians in the Celestial Empire in the Early Part of the Nineteenth Century and the War by Which They Forced Her Gates Ajar.* Chapel Hill: University of North Carolina Press, 1975.

Feng Liutang 馮柳堂. *Zhongguo lidai minshi zhengce shi* 中國歷代民食政策史 (A History of China's Policies during the Various Dynasties on the Question of Food Procurement for the Masses). 1934. repr., Beijing: Shangwu yinshuguan, 1993.

Ferguson, Niall. *The World's Banker: The History of the House of Rothschild.* London: Weidenfeld & Nicolson; New York: Viking, 1998.

Fichter, James R. *So Great a Proffit: How the East Indies Trade Transformed Anglo-American Capitalism*. Cambridge, MA: Harvard University Press, 2010.

Flynn, Dennis O., Arturo Giráldez, and Richard von Glahn, eds. *Global Connections and Monetary History, 1470–1800*. Aldershot UK: Ashgate, 2003.

Forbes, Robert B. *Personal Reminiscences*, 2nd rev. ed. Boston: Little, Brown, 1882.

Forbes, W. Cameron. "Houqua, the Merchant Prince of China, 1769–1843." *Bulletin of the American Asiatic Association* 6, no. 6 (1940): 9–18.

Frank, Andre Gunder. *ReOrient: Global Economy in the Asian Age*. Berkeley: University of California Press, 1998.

Fu, Lo-shu, comp. *A Documentary Chronicle of Sino-Western Relations (1644–1820)*. Tuscon: University of Arizona Press, 2 vols., 1966.

Gardella, Robert "The Boom Years of the Fukien Tea Trade, 1842–1888." In *America's China Trade in Historical Perspective: The Chinese and American Performance*, ed. Ernest R. May and John K. Fairbank, 33–75. Cambridge, MA: Committee on American–East Asian Relations, Department of History, Harvard University, 1986.

Harvesting Mountains: Fujian and the China Tea Trade, 1757–1937. Berkeley: University of California Press, 1994.

Gates, Hill. *China's Motor: A Thousand Years of Petty Capitalism*. Ithaca, NY: Cornell University Press, 1996.

Gibson, James R. *Otter Skins, Boston Ships, and China Goods: The Maritime Fur Trade of the Northwest Coast, 1785–1841*. Seattle: University of Washington Press, 1992.

Godley, Michael R. *The Mandarin-Capitalists from Nanyang: Overseas Chinese Enterprise in the Modernization of China, 1893–1911*. Cambridge: Cambridge University Press, 1981.

Goldstein, Jonathan. *Philadelphia and the China Trade, 1682–1846: Commercial, Cultural, and Attitudinal Effects*. University Park: Pennsylvania State University Press, 1978.

Stephen Girard's Trade with China, 1787–1824: The Norms Versus the Profits of Trade. Portland, ME: MerwinAsia, 2011.

Goodhard, C. A. E. *The Business of Banking, 1891–1914*. 1972. repr., Aldershot, UK: Gower, 1986.

Grace, Richard J. *Opium and Empire: The Lives and Careers of William Jardine and James Matheson*. Montreal: McGill-Queen's University Press, 2014.

Grant, Frederic Delano, Jr. *The Chinese Cornerstone of Modern Banking: The Canton Guaranty System and the Origins of Bank Deposit Insurance 1780–1933*. Leiden: Brill Nijhoff, 2014.

"Hong Merchants Litigation in the American Courts." *Proceedings of the Massachusetts Historical Society* 99 (1987): 44–62.

Greenberg, Michael. *British Trade and the Opening of China, 1800–42*. 1951. repr., Cambridge: University Press, 1969.

Greif, Avner. "Contract Enforceability and Economic Institutions in Early Trade: The Maghribi Traders' Coalition." *American Economic Review* 83, no. 3 (June 1993): 525–548.

Institutions and the Path to the Modern Economy: Lessons from Medieval Trade. Cambridge: Cambridge University Press, 2006.

"The Organization of Long-Distance Trade: Reputation and Coalitions in the Geniza Documents and Genoa During the Eleventh and Twelfth Centuries." *Journal of Economic History* 51, no. 2 (June 1991): 459–462.

"Reputation and Coalitions in Medieval Trade: Evidence on the Maghribi Traders." *Journal of Economic History* 49, no. 4 (December 1989): 857–882.

Guoli zhongyang yanjiuyuan 國立中央研究院 (Academic Sinica), ed. *Ming-Qing shiliao* 明清史料 (Historical Materials Relating to the Ming and Qing Dynasties). Taipei, 1960.

Guoshiguan 國史館(Academia Historica), ed. *Qingshigao jiaozhu* 清史稿校註 (A Draft of the Dynastic History of the Qing, with Annotations). Taipei. 1986–1990.

Hamilton, Gary, ed. *Business Networks and Economic Development in East and Southeast Asia*. Hong Kong: Centre of Asian Studies, University of Hong Kong, 1991.

Hampshire Advertiser & Salisbury Guardian Royal Yacht Club Gazette, Southampton Town and Country Herald, Isle of Wight Journal, Winchester Chronicle, and General Reporter (Southampton, UK). May 13, 1837.

Hao, Yen-p'ing. "Chinese Teas to America – a Synopsis." In *America's China Trade in Historical Perspective: The Chinese and American Performance*, ed. Ernest R. May and John K. Fairbank, 11–31. Cambridge, MA: Committee on American–East Asian Relations, Department of History, Harvard University, 1986.

The Commercial Revolution in Nineteenth-Century China: The Rise of Sino-Western Mercantile Capitalism. Berkeley: University of California Press, 1986.

Hazard, Samuel. *The Register of Pennsylvania, Devoted to the Preservation of Facts and Documents, and Every Other Kind of Useful Information Respecting the State of Pennsylvania*. Philadelphia: W.F. Geddes, 1828.

He Lie 何烈. *Qing Xian-Tong shiqi de caizheng* 清咸同時期的財政 (State Finances of the Qing Empire During the Reigns of Xianfeng and Tongzhi). Taipei: Guoli bianyiguan Zhonghua congshu bianshen weiyuanhui, 1981.

He, Sibing. "Russell and Company, 1818–1891: America's Trade and Diplomacy in Nineteenth-Century China." PhD diss., Department of History, Miami University, 1997.

Huang, Philip C. C. *The Peasant Family and Rural Development in the Yangzi Delta, 1350–1988*. Stanford, CA: Stanford University Press, 1990.

Hughes, Sarah Forbes, ed. *Letters and Recollections of John Murray Forbes in Two Volumes*. Boston: Houghton, Mifflin, 1899.

Hunter, William C. *The "Fan Kwae" at Canton before Treaty Days, 1825–1844 by an Old Resident*. London: K. Paul, Trench, 1882.

Hutcheon, Robin. *Chinnery: The Man and the Legend*. Hong Kong: South China Morning Post, 1974.

Ipswich Journal (Ipswich, UK). May 13, 1837.

Johnson, James. *An Account of a Voyage to India, China &c. in His Majesty's Ship Caroline, Performed in the Years 1803–4–5, Interspersed with Descriptive Sketches and Cursory Remarks by an Officer of the Caroline*. London: R. Phillips, 1806.

Journey to the Far East – George Chinnery and the Art of Canton, Macao and Hong Kong in the 19th Century. Tokyo: Tokyo Metropolitan Teien Art Museum, 1997.

Keller, Kevin Lane. *Strategic Brand Management: Building, Measuring, and Managing Brand Equity*, 2nd ed. Upper Saddle River, NJ: Prentice Hall, 2003.

Kishimoto Mio 岸本美緒. *Shindai Chūgoku no bukka to keizai hendō* 清代中国の物価と経済変動 (Fluctuations in Prices and Economic Conditions in China During the Qing Dynasty). Tōkyō: Kenbun Shuppan, 1997.

Kuhn, Philip A. *Chinese Among Others: Emigration in Modern Times*. Lanham, MD: Rowman & Littlefield, 2008.

Kun'gang 崑岡. *Qinding Da Qing huidian shili* 欽定大清會典事例 (Imperially Endorsed Collected Statutes of the Great Qing, with Administrative Precedents). 1899. repr., Shanghai: Shanghai guji chubanshe, 1995.

Kuroda, Akinobu. "Concurrent but Non-integrable Currency Circuits: Complementary Relationships Among Monies in Modern China and Other Regions." *Financial History Review* 15, no. 1 (2008): 17–36.

Lanning, G. and S. Couling. *The History of Shanghai*. Shanghai: Shanghai Municipal Council, Kelly and Walsh, 1921. repr., London: School of Oriental and African Studies, n.d.

Larson, Henrietta M. "A China Trader Turns Investor: A Biographical Chapter in American Business History." *Harvard Business Review* 12, no. 3 (1934): 345–358.

Lee, Jean Gordon. *Philadelphians and the China Trade, 1784–1844*. Philadelphia: Philadelphia Museum of Art, 1984.

Li, Bozhong. *Agricultural Development in Jiangnan, 1620–1850*. New York: St. Martin's Press, 1998.

Li Guangting 李光廷. *Guangxu Guangzhou fu zhi* 光緒廣州府志 (Gazetteer of the Prefecture of Guangzhou Compiled During the Reign of Guangxu). 1879. repr., Shanghai: Shanghai shudian, 2003.

Li Guorong 李国荣 and Lin Weisen 林伟森, eds. *Qingdai Guangzhou shisanhang jilüe* 清代广州十三行纪略 (Chronicle of the Hong Merchants in Canton During the Qing Dynasty). Guangzhou: Guangdong renmin chubanshe, 2006.

Liang Jiabin 梁嘉彬. *Guangdong shisanhang kao* 廣東十三行考 (An Investigation into the Guangzhou Hong Merchants). 1937. repr., Guangzhou: Guangdong renmin chubanshe, 1999.

Liang Tingnan 梁廷枏 et al., comps. *Yue haiguan zhi* 粤海關志 (Gazetteer of the Maritime Customs in Canton). repr., Taipei: Wenhai chubanshe, 1975.

Lin, Man-houng. *China Upside Down: Currency, Society, and Ideologies, 1808–1856*. Cambridge, MA: Harvard University Asia Center, 2006.

Liu Jianshao 劉建韶. *Fujian tongzhi zhengshi lüe* 福建通志政事略 (A Survey of Administrative Affairs for the Gazetteer of Fujian). China, 1920–1940?

Liu, Kwang-Ching. *Anglo-American Steamship Rivalry in China, 1862–1874*. Cambridge, MA: Harvard University Press, 1962.

Liu, Lydia H. *Clash of Empires: The Invention of China in Modern World Making.* Cambridge, MA: Harvard University Press, 2004.

Lockwood, Stephen Chapman. *Augustine Heard and Company, 1858–1862: American Merchants in China.* Cambridge, MA: East Asian Research Center, Harvard University, 1971.

Loines, Elma. "Houqua, Sometime Chief of the Co-Hong at Canton (1769–1843)." *Essex Institute Historical Collections* 84, no. 2 (April 1953): 99–108.

Macaulay, Frederick R. *Some Theoretical Problems Suggested by the Movements of Interest Rates, Bond Yields and Stock Prices in the United States Since 1856.* New York: National Bureau of Economic Research, 1938. repr., London: Risk Books, 1999.

Madame Tussaud's Exhibition: Catalogue. London: Printed for Madame Tussaud & Sons, Ltd., 1918, 1920, 1925.

Manchester Times and Gazette (Manchester, UK). May 13, 1837.

Marks, Robert B. *Tigers, Rice, Silk, and Silt: Environment and Economy in Late Imperial South China.* Cambridge: Cambridge University Press, 1997.

Master Houqua v. James Perkins et al., 3 Rec. Pt. 1, P.226 (U.S.C.C. D. Mass., May 1812). Minute Book References, October 1811 Term, N-23, and May 1812 Term, C-163.

McKeown, Adam. "Global Migration, 1846–1940." *Journal of World History* 15, no. 2 (June 2004): 155–189.

Miles, Steven B. *The Sea of Learning: Mobility and Identity in Nineteenth-Century Guangzhou.* Cambridge, MA: Harvard University Asia Center, 2006.

Morgan, E. Victor. *The Theory and Practice of Central Banking, 1797–1913.* Cambridge: Cambridge University Press, 1943.

Morning Post (London). June 15, 1831.

Morse, Hosea Ballou. *The Chronicles of the East India Company, Trading to China, 1635–1834.* Oxford: Clarendon Press, 1926–1929.

Nautical Magazine and Naval Chronicle, A Journal of Papers on Subjects Connected with Maritime Affairs, enlarged series, no. 8. London: Simpkin, Marshall, and Co., 1840.

New Madame Tussaud's Exhibition: Official Guide and Catalogue. London: Madame Tussaud and Sons, 1928.

New Madame Tussaud's Exhibition: Official Guide and Catalogue. London: Madame Tussaud and Sons, 1930.

New York Times. September 3, 1873. http://query.nytimes.com/mem/archive-free/pdf?_r=1&res=9A05E2DA1239EF34BC4B53DFBF668388669FDE&oref=slogin, accessed May 13, 2008.

Ng, Chin Keong. *Trade and Society: The Amoy Network on the China Coast, 1683–1735.* Singapore: Singapore University Press, 1983.

Nilsson, Jan-Erik and Cheryl Marie Cordeiro. "Walking the Streets of Old Canton," 2006. http://gotheborg.com/objectofthemonth/index.shtml, accessed November 12, 2010.

North, Douglass C. *Institutions, Institutional Change and Economic Performance.* Cambridge: Cambridge University Press, 1990.

North, Douglass C. and Barry R. Weingast. "Constitutions and Commitment: The Evolution of Institutions Governing Public Choice in Seventeenth-Century England." *Journal of Economic History* 49, no. 4 (December 1989): 803–832.

Oriental Navigator, or New Directions for Sailing to and from the East Indies: Also for the Use of Ships Trading in the Indian and China Seas to New Holland, &c &c Collected from the Manuscripts, Journals, Memoirs and Observations of the Most Experienced Officers in the Hon. East India Company's Service, and From the Last Edition of the French Neptune Oriental. London: Robert Laurie and James Whittle, 1794.

Oriental Navigator, or New Directions for Sailing to and from the East Indies: Also for the Use of Ships Trading in the Indian and China Seas to New Holland, &c &c Collected from the Manuscripts, Journals, Memoirs and Observations of the Most Experienced Officers in the Hon. East India Company's Service, and From the Last Edition of the French Neptune Oriental. 1794. repr., Philadelphia: James Humphreys, 1801.

Osborne, Anne. "Property, Taxes, and State Protection of Rights." In *Contract and Property in Early Modern China*, ed. Madeleine Zelin, Jonathan K. Ocko, and Robert Gardella, 120–158. Stanford, CA: Stanford University Press, 2004.

Pan Siyuan 潘思園. "Dai Yihe yanghang Wu Dunyuan zuo fenjiachan yiyue" 代怡和洋行伍敦元作分家產議約 (Negotiating an Agreement on the Division of the Family Assets on Behalf of Wu Dunyuan [Houqua] of the Yihe Company Which Handles Trade with the West). In *Siyuanzu yigao* 思園祖遺稿 (Surviving Manuscripts of the Ancestor Siyuan), ed. Pan Siyuan, 77–79. N.p.: n.p., 1880.

Pitkin, Timothy. *A Statistical View of the Commerce of the United States of America, Including Also an Account of Banks, Manufactures and Internal Trade and Improvements: Together with that of the Revenues and Expenditures of the General Government: Accompanied with Numerous Tables.* New Haven, CT: Durrie & Peck, 1835.

Pomeranz, Kenneth. *The Great Divergence: China, Europe, and the Making of the Modern World Economy.* Princeton, NJ: Princeton University Press, 2000.

——— "Ten Years After: Responses and Reconsiderations." *Historically Speaking: Bulletin of the Historical Society* 12, no. 4 (September 2011): 20–25.

Pritchard, Earl H. and Patrick J. N. Tuck. *The Crucial Years of Early Anglo-Chinese Relations, 1750–1800.* Pullman, WA, 1936. repr., London: Routledge, 2000.

Punch (London). "A Lass of Wax." July 8, 1848.

Qi Meiqin 祁美琴. *Qingdai neiwufu* 清代內务府 (Imperial Palace of the Qing Dynasty). Beijing: Zhongguo renmin daxue chubanshe, 1998.

Qinding Da Qing huidian tu (Jiaqing chao) 欽定大清會典圖(嘉慶朝) (Pictorial Section of the Collected Statutes of the Qing Compiled during the Reign of Jiaqing [1796–1820]). Taipei: Wenhai chubanshe, 1992.

Qing shi lu 清實錄 (Records of the Qing). Beijing: Zhonghua shuju, 1985–1987.

Qingchao wenxian tongkao 清朝文獻通考 (An Encyclopedic Collection of the Historical Records of the Qing Dynasty). Taipei: Xinxing shuju, 1963.

Roberts, Kevin. *Lovemarks: The Future beyond Brands.* New York: PowerHouse Books, 2005.

Rosenthal, Jean-Laurent and R. Bin Wong. *Before and Beyond Divergence: The Politics of Economic Change in China and Europe.* Cambridge, MA: Harvard University Press, 2011.

Rowe, William T. *Hankow: Commerce and Society in a Chinese City, 1796–1889.* Stanford, CA: Stanford University Press, 1984.

    Hankow: Conflict and Community in a Chinese City, 1796–1895. Stanford, CA: Stanford University Press, 1989.

Sala, George Augustus. *Madame Tussaud's Exhibition Guide.* London: Madame Tussaud and Sons, 1909.

Sayers, R. S. *Central Banking after Bagehot.* Oxford: Clarendon Press, 1957.

Scully, Eileen P. *Bargaining with the State from Afar: American Citizenship in Treaty Port China, 1844–1942.* New York: Columbia University Press, 2001.

Skinner, G. William. "Creolized Chinese Societies in Southeast Asia." In *Sojourners and Settlers: Histories of Southeast Asia and the Chinese: In Honour of Jennifer Cushman.* ed. Anthony Reid, 51–93. St. Leonards, Australia: Allen and Unwin, 1996.

"Some Account of the City of Canton, Part I." *Saturday Magazine* (London: John William Park West Strand) 10, no. 310 (April 1837): 162–168.

Standard (London). May 9, 1837.

Staunton, George. *An Authentic Account of an Embassy from the King of Great Britain to the Emperor of China, Including Cursory Observations Made, and Information Obtained, in Travelling Through that Ancient Empire and a Small Part of Chinese Tartary,* 2nd ed. London: Printed for G. Nicol, Bookseller to his Majesty, 1798.

Stuart, Jan and Evelyn S. Rawski. *Worshiping the Ancestors: Chinese Commemorative Portraits.* Washington, DC and Stanford, CA: Freer Gallery of Art and the Arthur M. Sackler Gallery, in association with Stanford University Press, 2001.

Sugihara, Kaoru. "Patterns of Chinese Emigration to Southeast Asia, 1869–1939." In *Japan, China, and the Growth of the Asian International Economy, 1850–1949,* ed. Kaoru Sugihara, 244–274. Oxford: Oxford University Press, 2005.

Thomson v. Houqua, Interrogatories, Case no. 34, December Term 1820. Records of the Supreme Court (Eastern District). Division of Archives and Manuscripts. Pennsylvania Historical and Museum Commission.

Tillotson, G. H. R. (Giles Henry Rupert). *Fan Kwae Pictures: Paintings and Drawings by George Chinnery and Other Artists in the Collection of the Hongkong and Shanghai Banking Corporation.* London: Spink & Son for the Hongkong and Shanghai Banking Corporation, 1987.

Torbert, Preston M. *The Ch'ing Imperial Household Department: A Study of its Organization and Principal Functions, 1662–1796.* Cambridge, MA: Council on East Asian Studies, Harvard University, 1977.

Trewman's Exeter Flying Post or Plymouth and Cornish Advertiser (Exeter, UK). May 18, 1837.

Trivellato, Francesca. *The Familiarity of Strangers: The Sephardic Diaspora, Livorno, and Cross-Cultural Trade in the Early Modern Period*. New Haven, CT: Yale University Press, 2009.

Van Dyke, Paul A. *The Canton Trade: Life and Enterprise on the China Coast, 1700–1845*. Hong Kong: Hong Kong University Press, 2007.

Merchants of Canton and Macao: Politics and Strategies in Eighteenth-Century Chinese Trade. Hong Kong: Hong Kong University Press, 2011.

Merchants of Canton and Macao: Success and Failure in Eighteenth-Century Chinese Trade. Hong Kong: Hong Kong University Press, 2016.

"New Sea Routes to Canton in the 18th Century and the Decline of China's Control over Trade." In *Haiyang shi yanjiu* 海洋史研究 (Studies of Maritime History), ed. Li Qingxin 李庆新, 1: 57–108. Beijing: Shehui kexue wenxian chubanshe, 2010.

"Operational Efficiencies and the Decline of the Chinese Junk Trade in the Eighteenth and Nineteenth Centuries: The Connection." In *Shipping and Economic Growth 1350–1850*, ed. Richard Unger, 223–246. Leiden: E.J. Brill, 2011.

Viraphol, Sarasin. *Tribute and Profit: Sino-Siamese Trade, 1652–1853*. Cambridge, MA: Council on East Asian Studies, Harvard University, 1977.

von Glahn, Richard. *Fountain of Fortune: Money and Monetary Policy in China, 1000–1700*. Berkeley: University of California Press, 1996.

Wakefield, David. *Fenjia: Household Division and Inheritance in Qing and Republican China*. Honolulu: University of Hawai'i Press, 1998.

Wakeman, Frederic, Jr. "The Canton Trade and the Opium War." In *The Cambridge History of China*, ed. John K. Fairbank and Kwang-Ching Liu, vol. 10, pt. 1, 163–212. Cambridge: Cambridge University Press, 1978.

Strangers at the Gate: Social Disorder in South China, 1839–1861. Berkeley: University of California Press, 1966.

Wang, Gungwu. "Merchants without Empires: The Hokkien Sojourning Communities." In *China and the Chinese Overseas*, 79–101. Singapore: Times Academic Press, 1991.

Wang Yongrui 王永瑞, ed. *Xinxiu Guangdong fu zhi* 新修廣東府志 (The Revised Gazetteer of Guangzhou Prefecture). 1673.

Wang Zhichun 王之春. *Guochao tongshang shimo ji* 國朝通商始末記 (The Complete Record of the Opening of Trade in the Present Dynasty). Taipei: Wenhai chubanshe, 1967.

Wilkins, Mira. "The Impacts of American Multinational Enterprise on American-Chinese Economic Relations, 1786–1949." In *America's China Trade in Historical Perspective: The Chinese and American Performance*, ed. Ernest R. May and John K. Fairbank, 259–292. Cambridge, MA: Committee on American–East Asian Relations, Department of History, Harvard University, 1986.

Wolf, Arthur P. and Chieh-shan Huang. *Marriage and Adoption in China, 1845–1945*. Stanford, CA: Stanford University Press, 1980.

Wong, R. Bin. *China Transformed: Historical Change and the Limits of European Experience*. Ithaca, NY: Cornell University Press, 1997.

Wong, Winnie. "Imagining the Great Painting Factory in the Studio of Lam Qua." Paper presented at "'China Trade' (1760–1860) Merchants and Artists: New Historical and Cultural Perspectives." Macau Ricci Institute. Macau, March 2–3, 2011.

Wu Bingyong 伍秉鏞. 1824 preface, in Wu Ziwei, ed. *Wushi ru Yue zupu* 伍氏入粵族譜 (Genealogy of the Wu Family that Moved to Canton), vol. 1. 1956.

Wu Chongyao 伍崇曜. *Lingnan yishu* 嶺南遺書 (The Surviving Works in the Region South of the Passes). Nanhai: Yueyatang, 1831–1863.

Wu Jiali 伍家澧. 1956 preface, in Wu Ziwei, ed. *Wushi ru Yue zupu* 伍氏入粵族譜 (Genealogy of the Wu Family that Moved to Canton), vol. 1. 1956.

Wu Lingli 伍凌立, ed. *Wushi Putianfang Fulonggong Guangzhou shisanhang zhimai zu yinpu* 伍氏莆田房符龙公广州十三行支脉族引谱 (Genealogy of the Wu Clan of Fulong, from the Putian Branch Extended to Those Involved in the Canton Trade). 2010.

Wu Quancui 伍詮萃, ed. *Lingnan Wushi hezu zongpu* 嶺南伍氏闔族總譜 (Complete Genealogy of the Entire Wu Clan in Lingnan). 1934.

Wu Ziwei 伍子偉, ed. *Wushi ru Yue zupu* 伍氏入粵族譜 (Genealogy of the Wu Family that Moved to Canton). 1956.

Xu Dishan 許地山. *Dazhongji: Yapian zhanzheng qian Zhong Ying jiaoshe shiliao* 達衷集: 鴉片戰爭前中英交涉史料 (*Dazhongji*: Sino-British Historical Representations Before the Opium War). 1928. repr., Hong Kong: Longmen shudian, 1969.

Yamamura, Kozo. "Japan, 1868–1930: A Revised View." In *Banking and Economic Development: Some Lessons of History*, ed. Rondo Cameron, 186–197. New York: Oxford University Press, 1972.

Zelin, Madeleine, Jonathan K. Ocko, and Robert Gardella, eds. *Contract and Property in Early Modern China*. Stanford, CA: Stanford University Press, 2004.

Zhao, Gang. *The Qing Opening to the Ocean: Chinese Maritime Policies, 1684–1757*. Honolulu: University of Hawai'i Press, 2013.

Zhongguo di 1 lishi dang'an guan 中国第一历史档案馆 (Number One Historical Archives of China). *Guangzhou lishi ditu jingcui* 广州历史地图精粹 (Selected Historical Maps of Guangzhou). Beijing: Zhongguo dabaike quanshu chubanshe, 2003.

Zhongguo di 1 lishi dang'an guan 中国第一历史档案馆 (Number One Historical Archives of China). *Qinggong Guangzhou shisanhang dang'an jingxuan* 清宫廣州十三行檔案精選 (Featured Archives on Thirteen Merchants in Guangzhou during the Qing). Guangzhou: Guangdong jingji chubanshe, 2002.

Zhongguo di 1 lishi dang'an guan 中国第一历史档案馆 (Number One Historical Archives of China). *Qinggong Yue Gang Ao shangmao dang'an quanji* 清宫粵港澳商貿檔案全集 (A Complete Collection of the Archival Documents on Trade in Canton, Hong Kong, and Macao from the Qing Palace). Beijing: Zhongguo shudian, 2002.

Zhuang Su'e 莊素娥. "Shijiu shiji Guangdong waixiaohua de zanzhuzhe: Guangdong shisanhang hangshang" 十九世紀廣東外銷畫的贊助者: 廣東十三行行

商" (The Sponsors of Export Paintings from Nineteenth-Century Guang-dong: The Merchants of the Canton Trade). In *Quyu yu wangluo: Jinqian-nianlai Zhongguo meishushi yanjiu guoji xueshu yantaohui lunwenji* 區域與網絡: 近千年來中國美術史研究國際學術研討會論文集 (Regions and Networks: A Collection of Essays Presented at the Academic Conference on Chinese Art History During the Last One Thousand Years), 533–578. Taipei: Guoli Taiwan daxue yishushi yanjiusuo, 2001.

Index